OUTSIDE SHOT

OUTSIDE SHOT

Big Dreams, Hard Times, and One County's Quest
for Basketball Greatness

KEITH O'BRIEN

ST. MARTIN'S PRESS ⧓ NEW YORK

www.stmartins.com

All interior photos are courtesy of Erik Jacobs/Jacobs Photographic, except page 51, courtesy of Teresa Haynes.

Design by Omar Chapa

ISBN 978-1-250-00033-0 (hardcover)
ISBN 978-1-250-02671-2 (e-book)

First Edition: January 2013

10 9 8 7 6 5 4 3 2 1

For Eva

Contents

Everything seemed so big . . . It seemed like the lights were much brighter. It seemed like you were just on this huge stage and the whole world was just watching.

—ALLAN HOUSTON,
   *former NBA star, on playing in the Kentucky state
   high school basketball tournament*

*Cheer, Cheer, for Scott County High,
We are the Red Birds flying on high.
Basketball is in our lives,
We have a good team every time.*

*Come on you Cardinals red and white,
Give us a victory, win one tonight.
This is all we ask of you,
So fight on with all your might.*

Fight, FIGHT!

—SCOTT COUNTY FIGHT SONG,
   written in 1956 by Velma Mason

Prologue

THE OLD-TIMERS WERE CLOSING IN NOW, reaching for the coach's elbow, clutching for the cotton of his shirtsleeve, hands moving down his forearm, grasping, as he tried to slip unnoticed through the crowded gymnasium.

Billy Hicks, reeking of the chili and barbecue that he had been cooking all week, didn't want the attention. The idea of having to talk about basketball with strangers seemed to make his frayed khakis cinch just a bit tighter around his waist and creep up his hips. But they had him now; Hicks knew it. As much as he may have wished to hole up in his windowless, cinder-block office near the basketball court and disappear amid the clutter of his desk, Hicks could not avoid the Scott County fans, thousands of them, surging through the gym over the course of the night.

"Where's Coach?" they kept asking. "Where's Coach at?"

Outside, a cold November darkness had fallen on the bluegrass of central Kentucky. Downtown, on Main Street, the antique stores, banks, and county offices had all been closed for hours. If you wanted a drink, you could get one at Galvin's, downtown's only bar. But tonight, most people were here in the gym, waiting for their first look at the Scott County High School basketball team, their beloved Cardinals, in the team's annual preseason intrasquad scrimmage. Never mind that the game didn't count or that the season wouldn't officially begin for three more weeks. Like Thanksgiving or Christmas, this night, Meet the Cards, was a notable event in the county, a holiday, really, circled on calendars for months in advance. The boys had been talking about it since August, itching to put on a show. One of them would play tonight with three broken bones in his face. "It hurts," said Zach Bryant, a backup point guard. "But I'd rather be out there playing." The scrimmage, many of them agreed, was more important than some of the actual games they would play in the months ahead. Because to suit up tonight meant that you were somebody, a county boy, a round ball star dressed in Cardinal red.

"Anybody grow since last year?" one fan asked Hicks now as the people cornered him near his office.

"How 'bout Ge'Lawn?"

"How's Dakotah doing?"

The boys had been practicing their dunks for days, hoping to impress the fans with rim-rattling tricks during warm-ups. "You gonna throw one down for me tonight or what?" students asked the ballplayers that day at school. And the players promised, yes—dunks would be thrown down, shout-outs would be given. "I'm gonna throw one down," one player told an inquiring student, "and then point at you." That made the student smile.

And now the time was growing closer, the people were gathering. The varsity scrimmage wouldn't start for another ninety minutes, but already the parking lot outside was full and the concession stand was bustling as people lined up to buy the chili and barbecue that Hicks had cooked to raise money for the school. The food was going fast while the questions kept coming.

"How's the bench, Coach? You got a lot of depth this year?"

"Any interest in retiring, Coach?"

"Sounds like you're still enjoying it, Coach."

"More so than I ever have," came Hicks's reply.

His answer was usually that he had ten years left in him, at least eight, no fewer than seven. He was only fifty-seven years old; what else would he do? But the truth was more complicated than that. These days, Hicks was always grousing about how the game was changing. The boys were different and the county was, too. Just over a decade earlier when Billy Hicks brought home Scott County's first state title, the coach had stood in this very gym and nearly wept before the crowd. Overcome by the moment, Hicks, standing at a podium beneath one of the basketball hoops, covered his large rectangular head with one of his thick hands and fought the tears that were coming.

The county adored him then—and with good reason. People here had always longed to win the Kentucky state basketball tournament, a contest unlike almost any other in the country. Here, there are no divisions—no 6A, 5A, and so on. In Lexington's Rupp Arena, home of the University of Kentucky Wildcats, where the tournament takes place, big schools face small schools and country boys from coal-mining hamlets take on inner-city kids from Louisville. It isn't about pitting same against same, or making sure kids take home trophies. Kentucky doesn't care so much about fairness. What people want here is excitement, to see who's best, plain and simple. And what they like about the format is its purity, its mathematical simplicity. Sixteen teams, playing for one title, over four days in March.

The crowds are known to exceed 20,000 people. And just making it to Rupp, just playing before these crowds, is considered a great achievement. In 1983, the first time Scott County ever made the Sweet 16, the team spent the week visiting every school in the county. Pep rallies became a daily event. And on the day of the county's first game at Rupp, the county courthouse shut down at noon and the schools at 10:30 in the morning. It was, according to one student, "the most exciting thing around here since electricity." And so, fifteen years later, when Hicks not only led the county back to Rupp, but actually took home the title, shocking just about everyone, people in Scott County did everything but declare a public holiday to mark the moment. "This is not a pep rally," said Gregory Figgs, the high school principal at the time, surveying a sea of jubilant students at one celebration that March. "This," he explained, "is an educational experience."

In the months that followed, Billy Hicks received enough fan mail to fill a large plastic bin. Old friends and total strangers, fellow coaches and former players, politicians and preachers, children and the elderly, county executives, fans from rival teams, the mentally ill, and even referees—they all wrote Billy Hicks to praise him or just thank him. "God bless you and all the boys," said one fan. "I will try to pray for you regularly," said another. "It really feels like we all won," wrote a local pastor at the time. For a rare moment, it seemed, people living in the rolling hills north of Lexington actually felt proud to call the county home. One letter put it this way: "You put Scott County on the map." And another told Hicks that, essentially, he had changed everything. "The people of Scott County now smile a little bigger, stand a little taller, and *look* for people they can tell where they are from," the fan wrote. "Here's to the one that will last *forever!*"

But now, just over a decade later, even as fans sought out Hicks at Meet the Cards to shake his hand and wish him well, some people were doubting him. In the hallways at the high school and the aisles of the local Walmart that fall, there were whispers: *The old coach didn't have it anymore . . . The county would lose this year, just like it had last year . . . These boys, this team—something just felt wrong.* People could feel it—perhaps Hicks most of all. Like a man standing in the surf and watching the sand around his feet being washed out to sea, Billy Hicks could almost feel the ground beneath him giving away. He was sinking, inching ever deeper into a world where child athletes called the shots and their parents demanded athletic greatness at seemingly any cost, while these fans, this county, longed for the innocence of a not-so-distant past.

"It'll be a good year," said one fan, nodding now. "It'll be a good year."

"Hope so," Hicks replied. "We'll see."

And then it was time. In the locker room, the boys were pushing for the door, shouting, their knees bouncing with nerves. On the court, the cheerleaders were waiting, lined up on the baseline, shrieking, fists in the air, growing louder by the minute.

Red! White! LET'S GO!

Red! White! LET'S GO!

The boys bounded onto the court. The county fans stood up and cheered. It was nearly winter in Kentucky. Soon, there would be snow in the hills and a blanket of frost laid out on the bluegrass. It was time to play basketball.

Part I

THE STRAW THAT STIRS THE DRINK

FOR MONTHS, Billy Hicks had asked the boys to remember the pain: the failure of not making it to Rupp Arena and the tears in that locker room the previous March. He urged them not to forget the ridicule: how opposing fans had mocked them that day, reveling in their collective failure and laughing at their disappointment. And now, with a new basketball season upon them, Hicks unearthed the past all over again, as if the boys had forgotten. "All of Kentucky rejoiced when we got beat," Hicks told them on the eve of the season. "But daggone, let's make all of Kentucky howl this year. Let's make 'em pay."

As he spoke, Hicks paced before them, one hand on his hip, the other on his head. He hoped his boys were ready. In quiet moments, huddled up with his assistant coaches in recent days, he admitted that he wasn't sure that they were. He wished they had another month to practice, another month to prepare.

But there was no use hoping and wishing anymore. It was time to play, time to win. Surely, they would win. The goal for the Scott County boys was simple: They were not to lose a single game to a Kentucky basketball team all season. Kentucky was theirs. Kentucky was Cardinal country. If they played like Hicks knew they could play, then no one would beat them. Billy Hicks was confident of that. They would win it all, every game, every time.

"Hey, guys," Hicks said. "We're going to make this *our* state."

And yet here they were just one night later, on the road, in the first game of the season, down three points with sixteen seconds to go, the undefeated year already unraveling, the boys staring at each other in the team huddle, and the opposing fans—some 1,500 strong—hollering themselves hoarse in the night.

"We are Ballard!"

Clap, clap, clap-clap-clap!

"We are Ballard!"

Clap, clap, clap-clap-clap!

Friggin' Ballard. Stomping his feet and throwing his arms into the air on the sideline, Hicks could barely believe what he was seeing. In his pregame speech two hours earlier, he had been the very portrait of calm—or as calm as he ever got—adjusting the fit of his red tie in the visitors' locker room and laying it, just so, against his blue-checkered, button-down shirt. His brown dress shoes shimmered in the lights as he stepped onto the floor in Ballard's gymnasium and his pleated beige slacks were perfectly pressed. But now it looked as if someone had set those slacks afire and that Hicks had leapt into the brown waters of the Elkhorn Creek to douse the flames. His face, smooth and creased like worn leather, burned bright red as he screamed at his boys in the final, frantic moments of the game. The veins in his neck were bulging as if pumping crude oil through his towering six-foot-four frame. And he wasn't merely sweating; Hicks was drenched, and his damp hair was disheveled from all the times he had grabbed his face in horror.

"How can you be out there, guys, and not rebound?" he asked the boys during one fourth-quarter time-out, shouting in an effort to be heard over the roar of the crowd. "Every time they miss, they get the ball back. *REBOUND!*"

In the team huddle, with the boys' chests heaving and sweat dripping to the floor, Hicks's eyes, small and nut-brown, darted from one boy to another. He turned to Dakotah Euton, the six-foot-eight, bearded man-child who had once been ranked among the top high school players in the country, but whose stock had fallen and now was among the most vilified players in the state. He turned to Chad Jackson, the county's quiet, sometimes confounding would-be hero who was as talented as any high school basketball player when he wanted to play. There was just one problem: The coaches weren't sure that Chad, with his distant gaze and proclivity for silence, really wanted it. And then, finally, Hicks turned to his star pupil, the No. 2 ranked player in all of Kentucky, with the father cheering in the stands and the handler, a distant relative, firing off e-mails to scouts about the boy's performances and statistics. More than anyone perhaps, Billy Hicks needed this player. To win, Hicks needed Ge'Lawn Guyn.

"Ge'Lawn," Hicks pleaded, slapping the boy's backside, *"c'mon now!"* The boy curled up his lower lip and just nodded.

THE DAY FOR GE'LAWN had begun that morning with sausage and scrambled eggs—a special pregame breakfast prepared by his father. By seven o'clock on typical mornings, George Guyn was already a couple miles into his route collecting garbage in Lexington, hauling away the debris of people's lives. But today was different. Today, George was going to be there for Ge'Lawn and make that breakfast on the first day of his son's last high school basketball season. The man stood in the kitchen in his sock feet, carefully slicing breakfast sausage and stirring the eggs in a skillet. Later, he'd ferry his boy some lunch—a McDonald's Quarter Pounder—to school. Whatever Ge'Lawn needed today, he would get.

"How you feeling?" George asked as Ge'Lawn came downstairs, sleepy-eyed in the dark.

Ge'Lawn yawned. The family's three dogs caged up in the living room were barking their snouts off. "Quiet!" his mama kept yelling. And one of his brothers was already on the Internet, reading the latest about Ballard, tonight's game, and his brother, who was, today, the most important Guyn of all. Between the barking and the shouting and the sizzling of the sausage in the kitchen—"Who wants some?" George called out—the house felt as if it had spun off its foundation. But Ge'Lawn—quiet and slumped over the breakfast table—paid the madness no mind.

He was dressed, nearly completely, in Scott County red. *(Red Heat! Big Red Nation!)* Ge'Lawn liked to give the fans who sat behind the county bench their props, turning to dap them up before he took the floor at game time. And so, of course, he was going to wear the red today. Hanging off his body was the team's warm-up suit: cozy fleece, red and black, and just a bit baggy. On his head, Ge'Lawn wore a matching red do-rag, and then, on top of that, a red fleece skier's hat with the earflaps flipped up. He couldn't be bothered to lace up his pristine white, size 13 Reeboks, and his earlobes sparkled with enough cubic zirconium to clog the bathroom sink. With hardly a word to anyone, Ge'Lawn sat at the kitchen table, waiting to be fed.

The house was the best place the Guyn family (pronounced *Gwinn*) had ever lived in, and still it wasn't much. You could find it in the new development of tract homes, just over the hill behind the high school, down the road past the tobacco field, and beneath the high-tension wires slicing toward Lexington. And if you found it there, you wouldn't find much else around. Despite all the optimism with which the developers had built the subdivision a couple years earlier—CHARLESTON VILLAGE, read the sign, welcoming people to the neighborhood—the people, and the money, simply had not followed.

The Guyns' was the only house on their block. Ge'Lawn's bedroom window on the second floor overlooked a ragged field, choked with weeds and the occasional children's bicycle tossed to the ground. Neighbors here were hard to find and the inside of the Guyns' home was nearly as empty as the outside. The living room was sparsely furnished and visits—from Ge'Lawn's teammates, anyway—were somewhat rare, which meant that few ever saw the empty living room, or the pile of trophies and plaques, Ge'Lawn's treasures, cascading off the mantel in the living room like a waterfall of plastic gold.

There he is, all region. There he is, all district. There he is, MVP, from the night one year ago, when he dropped twenty-nine points on soon-to-be-state-champs Holmes High with big-time college coaches in the house, watching, taking notes. The county lost that game by five, but it was a proud moment for the Guyns all the same. That was the night when people really began to take notice of their boy. And also the night, according to George, when Ge'Lawn's teammates, jealous of his son, began freezing him out. "After that game, he wouldn't never get the ball even if he was wide open," George complained to folks who would listen. "How in the hell could Coach Hicks not see that they were freezing him out?"

As he stirred the eggs in the kitchen, George worried that the same thing was about to happen this season, the most important season yet, Ge'Lawn's senior year, the year he'd finally land a college scholarship, and get out of Scott County. "That's the same stuff," George said, "that's going to cost us this year." But as he delivered breakfast to four of his seven children, George did so with a smile—trying to be positive, stay positive. It was a new season. Maybe things would be better this year. Still, it was probably worth a prayer or two. After shoveling down the eggs and sausage, the Guyn family circled up, joining hands in the living room where the furniture should have been.

"Hey, be quiet!" Ge'Lawn's mama, Rebecca Guyn, shouted at the yapping dogs caged up in the corner.

"Be quiet! Be quiet!"

And then she began to pray. She thanked God for what little they had and asked him to bless the team. She asked the Lord to give the boys good court awareness, to help them play together, to help them play as one. "Connect them," she pleaded, "and join them at the hip."

But mostly, she prayed for Ge'Lawn.

"Touch Ge'Lawn to be what he needs to be in the game, Lord God," she said, eyes closed and barely pausing for a breath between each sentence. "Lord God, bless his hands, bless his mind, bless his quickness, Lord God. Bless his feet to move, Lord God. Lord God, bless everyone to hit every basket, Lord God. In the name of Jesus, this we ask.

"Amen."

THE TELEVISION TRUCKS were waiting outside Ballard's gym when the Scott County team bus rolled into the parking lot that night. Everyone noticed them. With their satellite dishes angling toward the darkened sky, the trucks were impossible to miss. But no one mentioned the fact that the game was being carried live on cable television across the state. There was no need to make the game bigger than it already was. This was Ballard, a three-time state champion that had sent players to the NBA, including former New York Knick Allan Houston. This was Louisville, the state's largest city, with four television networks, a few of which would be here tonight. In Kentucky, this was the big time, about as big as it got. But the visitors' locker room, where the county boys were headed now, was nothing special whatsoever.

The locker room was located at the bottom of a concrete stairwell, twenty steps beneath the gym floor. Inside, it was dark and gray. Some of the fluorescent lights in the ceiling had burned out and the covering to one of the light fixtures was dangling overhead, looking like it might come crashing down at any moment. But Scott County had bigger problems than the lights. The team's new uniform jerseys had come in the day before, but the new shorts had not, which meant they were wearing last year's shorts with this year's jerseys, an ugly combination, at least upon close inspection.

"Sketchy," was the way Dakotah put it, examining himself in the mirror. But Ge'Lawn was so busy pulling on what appeared to be three layers of armor that he didn't seem to notice the wardrobe malfunction. Two pair of socks. One knee brace. And a pair of white, elastic, full-legged tights for good measure. The tights helped keep his legs warm, he said. Made him feel good. And tonight, Ge'Lawn needed to feel good.

"Hey, guys," Hicks told the boys in his pregame speech. "Let's get after them. *FIGHT* for every rebound. *FIGHT*. Hey, guys. *FIGHT* for every rebound. Don't ever get caught standing and watching. Go to the boards. And when you get inside, pump. They're all about ready to jump out of the gym. Pump—and then go up strong. Take them, the ball, and everything up with you. Let's go!"

"Let's go!" Ge'Lawn shouted in reply, grimacing and clapping his hands. He was ready. It was his time. As he hit the floor for warm-ups, his knees bouncing and his brown eyes cold, he kept whispering the same thing over and over again just loud enough so that he could hear it.

"My house," said Ge'Lawn.

"My house."

And then, out came the Ballard Bruins to the pleasure of the hometown Louisville fans. They hated Scott County. For beating their beloved Bruins in the state finals two years earlier in a stunning fourth-quarter comeback. For beating them—by twenty—in the season-opener last year. And for simply being from Scott County—a rural, backward place as far as many Ballard kids were concerned. One Ballard senior, Becca Balf, said she could describe the county fans in one word. "Trashy," she said. "But I mean that," she added, "from the bottom of my heart."

The crowd was roaring now. The Ballard student section, decked out in all white, was rocking in the stands. The Bruin cheerleaders, ponytails in their hair, were high kicking on the floor. Out in the lobby, an inflatable, two-story Chick-fil-A cow was quaking, like it might break free from its tethers and float away, while Chris Renner, Ballard's head coach, begged his team to rise to the occasion, to embrace this moment, to throttle Scott County, right here, tonight.

"In an atmosphere like this," Renner told his boys just before tipoff, "the communication on the floor is crucial. We're not good at that. Let's get started tonight because if we're communicating to one guy, and you expect everybody to hear it, you gotta make sure. '*Hey*, we're in hot! *Hey*, we're running strong this time! *Hey*, it's this play!' You gotta communicate on the floor. You gotta be looking at us. Don't be in the stands, listening to family, looking at girlfriends, boyfriends. Be into the game, the coaching staff, and your teammates, OK? Gonna be a great night, guys. Gonna be a *great* night. Bring it in. Lay it all on the line. Leave nothing left. Play like it's the state championship because we *will* play in the state championship."

The Ballard boys huddled up and prayed together. Then, having given it up to God, they began to whoop and holler.

"Let's go, baby!"

"Let's go, y'all!"

"Bruins on three, state on six."

"One, two, three . . . *BRUINS!*"

"Four, five, six . . . *STATE!*"

"DAP ME UP," Ge'Lawn had said that morning, arriving at school and finding his teammate Tamron Manning, a sophomore point guard, hanging out in the gym.

Ge'Lawn and Tamron bumped fists, and then stood around for a while, killing time and waiting for first bell at 8:45. School today was just a means to an end. Get through the day, then they could play. But that didn't mean they had to focus while they were there. In fact, today more than most days, the boys seemed to have very little interest in school at all. Before the first bell even rang, Ge'Lawn was off in his own world—his world of basketball.

He breezed through his first-hour gym class, goofing around on the court while the other kids actually tried to play basketball for a grade. Second hour was Spanish, held in an auxiliary trailer, built to accommodate the overpopulation of county students attending the high school. ELECTRONIC DEVICES WILL BE TAKEN, warned a sign on the plywood wall of the crowded trailer, AND YOU WILL RECEIVE A SATURDAY. But that didn't stop Ge'Lawn from texting girls all hour, fingering his phone under his desk while his teacher droned on.

"Ha ha."

"LOL."

"Watsup?"

Ge'Lawn might have done the same thing in his third-hour forensic science class, where the sign read, NO CELL PHONE ACTIVITY! It was a presentation day. The lights would be turned off. The kids were being asked to present brief PowerPoints about famous murderers; twenty points for a job well done. But then the teacher, Trevelin Conn, called on Ge'Lawn.

"Ge'Lawn," she said. "Go."

Ge'Lawn wasn't thinking about school now. "I'm thinking about winning," he said. "I want to win and play good. Play hard." And he certainly wasn't excited about speaking in front of the class. Just the thought of it made him wring his hands. But when Conn called on him, Ge'Lawn stood up to tell the class about his infamous murderer, a man accused of killing women in Wisconsin in 1957.

"How do you say his name?" Conn asked.

"Ed Gein."

"Geeeeen?"

"Yeah."

"All right. Here you go, Ge'Lawn."

Ge'Lawn.

His parents said the name meant warrior. But really, it was their own creation—with the "Ge" coming from his father's name, George, and the rest of it pulled from a Muslim name they had found in a book. Either way, it didn't matter. The name meant warrior and the story fit the boy's life well. Ge'Lawn wasn't afraid to fight. If pushed, he'd throw down with anyone, on or off the basketball court. He had always been that way even when he was a razor-thin child with arms like marsh reeds growing up in tough Lexington neighborhoods. But now Ge'Lawn Guyn had the body to match his will to rumble: rippling arm muscles, an angular jaw that seemed prepared to take a sucker punch at all times, and the tattoos that he had acquired that summer.

"Loyal to the Game," said the one on his shoulder.

"Psalm 144:1," said another one on his right breast. And then, on his left breast, came the accompanying Bible passage, which said just about everything Ge'Lawn wanted people to know about him.

"Blessed be the Lord, my strength," said the tattoo in dark, wobbly script, "which teacheth my hand to war and my fingers to fight."

Ge'Lawn had pulled this passage out of the Bible and then had someone burn it into his dark, mocha-brown skin at a classmate's house in the county. He was eighteen at the time and one of the most touted high school basketball prospects in the state of Kentucky. Mail from college coaches arrived from all over the country every day, piling up in his locker and spilling onto the floor. Text messages from girls—almost always girls—kept his cell phone bleating from morning till night. Ge'Lawn could do what he wanted—and he wanted the tattoos. In twenty-five words or less, they defined him, he believed. And the tattoos had a side benefit as well. They helped to announce his presence on the basketball court as a bad man—which wasn't a terrible thing, especially this year, his senior year. His parents were talking about following their boy wherever he went to play college basketball—even if the boy didn't plan on being on campus for long. "I could be one and done," Ge'Lawn said, dreaming out loud one day that fall about the possibility that he might play college ball for just one year before heading to the NBA. "Wouldn't that be tight?"

Such dreams were a bit far-fetched. Though it was often reported that he was six foot three, Ge'Lawn was at least a full inch shorter than that. And since he was nineteen by the time the season began, he was probably finished growing, too. If he played in college, it would have to be as a point guard—everyone recognized that. But after the summer he'd had on the AAU circuit, playing games across the country for his traveling team, who could blame the kid for dreaming big?

Coming out of the summer season, the basketball blogosphere was atwitter with awestruck accolades for Ge'Lawn—accolades which alone meant absolutely nothing, but when taken together somehow portended greatness for Ge'Lawn in the months to come.

"Best player on the floor . . ."

"Guyn is playing like the best senior in Kentucky . . ."

"Guyn is the straw that stirs the drink . . ."

The previous June, before all the buzz, he had briefly committed to play college ball for UNC Charlotte—a nice mid-major basketball program, where Ge'Lawn could have done just fine, perhaps making the NCAA tournament once or twice while getting a college education for free. But after his summer tearing up the AAU circuit, Ge'Lawn reneged on Charlotte, possibly believing he could do better, possibly for other reasons. All Ge'Lawn would say was that he'd made the decision too quickly. And so, he was a free agent, with no scholarship, nothing guaranteed, and everything riding on his senior season.

And, today, that season finally was here. At lunch in the school cafeteria hours before tipoff against Ballard, the students were talking about the game that night, and how good Ballard was supposed to be, and how intimidating it was to play in the Bruins' gym, before their crowd. Even the way that Ballard introduced its players—turning off the lights in the gym, NBA-style, as each player heard his name announced—seemed to have the county kids rattled.

"Do they really turn off the lights?" Dakotah asked.

"Yeah." Ge'Lawn nodded. "It's bad."

But Scott County, ranked No. 2 in the state's preseason polls, could not lose. That simply wasn't an option. Students reminded Ge'Lawn of that again and again as he finished the lunch that his father had delivered to him and started to meander back to class in his Reeboks—up, up on his tippy-toes—gliding down the halls of the school.

"Y'all lose and it's going to be trouble," said Ali Cecil, a blond-haired senior who would be in Louisville that night for the game. "I'm just telling you."

Ge'Lawn didn't reply. He just kept walking down the hall.

"Y'all lose your *first game*?" Ali continued, amped up and obviously ready to keep going. But Ge'Lawn had heard enough and cut her off right there.

"Ali," Ge'Lawn snapped. "Will you stop? *Please?*"

SCOTT COUNTY lost the opening tip, but the Bruins missed a couple of easy baskets and, forty-five seconds into the game, Ge'Lawn notched the county's first points of the season, draining two free throws. Scott County was up, 2–0. But Ge'Lawn then proceeded to miss his next three shots while the man he was covering nailed back-to-back three-pointers at the other end. It wasn't even ninety seconds into the season and already Hicks was hollering at the boy in the white tights.

"Gawwwwsssshh almighty!" he yelled.

He yanked Ge'Lawn from the game to ask him if he planned on playing defense tonight and then inserted him back in. But things on the floor didn't get any better after Ge'Lawn returned. Ballard reeled off ten unanswered points while Ge'Lawn sputtered, even managing, at one point, to dribble the ball off his left foot and out of bounds. He threw his hands in the air, asking the ref for a foul call, but he didn't get one. And there was no stopping Ballard in the early goings. The Bruins were up 16–4 before Ge'Lawn hit his first jumper of the season, from the top of the key.

"Nice jump shot," the color commentator said on TV.

"He'll take that," agreed the play-by-play man.

Chad Jackson came right back with a nifty steal and an easy layup at the other end. It was 16–8 now, the gap closing. But the Cardinals would not score for another two minutes. Even layups, gimmes, wouldn't fall. When Tamron Manning stole the ball late in the first quarter and flung it down the court to a wide-open Ge'Lawn streaking to the hoop, it looked like an easy two. But Ge'Lawn was a moment too slow and a Ballard player, soaring to the rim, swatted the shot back into Ge'Lawn's face. The Bruins were rolling now. With the Ballard faithful still roaring over the blocked shot, a Bruin guard cut to the baseline with the ball, hustling past Dakotah, Chad, and another Scott County player, before flipping a reverse layup into the hoop, right in front of Ge'Lawn.

"Let's take a look at this again," said the play-by-play man, sitting court-side and calling up a replay of Ge'Lawn's shot getting swatted toward Lexington. "Watch this block . . . *Get outta here!*"

Just like that, it was 21–8.

"We've got eight points?" Hicks yelled. *"Eight?"*

This was not the game plan that he had drawn up. Scott County's calling card under Billy Hicks for the last fifteen seasons was speed. The Cardinals wanted to push the ball on offense and wreak havoc on defense; a fast game, up and down the floor, was their kind of game. But not tonight, not with the way they were playing in the first half. An entire quarter had nearly elapsed before Dakotah hit his first shot of the season—a three-pointer from the left wing. Chad and Tamron got into foul trouble early. The county's reserves, forced to play due to all the fouls, seemed rattled by the din of the crowd. "Some of you guys," Hicks said, "look like you're scared to death out here." And Ge'Lawn? Hicks had no idea what was wrong with Ge'Lawn.

"Dadburnit!" he yelled in a time-out late in the first half. "We gotta re-bound *the ball.* Ge'Lawn, you're just sitting there, watching."

Yet the county boys began to creep back into the game. Ge'Lawn hit two free throws. Dakotah knocked down another three. Chad forced one steal, then another. Moving like water over a rock, slippery in a pair of red high-tops, Chad scored nine of the county's last sixteen points in the first half, saying nothing as usual, but willing his way to the basket. And there they were at halftime, only six points down.

"We're good . . . we're good . . . we're good," muttered Dakotah down in the locker room at half as if trying to convince himself of the fact. But the county's center, sporting a trim goatee on his formidable chin, was serious. "We're gonna win this game," he told his teammates as they took the floor for the second half. Then the county boys huddled up and reached for the lights.

"One, two, three . . . *RUPP!*"

IT WAS A STUPID, no-good shot. That was about all that had kept Scott County from going to Rupp Arena last season: one bad shot in the waning seconds of the regional final, followed by one very mysterious foul call, which handed the other team the game. Both issues—the shot and the foul—had irritated Scott County fans for nine months now, like a wound that would not heal. The foul, at least, could be explained. That was cheating, plain and simple, fans believed. A cowardly referee from Lexington had cheated the county out of its rightful victory, so that the Cards' nemesis, Lexington Catholic, could win the game, take the region, and go on to Rupp. On this point, for many people, there was no doubt. But the shot—Ge'Lawn's ill-conceived and poorly aimed shot—was something that county fans could not explain as easily.

Up until that moment, it had been one of the greatest games of Ge'Lawn's life. With the county's best player and senior leader knocked out in the regional semifinals with torn knee ligaments, someone else needed to lead the team to Rupp. And Ge'Lawn, still just a junior, was determined to be that guy. Wearing his hair long and braided into rows, he was scowling before he even stepped onto the floor for the game. And once he got the ball in his hands he was almost unstoppable.

He dropped thirty-one points on Catholic—more than double his season's average—scoring six of the county's first seven points to keep them in the game when his teammates came out flat. And by the fourth quarter, he was working so hard that his jersey had come untucked, giving him the illusion of wearing a cape as he bounded down the floor. His thirty-first point gave the Cardinals a one-point lead over Catholic with 4:15 to go. And then Ge'Lawn vanished. He missed a turnaround jumper on the baseline. He turned the ball over, and then turned it over again.

Scott County was clinging to its one-point lead now, barely hanging on against an all-out, full-court Catholic assault, but the Cards had the ball and they had time on their side. With no shot clock in Kentucky high school basketball, and just 1:30 left in the game, the boys seemed intent on running out the clock and force Catholic to foul. Chad dribbled it around some. One minute to go. Dakotah dribbled it around some. Forty-five seconds to go.

On the Catholic bench, Knights coach Brandon Salsman was getting ready to ask his boys to foul, stop the clock, and put Scott County on the line. But then Dakotah, trapped against the far sideline, threw a cross-court pass to a wide-open Ge'Lawn on the edge of the paint. Ge'Lawn could have easily pulled it back, dribbled around, and waited for the foul to come, as it was surely coming. But Ge'Lawn saw an opening. He thought for a moment that he had a path to the basket, so he took it. Four dribbles down the court and he was right there, maybe four feet from the hoop on the baseline. But the defense had collapsed on him now. Two Catholic players were all over him, forming a wall between Ge'Lawn and the rim, and a third was waiting behind them. Ge'Lawn didn't have a clear look at the hoop. He was falling behind the backboard now, but he fired up the shot, anyway—a one-handed half-hook that kissed the side of the rim as he stumbled out of bounds. It wasn't even close. And that was it.

The Knights ultimately collected the ball, got that questionable foul call on the next possession, drained two foul shots, and went on to win by one.

Months later, folks in the county still clicked their tongues and wagged their heads over that one. *What was Ge'Lawn thinking?* No one knew. Not his coaches, not his teammates. "That," suggested teammate Tanner Shotwell, "was the dumbest shot you could possibly take." Even the opposing coach was stunned. It was a gift was all Salsman could figure. Ge'Lawn had given Catholic a gift. And, of course, Ge'Lawn thought about it, too.

Not all the time. The kid was moving on, even changing his look, cutting his long hair short and acquiring those new tattoos. But Ge'Lawn thought of the missed opportunity often enough that he kept a reminder pinned to the wall inside his locker. It was a quote from Michael Jordan—part of a recruiting letter from Oklahoma State University—and it spoke to Ge'Lawn. It read:

> I've missed more than 9,000 shots in my career. I've lost almost 300 games. Twenty-six times I've been trusted to take the game-winning shot and missed. I've failed over, and over, and over again in my life. And that is why I succeed.

Ge'Lawn liked the sound of that: to fail only to succeed; to lose only to win another day. And now he had that chance. It was seven hours before tip-off against Ballard, and he and Dakotah were getting pumped up in the school cafeteria, talking about how they should huddle up before the game and do a sort of dance on the court, even though they knew Hicks didn't like any showboating.

"Let's do it, anyway," Ge'Lawn said. "It's our senior season, man."

"I know," Dakotah replied.

"Let's do it. It's not like we're out there horsing around."

Dakotah nodded. "You think I should ask Coach or not?" he asked.

"Don't ask him," Ge'Lawn replied. "Just do it."

Dakotah nodded again and looked up at the clock. "You even supposed to be in here?" he asked.

"I dunno," Ge'Lawn replied. "I can't even focus on class."

He strolled off to fourth-hour English, where he promptly asked to use the restroom and disappeared for ten minutes. While the other kids were forced to learn their Chaucer—deciphering the meaning of words like "victuals" and "verity"—the teacher wondered aloud about the whereabouts of her missing student. "I wonder what's taking Ge'Lawn so long to get back," Erin Wilson asked her class.

But the kids knew the answer. It was almost game time. "Closer and closer to game time," Ge'Lawn whispered. With each tick of the clock on the wall, Ge'Lawn seemed to be focusing more on the game and less on his lecturing teachers. In his fifth-hour psychology class, he stared across the room, cell phone in hand, while the teacher spoke about the effect of drugs on the brain. And in his sixth-hour math class, while his teacher, Ivon Mucio, talked about factoring trinomials, Ge'Lawn did his best Billy Hicks impersonation.

"Hey, guys!" he bellowed for the benefit of his teammates, Chad and Dakotah, sitting near the door. "What's going on?" he said, his voice high-pitched and raspy, while waving his arms as if pleading with the heavens. "You're in here barking like a *bunch of dawgs!*"

The boys laughed while the other students—at least a few—tried to work. Finally, mercifully, the teacher agreed to let Ge'Lawn, Chad, and Dakotah leave class fifteen minutes early, so that they could grab a sandwich and board the bus for Ballard before the rest of the school buses lurched onto Route 25, clogging the roads to bluegrass outposts like Stamping Ground and New Zion.

"As long as you all win," Mucio told the boys as they left. "The first time you lose, you're going to have to eat on the run."

Ge'Lawn smiled and wagged a finger in the air, speaking in his own voice this time, steely and strong. "Let's get this dub," he said.

DON'T BE AFRAID to take your jump shot, honey," Hicks implored Ge'Lawn before the second half began. "You can't miss a couple shots and then just forget your jump shot. You gotta have confidence in those things."

It was easy for Hicks to say. He wasn't the one who was 3-for-11 from the floor in the first half against Ballard. He wasn't the one who had watched an easy layup swatted away to the delight of the crowd. But Ge'Lawn nodded. Ge'Lawn was listening.

The first time he touched the ball in the second half he fired up a three-pointer. It missed. Dakotah got the rebound and pulled up for a jumper. *Air-ball.* Ballard scored quickly in transition to extend its lead to eight. But the two basketball powerhouses began trading punches now. Ge'Lawn drove to the basket and scored. Ballard answered with a three. Ge'Lawn scored again, and Ballard countered with a bucket of its own. Chad picked up his third foul midway through the third quarter and Hicks complained about the call.

But instead of benching Chad, he kept him in the game, and Scott County gradually began to close the gap. Even as Ge'Lawn picked up his third foul, and then his fourth. And even as the county teammates bickered among themselves. At one point, Dakotah lingered on the bench, a hand on his forehead, asking God for forgiveness because, in a moment of frustration, he had cursed on the floor.

Apparently, God was listening. With less than six minutes to go in the game, Ge'Lawn tied it up, 66–66, with a jumper from the right wing. Ballard answered with a dunk. Ge'Lawn came right back with a drive and another bucket. And then Ballard managed to scrape its way back out in front. The Bruins went up three, then five. But here came Ge'Lawn, driving and scoring. Here came Ge'Lawn, pulling down a rebound, pushing the ball up the court and then dishing it to the county's sharpshooter, Austin Flannery, who was standing alone in the left corner. Austin took the ball and let it fly. *Three-pointer!* Nothing but net. It was a tie game now with less than a minute to go. Time-out Ballard.

"Take the drive away!" Hicks hollered in the huddle, kneeling down and placing one hand on Dakotah's knee. "Guard the ball hard!"

"Let's go, y'all!" Ge'Lawn yelled, pointing in his teammates' faces. "Let's get a stop! Let's go!"

As Ballard inbounded the ball, Ge'Lawn hitched up his baggy red uniform shorts, squatted down, butt to the floor, clapped his hands twice and met Ballard's point guard at midcourt, his arms spread wide. There was no way anyone was scoring on him now—bring it. But as usual, the Bruins found a way, missing their first shot but tipping in the put-back while three county players, including Dakotah and Ge'Lawn, stood around, boxing out nothing but air. Scott County was down two now, then three. With sixteen seconds left—and Chad fouled out of the game—Hicks called a time-out and asked Ge'Lawn to drive to the hoop, score, cut Ballard's lead to one, and then call a quick time-out.

"We've got time," Hicks promised him.

But once on the floor, Ge'Lawn didn't listen. Instead of driving to the basket for an easy two—a shot that Ballard seemed willing to concede—Ge'Lawn stopped short at the three-point line and just sort of lingered there.

Ten seconds to go.

With his left hand, he flipped the ball to Dakotah, who was standing flat-footed outside the three-point arc. Dakotah, with the ball in his hand, dribbled once, and tried to pull up for an off-balance three with a Ballard player screaming in his face.

Seven seconds to go.

Dakotah's shot missed, bricking off the backboard and sparking a wild scrum for the loose ball beneath the basket.

Three seconds now.

A Ballard player scooped up the ball and raced up the court. Ge'Lawn pushed him, fouling out in the process, and none of it mattered.

"Do something!" a frantic Scott County fan shrieked. *"Do something!"*

But it was too late. Ballard had won, 84–81.

ANYBODY GOT A TOWEL?" Hicks asked moments later as he stripped off his sport coat down in the locker room, pacing on the concrete floor beneath the broken lights. He had sweated clear through his shirt, drenched from his shoulders to his navel, as if he had played the game himself. One of the managers tossed a towel to Hicks, who barely had a chance to utter another word before a throng of Ballard fans started pounding on the solid metal locker-room door outside, hooting and hollering, drunk on victory and emboldened by their own obvious greatness.

No one moved to stop the banging horde of Ballard kids, least of all Hicks.

His team had earned this particular indignity. While the Ballard fans yelped outside, scratching at the door like wild dogs set loose in the night, Hicks just stood there, towel in hand, letting the gravity of the loss sink in with each echoing thud of fist against metal.

Upstairs, back in the gym, Ballard's pep band was playing the theme to *Mission: Impossible* while the cheerleaders danced and swayed. And down the hall, in the home locker room, the Ballard players were roaring—"Let's blow 'em out next time, boys!" one player screamed again and again—as their coach pulled out two celebratory cigars: one for tonight and one for the state finals.

"We made some noise tonight," Renner declared. *"I'm tellin' you."*

"Yeahhhhhh!" the Ballard players screamed.

"Get it in, y'all!"

"Get it in, baby!"

"Wooo-OOOOOOO!"

As Renner lit up his stogie, savoring the taste of the tobacco on his tongue, Billy Hicks was still down in his locker room, silently waiting out the banging. After a while, the Ballard kids tired of the exercise, skipping off into the yellow lights of the parking lot, while Hicks, a hand on his forehead, began to break down everything the county boys had done wrong that night: how they hadn't rebounded, how they had quit playing defense down the stretch, how some of them looked like they had never played in a big game in their lives. When Hicks caught one of the boys hanging his head, he snapped. "Get your head up!" he said. "When I'm talking, I want to see your eyes!" And when he considered how close his Cardinals had actually come to winning the game—despite their best efforts to lose—he just sighed. "They was ready to crack, guys," Hicks said. "We could have busted 'em." He stood there, just shaking his head while the boys sat before him, elbows on their knees, taking their tongue-lashing in silence. They had heard such things before.

It was what Hicks said the next day back in Georgetown that revealed the most about what it meant to be a Scott County basketball player. It was about far more than perfecting the skill of shooting a round ball into an orange hoop, far more than representing the school or even the county, far more than learning the fundamentals of the game, hustling, working as a team, or just having fun in the sunset of their youth. Although all of those things mattered, there was much more at stake for the boys than just that.

"Guys," Hicks told them, "don't ever think losing is acceptable here.

"It's not," he explained. "It's not."

2

THE FARMER AND THE BEAUTY QUEEN

IN SOME PLACES, it's considered a weed: not just unnecessary, but invasive and unwelcome. People who live out west on the plains, or in parts of Canada, have been known to bury it in sawdust or burn it off the prairies—anything to get rid of the Kentucky bluegrass, which spreads, often at will, threatening wildflowers, choking out the prairie drop seed, and consuming acre upon acre of North American soil. And yet this grass, this so-called bluegrass, is believed to be neither native to America nor to Kentucky. As well as experts can determine, Kentucky bluegrass, known as *Poa pratensis*, is most likely Eurasian by origin, ferried to the New World centuries ago by wide-eyed settlers who thought it best to bring their own seed, a grass they could trust and knew how to grow for their cattle and other livestock.

Once here, especially in cooler climates up north, the bluegrass flourished, moving out of the pastures and into the hills, valleys, and flat stretches of nothingness from the colonies to the Pacific Northwest. Its seeds moved not just on shoes, hooves, and wagon wheels, but underground in the soil, claiming new turf like crabgrass. If there was a hole, bluegrass would fill it, bearing small blue flowers and growing up to two feet tall when left alone. Some people called it English grass or meadow grass. Even the Native Americans gave the plentiful new vegetation a name. They dubbed it "White man's foot grass," said early traveler William Strickland in 1794. "Wherever he has trodden, it grows."

And so, it was not special at all, but somewhat inevitable perhaps, that bluegrass would find its way to Kentucky and, specifically, to a slice of land that early settlers would come to call Scott County. The grass thrived so well here, laying down roots in the rich limestone soil, that Kentucky's pioneers marveled at the sight of it blanketing the meadows. Where there was bluegrass, there were often animals: buffalo, turkey, and deer. And soon, the people followed.

By the late 1700s, all Kentucky towns were either in, or on the fringes of, a region that people called the Bluegrass—and Georgetown, in Scott County, was one of them, founded by strong, God-fearing Baptists.

Those living here today will say, simply, that they live in the Bluegrass, as if it is of them, which in a way it is. As detestable as *Poa pratensis* might be elsewhere, the grass is a nutritious feast for the pasture animals that make their home in Scott County. Kentucky thoroughbreds and short-horned cattle love to munch on its tender leaves. And for that, county folks love it—even though the grass can't stand Kentucky's sweltering summers, even though it will go dormant during droughts and at the first gust of winter, and even though it's not from here, not native, and, in fact, not really suited for Kentucky's climate in the first place. Burn it in Wisconsin, if you must, or dump sawdust on it out west. Scott Countians will keep their temperamental grass, which appropriately begins to thrive in these hills around March, just as Billy Hicks is usually leading his boys back to Rupp Arena for another shot at basketball greatness.

But for a long time, grass was just about all the county had—and as lovely as it might be, it simply wasn't enough. By the 1980s, despite Interstate 75 roaring straight through the county on its way to Lexington and Cincinnati, there were few jobs to be had. Employers were leaving Scott County, not coming. Young people who wanted to stay often had one career choice: farming. And, to many, it didn't seem like such a promising choice anymore. Recent dry summers had not only browned out the bluegrass, but destroyed the harvest. Farmers were scrambling, and people here were beginning to worry about the future.

There was anxiety on Main Street. People complained of the unemployed youngsters—"rowdies," they called them—toting ghetto blasters downtown, disturbing residents, harassing pedestrians, and cursing. One local man described the corner of College and Mulberry streets as a pit. "There is going to be a war on that corner," Kenneth Fendley warned. And others complained of empty whiskey bottles being discarded in their yards. School enrollment was down—again—and absenteeism was soaring. "Senior skip day has now become high school skip day," complained James "Buddy" Johnson, the county's director of pupil personnel, "and goes on each Friday for a month."

It was the spring of 1983. And people living in Scott County, population

22,000, could feel it: a way of life was dying, something large and indefinable was changing, and not for the better. County residents didn't even seem to trust each other anymore. That Halloween, Georgetown officials voted to cancel trick-or-treating for the second year in a row—a decision that the local newspaper didn't criticize, but lauded. "The risk of one child being poisoned or harmed," wrote the editors, "is too much of a chance to take." Something needed to change, many believed. What they needed was opportunity, not unlike the one Lexington had enjoyed decades earlier, when IBM built offices there. In other words, what they needed was an act of faith—a miracle. It could be the difference, some people believed, between losing and keeping the family farm.

It was a folly of a wish, like praying for snow in the tropics. The county's unemployment rate that spring was hovering around 9 percent. Job lines had formed outside local businesses. "Look at all these people," marveled Brenda Isaacs, standing in one of those lines, "and tell me things are getting better." No company was moving here. And then, that summer, it got worse.

The problems for Scott County began with one hot day.

BILLY SINGER HAD A BAD FEELING from the start. The tobacco plants in his fields were abnormally small that June—yellowed and eaten, apparently, by flea beetles. Scott County extension agent, Mark Reese, couldn't tell him and other farmers why it was happening. "The answer," Reese reported bleakly, "is no one really knows." Plants were going to have to be sent to a diagnostic lab and studied. Singer would just have to wait—and hope.

The fifty-three-year-old man and fourth-generation Scott Countian was accustomed to living with the whims of nature. He had been farming all his life on land near one of the county's most recognizable houses. By county standards, Singer's three-story mansion, north of downtown, was a pretentious structure with its large bay windows, wood-trimmed balconies, and dome-shaped roof. But to Singer, it was just home: where his mother raised him after his father left them and where, even now, Singer would work, tending to his hogs, cattle, tobacco, and corn, with an old ball cap pulled down over his brow.

Even with the tobacco problems that summer, the father of three figured they'd be all right, just fine. He had battled pests and disease in his fields before.

But just after the county's Fourth of July festivities that summer, temperatures began to rise. One hot, stifling day bled into another. Ninety degrees became the norm, except for the days when the heat reached—and topped—100, baking the earth, the crops, and the people, too.

Singer was now scanning the horizon from his scorched fields, looking for rain clouds. But the clouds did not materialize—for days at first, then weeks. No rain, not a drop in many places. Crops began to shrivel. Scott County tobacco fields soon had "all the lushness of a burnt marshmallow," reported local columnist, Paul F. Power. Fields were burning and fish were dying. Bass, catfish, bluegills, long-eared sunfish, and even one thirty-seven-pound carp were all found dead that summer in the Elkhorn Creek in Scott County, deprived of oxygen, apparently, in the low, stagnant water and decomposing in the heat.

Some blamed the farmers who were pumping the creek water to irrigate their fields. But the county's conservation officer wouldn't hear of it. He could always replace the fish, he figured. The farmers were losing everything. Seventy-five percent of the county's corn crop—gone. Fifty percent of the tobacco—useless. Even the livestock was suffering. Singer's short-horned cattle struggled to find pasture worth eating that summer during a drought that farmers were now calling one of the worst they had ever seen. "This one," said Scott County farmer Randy Rains, "is a fast-approaching disaster."

Folks were told to imagine colder weather. And there were diversions to take their minds off the heat. The county's two-day Bluegrass Tobacco Festival went on as planned that August with its greased-pig and tobacco-spitting competitions. A Miss Burley Leaf beauty queen would be named, and so would a Farmer of the Year. There was joy, to be sure, in watching a Bourbon County man finally take down the slick, 230-pound pig that was chosen for the day's entertainment. But in this heat—this brow-wiping, sun-scorching misery—it would not last.

Rivers and ponds weren't just drying up now; the body count was rising. From Lexington to Paducah, Ashland to Louisville, people, mostly the elderly, were succumbing to the heat, some literally baking to death as temperatures in homes without air-conditioning hit 120 degrees. Some heat victims had been dead for days before neighbors or loved ones found their bodies decomposing.

One victim, inexplicably, died with the furnace on; another was wearing thermal long johns. In Louisville, people tried to convince one ninety-four-year-old woman to leave her oven of a home for a few nights and move to a place with central air. Pearl Price wouldn't listen, though, and people found her the next morning sitting in a chair in her living room—dead, apparently for hours.

State and local officials scrambled to hand out free fans to Kentucky's poorest people, and folks without air-conditioning were told to keep their windows open. But people living in housing projects refused to listen. To open the windows was to increase their chances of being robbed, raped, or murdered. Better to take your chances with the heat, they figured, as bad as that might be. "You're caught betwixt and between," said Mary Adams, a woman who lived alone in Louisville. But that summer Mother Nature was often more deadly than any thug. In one apartment, where a seventy-four-year-old woman refused to open the windows and later died of heat-related causes, the walls were found to be hot to the touch. "The brick," marveled the woman's sister-in-law, Evelyn Trevis, "oh, you could have cooked an egg."

August was oppressive and September hardly better. The heat buckled the roads at times, leaving craters in the asphalt. Soldiers training near Scott County thought they could feel their combat boots sinking into the pavement as they marched. And there were other, less expected, complications. At one outdoor Shakespeare production, organizers worried that the stage lights might actually burn up in the heat and set up a fan to cool the lighting equipment.

And so it went—week after hot, steamy, miserable week. The chances of the heat wave breaking anytime soon, Kentuckians were often told, were absolutely none. And then, in mid-October, it finally happened. Storm clouds gathered over Scott County and let loose with a torrent of water, the likes of which had not been seen in months. Nearly three inches of rain, wet and cold, fell from the sky and seeped into the thirsty soil. Prayers had been answered. But Scott County's economic problems were far from over. People living here were going to need help from an unlikely savior. She was—as the newspapermen enjoyed calling her—an ash-blond beauty queen.

ARTHA LAYNE COLLINS bristled at the description. Beauty queen? Couldn't they just call her Governor? Sure, the blue-eyed, fair-skinned funeral director's daughter had competed in beauty pageants in her youth, being crowned Derby Festival queen before the state's famous horse race in 1959. But those days were behind her now. The unlikely politician—she was a home economics major in college—had won the governor's race in 1983 in a landslide, easily carrying Scott County and every other county in the Bluegrass. Her Republican foe, future baseball Hall of Famer Jim Bunning, was bespectacled and square-jawed—all man. But he was no match for the forty-six-year-old woman still known, by and large, for her sorority girl good looks. "We need that woman," former governor and fellow Democrat Bert Combs told voters that fall. "That pretty woman."

Collins made economic development a top priority and boasted that she created more than 22,000 jobs during her first year in office. But any gains she may have made in 1984 were overshadowed by her losses—and there were many of them. Lawmakers in Frankfort claimed that Collins was weak. Unlike past governors who implemented their agendas by threatening state legislators with political harm, or by buttering them up at college basketball games, Collins was neither confrontational nor especially chummy. In attempting to pass a $324 million tax package to improve education, she chose to meet with lawmakers one on one—a fine idea except that some lawmakers said she didn't even ask for their vote. She was called naïve and unprepared, good at winning elections perhaps, but not skilled at governing. Her tax plan went down in flames. And even the simple things weren't going right. While on a tour of Great Britain in November that year, Collins somehow swallowed a shard of glass, suffered a pierced intestine, required emergency surgery, and was laid up for weeks, unable early on to eat solid food. "After a while," the weary governor told the press from her hospital room in London, "water gets a little old."

In 1985, determined to do better, Collins set her sights on landing a big fish: General Motors' new Saturn factory, projected to employ six thousand people. Nearly every state wanted it. Michigan's governor vowed to best any offer to win the factory. But Collins was undeterred. Traveling to Detroit in February 1985, she made her pitch. It went well. "*Fan*-tastic," she announced

upon returning. And apparently, she was right. The state was among the finalists for the factory. But yet again, Collins fell short. GM chose Tennessee for
the Saturn plant that July at least in part, it was reported, due to concerns over
Kentucky's educational system, where all too often students didn't want to
learn and teachers didn't want to teach. The problems in the schools were laid
bare the year before in an eight-part series in the *Louisville Courier-Journal*,
which documented one case where a teacher crocheted during class and another where a science teacher had the kids just play basketball. But when these
issues earned mention in the national press after GM snubbed Kentucky,
people lashed out, attacking the media and Collins alike, perplexed how they
had lost the prized car factory.

"Is Tennessee a better place to live than Kentucky?" asked Larry Forgy, a
Lexington lawyer as he spoke to a crowd that August. "Does Tennessee have
better people than Kentucky?"

"No," the crowd replied.

"We need a change," Forgy demanded.

Back in Frankfort, Collins's staffers were feeling the pressure now. One
top economic adviser was so stressed that he was developing an ulcer. But even
as the staffers began to sweat, Collins wasn't giving up. Just a few days after
Forgy leveled his criticism at her, the governor received a confidential letter
from the executive vice president of the Toyota Motor Corporation in Japan.
"Dear Ms. Collins," it began, going on to inform her that Toyota was interested
in building a plant in the United States—the company's first in America—and
Kentucky was on the carmaker's list. "We would appreciate your informing us
of the normal incentives afforded to businesses who establish new enterprises in
your state," the letter said, "as well as those which might be offered specifically
to Toyota, if any."

Good news—for once. And this time, the governor was ready. Months
earlier, at the invitation of the Japanese foreign ministry, Collins had embarked
on a two-week visit to Japan that had all the appearances of your typical political junket: dinner with the youngest daughter of the Japanese emperor; interviews with Japanese television stations; tourist stops; and meetings with Japanese
businesses said to be interested in investing in Kentucky. "Especially during

this time of transition in our economy," Collins declared, "Japan offers a promising means of bringing new and better jobs to Kentucky." She then made her itinerary available to the press. "There is a full schedule," she assured reporters.

But the calendar of events did not mention the most important meeting of all: a sit-down with Shigenobu Yamamoto, then vice chairman of Toyota. Some staffers were worried about the meeting, concerned how the governor, as a woman, would play to Japanese executives. The state's head of international economic development, Ted Sauer, who was soon to be nursing that ulcer, recalls wondering whether the Japanese would dismiss her simply because she was wearing sensible pumps.

But inside the Japanese boardrooms, Sauer watched as the exact opposite took place. The Japanese men loved Collins as she worked the room: firm and professional, focused and organized, but feminine, a blonde and still something of a beauty. "A blonde in Japan," Sauer said, "particularly one as pretty as she is, commanded their attention in a room."

Jiro Hashimoto, Kentucky's foreign representative in Japan, had struggled at times in the past two years to get Japanese investors interested in Kentucky—a state that most Japanese equated with fried chicken or horse racing. But the foreign rep had no problems booking meetings for Collins. People wanted to sit down with her. And the meeting with Toyota's Yamamoto, Hashimoto recalled, went especially well. It was clear, he said, that the Toyota executive liked Martha Layne. "Maybe it was love at first sight for him," Hashimoto suggested. "Whenever he went to a party, he told everybody he had met with a beautiful governor from Kentucky. And he was very, very proud to say that."

Collins, it seemed, still knew how to use what she had, when she had to, and now her pageantry was paying off in the form of that letter from Toyota. The company wanted as much as 1,600 acres, ideally on flat land near the interstate and a major airport—and quickly. Toyota wanted construction to begin by the spring of 1986, hoped to be producing Camrys within two years, and planned on employing at least three thousand people, which would instantly make Toyota one of the largest manufacturing employers in the state. The governor's staff quickly identified four potential sites, including one in Collins's native Shelbyville, and Sauer was dispatched to Japan to hand-deliver written answers to Toyota's many questions. The feeling was, the Japanese were going to like Shelbyville—and if not Shelbyville, perhaps Winchester.

But Toyota set its sights on a different location: a swath of farmland in a place called Scott County. They visited the county—once in October and again in November. Yes, the county was the frontrunner now: twenty-five minutes north of Lexington, right off I-75, with plenty of land for an enormous factory—perfect. There was just one problem. The state had no claim to 1,600 acres there, no land to give. Nor could Collins, under state law, buy the land outright and give it to Toyota. So a corporation secured options to the necessary land. Railroad land agents were called in to do the job, going door to door in the county, asking people for the rights to their property but telling them little else. Secrecy was key. If word got out that Toyota was behind the requests—not the railroad—land prices could soar. So quietly, in early November 1985, a list was created, documenting the land that the state needed to acquire. The first property on that list, plot 57-07, was owned by a farmer and county native.

His name was Billy Singer.

SINGER WAS NO FOOL. The moment representatives showed up on his doorstep asking for 136 acres of his family's long-held land north of Georgetown, he figured Toyota was behind it. Reporters had been writing about the possibility for weeks. And when officials began to pressure Singer to sell—and sell now—the farmer went public, telling reporters exactly what was happening. He said he wouldn't deal with a third party and demanded to speak directly with Toyota. He said the state was trying to isolate landowners. "If they can isolate you," he warned, "they can get the land cheaper." Both he and his wife, Marilyn, were of the same mind: They weren't selling. The land had been in Singer's family for two centuries, and he wasn't going to part with it now. Certainly not for Martha Layne Collins; he'd supported Jim Bunning. And not for Toyota; he drove Chevy trucks. He was old enough to remember Pearl Harbor.

The phone in his house was ringing now, with some begging Singer to sell and a few asking him not to. Suddenly, it seemed, everything hinged on Billy Singer. Toyota was ready to announce its decision. It had narrowed down the finalists for the new plant to Tennessee and Kentucky—yet again. The carmaker's president, Shoichiro Toyoda, was in the United States, riding around New York City in a silver limousine, increasing speculation that a deal might come down at any moment. And here were the reporters, outside the farmer's house, chasing scraps of information. They even interviewed the Singers' twelve-year-old son. Mostly, though, they just waited.

The morning Billy Singer's defiant comments first hit the newspaper he went to his farm as usual to tend to his hogs, but he didn't stay there long. Soon, local officials had him sitting in a room downtown on Main Street, where after a while, under pressure, Singer began to think about the money—he stood to make close to $1 million for his land. And he started to consider all the recent troubles, too: the drought and the lost crops, the heat and his dying way of life. Maybe selling was the right thing to do, best for the county and best for him. Maybe he couldn't afford not to sell. "Quite simply, I'm broke," he admitted finally.

Billy Singer agreed to sign away the acreage, but his wife, Marilyn, refused. Believing that they were being bamboozled, she decided she'd had enough. "They say it's now or never," Marilyn declared. "Maybe it's never. I'm not doing anything tonight." She left the bank downtown to watch her son's middle school basketball game. Toyota could wait another day. But attorneys quickly found a loophole. If they had Billy, they determined, they didn't need Marilyn after all. Toyota's path into the county had been cleared and the next day Billy Singer held court in his living room, speaking with reporters and watching the news on television. "Why should I stand in the way of something," he said, "that will be worth a billion dollars to the state of Kentucky?"

Three days later, on a cold December day, Toyota made it official: The Japanese company was coming to the Bluegrass, and many Scott Countians celebrated the news. Overnight, it was the biggest thing to ever happen here. And the national media soon descended upon Lexington for a bilingual press conference. Inside a packed ballroom at the Hyatt Regency, Scott County's judge executive welcomed the company by speaking in Japanese. Toyoda himself was there and received not one, but two standing ovations. People snatched up buttons that read, KENTUCKY . . . OH, WHAT A FEELING. And then civic leaders and politicos all retired to a high-end restaurant for a lunch of baked scrod, roast beef, and chicken Florentine. Everyone got gifts: Toyota letter openers for the important people; dashboard compasses for the reporters. Then, with the baubles in hand, it was off to Scott County for photo-ops with Martha Layne and her new Japanese friends. "I don't know about all this automobile making," said Bill Beckett, one curious farmer who came out in the rain to witness the moment. "But I know that farming is the pits."

The next day, Collins returned to the county for a pep rally in the high school gymnasium. The county kids didn't just greet Collins by playing "My Old Kentucky Home" and the Toyota jingle—"Oh, what a feeling!" Carried away by the moment, they played the school's fight song, too. A minister prayed over the congregation and local officials showered the governor with presents: a gift basket, a painting, the key to the city of Georgetown. "This is a community on the move," Collins told the crowd from the stage. "You already have the state's number one ranked basketball team, and now we're moving ahead."

The crowd roared. Six times the people gave Collins standing ovations before she hopped aboard a helicopter and flitted off to Louisville. Nearly two thousand people were estimated to have been there—roughly 10 percent of the county's population at the time. But one notable resident wasn't among them: Billy Singer. He had taken the money, but couldn't bear to watch the celebration.

"Will the town be wide-open tonight?" asked Thomas Risk, a customer at the Scott County Pharmacy on Main Street that week. "Will people be carryin' on all night, going up and down the street, drinking beer and all?"

Probably not came the reply from Gary Perry, the pharmacy's co-owner. After all, it was Wednesday.

"It's prayer meetin' night, Tom."

BUT CHANGES WERE COMING—of this, the people were sure— and questions were coming, too. The honeymoon lasted all of a week before people began attacking Collins for the $125-million incentive package the state had crafted to lure Toyota to Kentucky. Labor unions were livid. They knew Toyota wouldn't accept them at the plant. Others mocked the deal. One registered nurse sarcastically asked the state for $2 million in incentives so she could buy some land and build a first-class nursing home—her own dream. "I do realize I am under a handicap," Beth E. Page added. "I am a taxpayer and an American citizen." And some World War II veterans took it personally, staging anti-Toyota protests and making it clear that the foreigners weren't welcome. JAPS, GO HOME, read one bumper sticker. Martha Layne, it was said, was the best governor that Japan had ever had, and she had been played like a sucker.

The xenophobia was perhaps to be expected. As recently as the late 1970s, the Ku Klux Klan met openly in Kentucky, assembling in pastures not far from Scott County, condemning blacks, homosexuals, and Jews. Thousands attended the rallies at times, many in white hoods and robes. Refreshments— soft drinks and hot dogs—were served as if the events were church festivals, and the press sometimes covered them like any other political rally, quoting grand dragons and imperial wizards—at least until the hooded men slipped away to meet in private. At one such private meeting inside a barn, a man guarded the entryway armed with an automatic rifle while a forty-six-foot, kerosene-soaked wooden cross burned and crackled in the hot summer darkness. "Too bad they used kerosene," observed one man as the flames licked the wood. "The best thing I ever saw to light a cross with is diesel fuel."

In the months before Toyota announced it was coming to Kentucky, such racism persisted. In Louisville that summer, with the drought looming, an unidentified assailant firebombed a black family's home in a predominantly white neighborhood, tossing a flammable substance through an open window in the night. A police spokesman said it was a rare occurrence, at least in part because very few black families dared to move into that neighborhood. "I never thought that something like this could happen in 1985," said Robert Marshall, the young black homeowner. "My wife doesn't ever want to come back." And it was easy to understand why. The day after the fire, someone posted a prominent sign on a tree near the scorched home. The message: "Join the Klan."

Many were still doing just that. Klan members across the state served on police forces at times in the 1980s. A few debated whether such membership was even cause for dismissal and others used personal prejudices as justification not to work. In April 1985, eight months before the Toyota announcement, a thirty-seven-year-old sanitation supervisor in Louisville claimed he had suffered from "recurring depression," in part, because he was forced to work with black sanitation workers. Testimony showed that the supervisor did indeed have a difficult time accepting black people. And ultimately, the state Worker's Compensation Board found in his favor, awarding him a "100 percent permanent occupational disability" and ordering that "exhaustive efforts be made to return the plaintiff to gainful employment, in an all-white setting."

Such people could not have been pleased with all the attention—and money—that Collins was now lavishing on the Japanese. Others filed suit against the state, trying to stop the Toyota project on constitutional or environmental grounds. One plaintiff's attorney even had the gall to depose the governor herself, trying to get Collins to admit that the proposed incentives, like making improvements to U.S. 62 to accommodate more traffic near the car factory, only benefited Toyota—not anyone else.

"It serves the people of Kentucky," Collins insisted.

"How?" the attorney shot back. "There is an existing U.S. 62, is there not?"

"That's an insult," Collins's lawyer objected.

"Total harassment," Collins agreed. "I can't believe these people."

But one by one, judges dismissed the court challenges. Up went the plant and in came the job applications by the thousands. With the assembly-line jobs came prosperity—or at least some measure of it. Car-parts suppliers moved in, offering still more jobs. And then came the chain restaurants, strip malls, and big-box stores. It was what people had wanted. And yet soon, some began longing for the past, for a time when they knew their neighbors and still said hello to each other on Main Street. It was hard to get a smile out of people today. Too many outsiders, folks complained, too many Yankees. These days, Billy Singer worried that he had made the wrong decision all those years ago.

"Today, I feel like Judas, only with inflation," said Singer, now eighty but still farming on what was left of his family's land. "Judas sold out Christ for thirty pieces of silver. I sold out Scott County for one million dollars."

BUT THERE IS ONE POINT on which most everyone can agree. Without Toyota's sprawling plant, the county probably would not have grown like it has in the last two decades, doubling in size to about 45,000 people.

There would have been no need for a new high school, no money for a new sparkling gymnasium with a seating capacity of 2,500, and little chance that Billy Hicks would have quit his coaching job at Corbin High, 100 miles south. Hicks could have just stayed there, which would have been just fine with his high school sweetheart, and now wife, Betsy Hicks.

In May 1994, with Scott County school administrators angling to hire Hicks—he was Coach of the Year in Kentucky that season—Billy drove Betsy to Georgetown one weekend to show her around. The tour went fine, but Betsy didn't want to leave Corbin and move there. The greatest thing that had ever happened there was the governor's announcement that Toyota was coming. This was no place for basketball, Billy's wife told him, no place for him, no place to be moving his family, not now. Sitting in their car outside the sad, little gym, soon to be replaced by a bigger one, Betsy Hicks begged her husband not to take the coaching job, crying at times to make her point.

But Billy, as usual, was not listening.

"I know what I'm doing," he said.

OFFENSE
① Carolina Break
- Down screen for
② Thumbs Up
③ 4 out Motion
④ Double screens
baseline
Keys
Rebound
Rebound
hard in
Play hard & physical
easy baskets
11
ball out
BUMP

COAL DUST AND DREAMS

YOU'VE GOT TO MOVE!" he shouted. *"MOVE!"*

Hicks was angry even before he set foot in the gymnasium for practice the day after Scott County lost its season opener to Ballard. He didn't like to hold on to losses, to let them to fester inside of him. But sometimes, it was hard to let go. This was one of those times.

It wasn't just that his boys had lost; it was how they had lost. Standing around. Being outhustled. Taking a lead in the fourth quarter only to give it away. Hicks was in his office early the next morning to watch the game on tape and it was even worse than he had feared. Scott County had outrebounded Ballard, committed fewer turnovers, and made twice as many free throws. But Ballard fought and scrapped—while the county so often stood and watched. By Hicks's count, Ballard had won thirteen of the game's fifteen loose balls—an unacceptable margin for any coach, but especially for one who had built a reputation for assembling tough teams. He told the boys that he had been calling around that day, asking other coaches what people were saying about this particular team. The answer, Hicks said, wasn't pleasant. "Everybody says y'all are soft," he announced. And he was inclined to agree with that assessment. "We are without a doubt," he told the boys, "the softest basketball team to ever be ranked in the top ten in the state of Kentucky."

The season had begun a mere twenty-four hours earlier with the loftiest of expectations: an eleventh region title for Scott County, a trip to Rupp Arena, a state championship. And they had a legitimate chance at all of it, especially that trip to Rupp Arena. For months, when the boys huddled up after practice, their fingers reaching for the rafters, they called out its name: *"One, two, three . . . RUPP!"* But Hicks was going to put an end to that right now. Rupp Arena? *Really?* At this point, it seemed, the boys would be lucky to win a game. "Let's just

quit saying that," he told the boys. "I don't even want hear that Rupp crap no
more."

Crap . . .

Cursing was common in high school locker rooms and sideline huddles.
Some coaches made a craft out of it, somehow turning obscenities into artistry.
But Hicks wasn't one of them. As a rule, he never swore. It was always *daggone
it, dadburnit, gosh almighty.* And so, as the word slipped past his mustache and
echoed down the court—*crap*—the boys duly noted it.

This was serious.

"We're gonna holler 'defense' or something like that," Hicks continued.
"Rupp is something down the road. We gotta work for that. I guarantee you, the
way we're playing right now, we ain't going to Rupp Arena. You're crazy if you
think we can win the eleventh region without playing defense, guys, and not
being tough.

"We don't even play hard, guys," he added. "We are *soft. Gaaaawwwwsh
almighty.*"

Hicks asked them to start changing those habits today and sent them onto
the practice court for a series of 4-on-4 drills. With a whistle in one hand and the
day's practice schedule rolled up in the other, he was pacing now, up and down
the court, shouting, begging, pleading.

"Let's be tough right here!" he bellowed.

"Trap, trap, trap!"

"Run hard, run hard! . . . C'mon! . . . *Move!*"

And then, to Dakotah personally, some advice. Dakotah was a great outside shooter with a mind for the game, but a lumbering giant who was simply
not designed for Hicks's swarming style of defense. To compete, Dakotah was
not only going to have to be smarter, but he had to work harder than everyone
else. And Hicks pulled the kid aside now to remind him of that fact once more.

"Dakotah," Hicks said, "you gotta work your tail off."

"Yes, sir." He nodded.

"You gotta work your butt off."

"Yes, sir," he said again.

But speed was almost impossible to teach and the old habits that many of the boys had acquired elsewhere—before they'd moved to the county, transfer-ring in to play here—were hard to break. And soon enough that afternoon, they were making the same mistakes in practice that they'd made the night before against Ballard: not keeping their butts to the baseline; following their man, not the ball; standing around or failing to collapse to the help side when the other team flicked a pass across the court. Hicks slapped a hand against his forehead, disgusted.

"You guys take a lap," he muttered finally. *"Run!"*

The boys made a loop around the gym, with more than a few of them taking their time doing it. But Hicks didn't let them off easy. "You hurt?" he barked, singling out one of the loafing boys. "You hurt?" he said again. "Take another lap around. Hurry. You're holding this team up. You're *holding this team up!*"

Scott County was just 0-1 on the year. It was early December, three weeks before Christmas and almost three months before the outcomes of the games really mattered. There were at least thirty games left on the schedule, and yet Hicks and his fellow Scott County coaches were sick already, troubled by what they had seen—or rather, had not seen—the night before. "I had to pray to go to sleep last night," admitted assistant coach and Scott County graduate Tim Glenn. "Lord," he said, "don't let me hold on to it."

But Billy Hicks wasn't holding on to anything anymore. He was just con-fused. He had made a career of getting the most out of his players: 729 wins, 8 trips to Rupp Arena, 18 victories in the state tournament—a couple shy of the record—2 state titles, and counting. Opposing coaches always marveled at how hard Hicks's teams played, pressing, pushing, fighting, and winning, always winning—even when they didn't always have the God-given talent to do so.

This year, though, they had the players. They were supposed to win. And yet, already, they weren't. Hicks was lost; in thirty years of coaching, he had never had so much talent and so few answers at the same time. "What else can I do," he asked his assistants after practice that night, "to teach them how to play?"

THE NAME WAS JUST BILLY, not William. Billy Wayne to his mama. And he had learned the game of basketball on the other end of the state: down a hollow deep in eastern Kentucky, hemmed in by the mountains, just across the Clover Fork River, in a remote Appalachian outpost called Ages Bottom. This was Harlan County, just a few miles from the Virginia border, on the outskirts of America—the backwoods of the backwoods where the trees climbed up the lonely ridges and visitors were both rare and, often, unwelcome among the moonshiners and mountaineers. There was just one road into Ages, one road out, and one reason primarily for being there: thick, black seams of rich American coal.

Pioneers had noted the presence of coal here from the moment they arrived. So plentiful was it, coal could be found lying on the ground in large chunks, or just beneath the surface, twelve inches thick in some places. It was, as one early explorer described it, "the Coal Land." And as soon as the railroads could get here, hacking through the mountains, people became convinced that something grand was about to happen in these hills. "This section of Kentucky," declared one confident writer in the London, Kentucky, *Mountain Echo* in 1888, "is destined at no distant date to become the richest part of the state."

Coal camps sprung up, built around the mines, for the mines, and people were soon lining up to live in the small, batten-board shacks. The homes usually weren't much—sometimes just three rooms, lit by a single lightbulb dangling from the ceiling. But the money in the mines was good. By the mid-1920s, a coal miner could make seven dollars a day—a magnificent sum—and word was spreading of the riches that could be made in Kentucky, if a man was willing to work underground, often on his hands and knees, in squat, damp, inky-black tunnels that sometimes collapsed without warning.

In Harlan County in the 1920s, with seventy-two coal mining operations in full swing—more operations than almost any other county in the state—the accident reports began to pile up, detailing in dry, dispassionate accounts snapped femurs, crushed pelvises, and inescapable deaths. ACCIDENT NUMBER 288—A. B. McKnight, tippleman: "Killed by being run over by railroad cars . . . Widow remarried." ACCIDENT NUMBER 664—Alex Roman, miner: "Injured was loading coal in place by himself and slate fell on him. Dead when found." Men were injured in coal "heaves" or "bumps" as the mountain shifted beneath their feet, resettling its weight as coal was pulled from its belly. The bumps were impossible to predict and random rockfalls were just as hard to avoid. Huge slabs of slate—as big as pickup trucks at times and just as heavy—could peel away from the mountain and crush miners unlucky enough to be working below. Sometimes the remains of the dead were so badly mangled, so flattened by the falling rock, that other miners were forced to scrape them up with shovels. Other times men were killed in rockfalls even when they dodged the worst of it.

In September 1922, poor Briscoe Washington managed for the most part to avoid a falling five-by-six-foot chunk of slate as he shoveled coal on the job in Harlan County. But as Washington toppled to the ground, his shovel handle caught him in the throat, jerking his head backward, and breaking his neck at the base of his skull. "I am convinced," the safety inspector said afterward, "that this man would not have been killed by the fall of slate, or even seriously injured, if it had not been for the position of the shovel handle which struck his neck." Still, the inspector managed to find the dead miner at fault in the accident—acquitting the mine company of any wrongdoing. "I attach all blame for the accident to Washington himself," the inspector concluded, going on to recommend that compensation to his loved ones be reduced due to Washington's "gross negligence and disobedience." It was Washington, after all, who had chosen to stand in that particular spot, with that particular shovel, angled just so. "No one," the inspector said, "could help him."

And then there were the mass deaths and the pulverizing methane gas explosions, which burned miners beyond recognition, entombed them underground, and literally shook communities, sending coal cars, mules, and human body parts spewing out of the mouth of the mine. At times, in the wake of such explosions, rescuers were forced to remove the dead animals first, so bad was the stench of decaying flesh. And, of course, the miners noticed the concern for the animals, acutely aware of their place in the hierarchy. Some miners believed that even the mules outranked them. In Harlan County, there was a saying about it. Get a man killed; hire a man. Get a mule killed; buy a mule.

With such threats looming over them, miners lived like soot-covered rabbits in underground tunnels, always ready to jump. Still, desperate people wanted in, and Orie Hicks, a young widower and father of two, was one of them. A farmer's son raised in Tennessee, Hicks came to eastern Kentucky with his motherless children in the wake of the Great Depression, seeking a job in the mines and, if possible, a good woman to help him raise his kids. Orie quickly found both, marrying a coal-miner's widow, Maggie, landing a job with the mines, and building a small three-bedroom house in Ages Bottom. From the cinder-block porch at the house, Orie could see the earth rolling away, down to the river below, before sweeping back up into the mountains on the other side, and Maggie Hicks—working as hard as any man—did everything she could to make it a home, growing beans and potatoes in the weak soil outside in order to feed her family. Few in Ages had a garden like hers. But the family's timing—building this tenuous life in Harlan County—hardly could have been worse.

By the 1930s, Harlan County's boom years were finished, and so were the good wages. With oil and electricity on the rise, coal prices were tumbling. And with mines in other states able to ship their coal at lower rates, Kentucky companies were especially troubled. In the span of five years, miners in places like Harlan County saw their wages almost cut in half. Panicked now, coal miners took up arms, raided local stores for food, and prepared for war against the coal companies. "All we need to settle this thing and mighty quick," said one miner, "is about six hundred more guns and we'd wipe 'em off the earth." But by May 1931, they were tired of waiting for the arsenal and gunned down three deputies in Evarts, near Ages. Down came the indictments, in came the National Guard, and then, for a while, begrudgingly, a sort of peace took hold.

But the poverty persisted. Soon, in eastern Kentucky, officials were trying to explain how it was possible to feed a family of five on just $8.83 a week—difficult at best and a starvation diet at worst. Children were dying now, malnourished and plagued by disease, and reporters who traveled from elsewhere to report on the crisis were often threatened, harassed, followed, or worse. "When you go to Harlan County, you are not welcome," wrote Boris Israel in *The New Republic* at the time. "It is not a place for tourists. The fewer sights you see there, the better they will like you. The fewer people you speak to, the safer you will be." Israel knew about the dangers firsthand. While reporting in Harlan County in 1931, he was driven into the mountains by deputies and given a warning: "Never show your face around here again." Then, for good measure, as Israel was running down the mountain, heading for the highway as he'd been told to do, a deputy pulled out his gun and began shooting, striking him in the leg. Perhaps, Israel should have listened to the deputy who had given him this warning earlier that same day: "If I was you, I wouldn't let the sun set on me in Harlan County."

But amid the violence and the hunger, the poverty and the tragedy, Orie Hicks was convinced he could make a life here. Blue-eyed with big ears and a long slope of a nose, Orie was a small man—well under six feet tall. Even his bride, Maggie, was about as tall as he was. Yet Orie's stature belied his strength—and his will. He might have been small, but he could outwork anyone, and he often did just that. He and Maggie built that house into the mountainside. They had seven children together—four boys and three girls, plus the two from Orie's first marriage—and raised them right, taking them to Ages Baptist Church on Wednesdays and Sundays. When falling rocks killed neighbors in the mines in one of those unpredictable coal bumps, Orie was there to console the families. When falling rocks struck him, injuring his back and laying him up for weeks, Orie did not despair, but instead struck out on his own, starting a hauling company. Unable—or unwilling—to go back into the mines, Orie would haul coal for years, delivering it across the county. People knew him, most respected him, and his boys would follow him, taking work inside the mines.

All of the boys, that is, except one.

ORCE HIM WIDE!" Billy Hicks was yelling. "Force him wide! Stay with it, stay with it. Be tough, be tough!"

The Scott County players were sweating now, gasping for breath, and wiping their faces with their red-mesh practice jerseys. On days between basketball games, practices were supposed to be light, but not today, not with the way they had played the night before. Hicks was pushing them, pairing them up against each other, one on one. Scores would be kept and the losers would run, and no one wanted to run. "This practice right here, it's no joke," Chad Jackson whispered during a brief water break. "It's a no-joke practice right here." His teammates nodded while Hicks kept coaching, trying to get past the Ballard loss, get better, get tougher. Twenty minutes after telling the boys they were soft, he turned around and told them he refused to believe it. He refused to believe that they couldn't guard people, despite all the immediate evidence to the contrary. "Guys," he said, "there's a lot of playing time on this basketball team for somebody who wants to step up and play defense, who shows they can hustle and get after people."

No one hustled more than Orie Hicks's youngest son, Billy Wayne. Quiet as a child, Billy made his noise on a ragged patch of dirt in Ages that the kids called the basketball court. Local vandals, drunk on moonshine, were always tearing it up, it seemed, knocking down the goals. But Billy and his brothers would simply rebuild them. Go up into the hills, cut down a couple of poplar trees, build backboards out of plywood, coat them with mud-flap rubber or mine belts, and hopefully rustle up a rim from somewhere. In the rain, they got muddy. In the winter, they warmed their basketball by a fire so it would still bounce. Billy would be in sixth grade before he ever wore a uniform or played inside a gym. It was here, in the dirt, where he learned to shoot a layup, dive for loose balls, crash the plywood boards, and fight, always fight, to win.

By the fall of 1966 when Billy enrolled at Evarts High School, the boy, tall and lean, had managed to craft a beautiful jump shot. With the ball cupped in his large right hand and guided by his left, his eyes focused on the rim and his knees bent just enough to pull his left heel off the floor, Billy Hicks was a shooter and soon to be a starter in the Evarts gold and blue. The small mountain school wasn't very good at basketball. The Wildcats had taken home just one district title in their entire history and had never made it to the state tournament. But with Billy pushing six foot four by the time he was a senior, Evarts could compete. In three of the first four games of the 1969–70 season, Billy scored more than thirty points. And on it went: twenty-nine against Pineville, twenty-three versus Cumberland, thirty-five over Lone Jack. Evarts was 6-0 before the Wildcats' lack of talent and depth caught up with them. They finished the season 12-9 and failed, once more, to win the region—just another mediocre year in a history of mediocre years.

But people here wouldn't soon forget the kid who wore number 14. Bob Howard, one of Billy's former teammates, can still recall the night the Evarts coach asked him to keep a log of the team's shot selection—an easy job. But Howard, sitting on the bench, got distracted as Billy got hot, hitting shot after shot.

Suddenly, the clipboard didn't matter. Howard couldn't take his eyes off Billy whose shots kept finding the bottom of the net. As Howard would recall decades later, still with awe in his voice, "Everything he threw at the basket was a'fallin'."

That season, Billy took home all-Cumberland Valley Conference honors, earned honorable mention all-state, and was recruited to play basketball at North Greenville Junior College in Tigerville, South Carolina—exciting for Billy, but not exactly cause for celebration in the Hicks' house. College, to Orie, didn't make much sense. His other boys had gone away on athletic scholarships, only to leave school and work in the mines. And basketball, in particular, was just plain folly. Better to be productive, Orie believed, better to be working. The aging coal man didn't understand why Billy would want to play ball at North Greenville or, a year later, at Wofford College, a four-year school in hot, flat Spartanburg. Dropping Billy off at Wofford in the fall of 1971, Orie Hicks told his youngest son that he'd have a job waiting for him at the mine in a few weeks. Billy Hicks was never going to make it at college.

But the young man was determined to prove his father wrong and began approaching the game of basketball like a trapped miner shoveling for daylight. He'd do anything to make the team better, sprawling across the floor for loose balls, scrapping to win every rebound, and practicing long after the coaches had gone home. His college teammates would find him in the gym at all hours of the day and night. Billy might doze off in an early-morning Bible history class, but it was only because he'd been practicing past midnight the night before. At times, he called out his teammates for not joining him in the gym, for not caring as much as he did. And, like any self-respecting Harlan boy, Billy never backed down from a fight. While playing two-on-two in the gym during his freshman year at North Greenville, one of Billy's teammates, a larger man, elbowed him, then shoved him. Billy responded by rearing back and punching his teammate square in the face. "It sounded like a shotgun went off when he hit him," recalled Billy's teammate Javon Robinson, who was on the floor at the time of the fight. "Blood went everywhere; it was a bloody mess. He broke his nose right on the spot. His nose was crooked, right on the spot."

Basketball, at this point, was more than just a game; it was a way to stay out of the mines and away from Harlan County, where work was harder to find by the day. Coal miners, 12,500 strong in the county in 1950, numbered just 2,600 by the time Billy graduated from high school. A massive migration was taking place. People, especially young folks, were leaving the Kentucky coal-fields in droves. "If I was a young man, I'd get me a hoe and hoe corn, before I'd go in there," said one old coal miner around that time.

That man, Hiram Maggard, had spent forty-seven years mining coal and he conceded there was some money to be made in the job. But there was no real wealth in it, no true riches. For miners, there were only a few promises in life: that they'd get hurt or killed, walk away with lungs so black that they would struggle to breathe, or legs so stiff that they would limp to walk. No, Maggard said, advising the younger generation. "I wouldn't go. I'd hunt me something else."

Even Orie Hicks was taking that advice now. A friend had been elected sheriff and Orie, a longtime volunteer on the force, had been asked to serve as chief deputy. He stopped hauling coal and started serving arrest warrants and collaring angry drunks. Maggie and the kids didn't like the idea of it. Orie was fifty-eight now, his back hunched over and his small body breaking down. But still, few would mess with him. Even at this age, he could disarm a drunk wielding a .38-caliber pistol. He proved it once—and that was enough for most people. If he showed up at your door with a warrant, you went with him—simple as that.

But late one night in October 1972, with Billy about to begin his junior season at Wofford, Orie Hicks was met with resistance while attempting to arrest two men who had escaped custody at a car wreck earlier in the day. Back home that night, near the top of a hill in a place called Cemetery Hollow, the men sat in their dining room, drinking beer, and laughing about how they had taken flight, using chisels to break their handcuffs after slipping out of the deputy's squad car.

There was at least one gun in the room: a .22-caliber automatic rifle. And a shotgun wasn't far away, either. They figured the sheriff might send people to find them. And they were right about that. Just before eleven o'clock that night, two sheriff's deputies and two Evarts city police officers made their way down the dirt road leading up to the house. While two of the officers waited outside, expecting the men might try to escape yet again, another lawman and Orie Hicks, armed with a .38-caliber revolver, went to the door near the kitchen.

What happened next isn't clear. By one account, Hicks knocked on the door and declared, "You're under arrest." By another, Hicks and the other officer just busted right in. The only thing agreed upon was that if anyone was talking, it was Orie Hicks, saying something to the effect of, "Hold it . . . Everybody hold it."

A moment passed, a beat, maybe less. At least one of the men inside stood up from the table, confronting Hicks and the other officer. "And then," a sixteen-year-old eyewitness told police, "all the guns started shooting . . . It sounded like the whole world was shooting."

To dodge the gunfire, some hid in a bedroom and others in a backroom. One man even dove into a closet and covered himself with old clothes. But there was nowhere for Orie Hicks to go. He went down just inside the doorway, crumpling to the floor, faceup near the stove in the kitchen. He had been shot three times in the chest, the bullets slicing through his rib cage from right to left, and there was little that the other officers could do to help him. After the shoot-out had stopped, one of them knelt down beside Orie and felt for a pulse.

There wasn't one. Orie Hicks was dead.

BILLY CAME HOME FOR THE FUNERAL, but returned to Wofford a few days later, speaking little about his father's death even with close friends. He just went back to work, back to basketball. He'd end his playing career two years later, averaging nine points and five rebounds a game, and unlike many college graduates Hicks knew exactly what he wanted to do. He returned to Harlan County and began coaching basketball: middle school, then high school at his alma mater, Evarts. He was 10-16 his first season—the only losing season he'd ever have as a coach. And his career almost ended there. In a 1978 Christmas tournament, Hicks permitted a player who was still enrolled at another high school to suit up for Evarts. It was an innocent mistake, he said after the fact, and offered to resign if it would help the school keep its eligibility. "I would do anything reasonable," he announced, "if it would help the kids." The school district took him up on the offer, Hicks left basketball, briefly lost his way, and considered the previously unthinkable: going to work full-time in the mines. But his wife and his mother came down against it, and Evarts soon rehired him. From now on, there would be no more losing seasons.

He led the Wildcats to the district title in 1983—Evarts' second title ever—in his second year back as coach, pulling off upset after stunning upset, with a team that had little business winning anything. The boys simply believed in their coach: a Harlan kid who proved it was possible to do something other than mine coal. To these kids, he wasn't just a coach; he was Billy Hicks, a six-foot-four tower of mustached inspiration stalking the sidelines and demanding intensity. "You wanted to play for the man," recalled Kerry Vanover, one of the stars on the '83 Evarts squad who would become an army infantryman after high school and serve in Iraq during Desert Storm, before winding up disabled. "It was probably the best time in my life."

Hicks was moving up now, to larger schools. He coached the Harlan Green Dragons, then the Corbin Redhounds. In 1991, he led the Redhounds to their first state tournament in four decades: toppling their mountain nemesis, Clay County, in the regional semifinals; staging a frantic thirteen-point comeback in the last five minutes of the regional finals to earn that trip to Rupp; and shocking just about everyone along the way, including himself.

"Is this real?" he asked.

It was—and it was only just the beginning. After being persuaded to coach at Scott County in 1994, Hicks would make trips to Rupp Arena so often, so routinely, that students would lay claim to the arena itself. "Rupp," said one hand-painted sign, "is our house." Losses became so rare that Hicks almost made it look easy. People didn't realize that he was in the gym at 7 A.M. and sometimes at midnight, too. During basketball season, he was so focused on the games that it was hard for him to think about anything else. On a couple of occasions, he locked the team's student manager in the laundry room and went home, forgetting that the boy was inside. Inevitably, when doing the laundry himself, he'd throw the red and white jerseys into the washing machine together, turning the whites a fine shade of pink. And his office—always cluttered with mounds of trophies, plaques, game tapes, and letters from college coaches recruiting his boys—would grow messier as the season marched on. One year, students found mice living in his desk drawers, most likely attracted to his stash of snack cakes, available at any hour to any student who wanted one.

He couldn't be bothered to tidy up, though. He was too focused on the next game, which, almost surely, he'd win, or the next practice, which he had planned down to the minute. The focus was always individual improvement—not scripted plays or the next opponent. He wanted each boy to have a ball in his hand for as many hours of the day as possible. If they didn't have a ball, he figured, they couldn't be really learning the game, and college coaches noticed the difference. The first time Dale Brown, the longtime coach at Louisiana State University, saw one of Hicks's practices in the 1990s, he was mesmerized by the long-armed man whirling across the floor. It was clear to Brown that Hicks just wanted to work and wasn't looking to impress anybody. While some high school coaches seem to take great care in how they dress—sporting fine warm-up suits in the team's colors—Hicks is apt to wear the same Scott County pullover day after day. And he isn't bashful about sending visiting college coaches home with odd, culinary souvenirs. Once, when North Carolina head coach Roy Williams visited the county on a recruiting trip, Hicks proudly retrieved two large Ziploc bags full of chili and barbecue from his office bathroom and handed the soggy, plastic sacks of homemade food to a mystified Williams. "Eat it after practice tomorrow," Hicks said, bidding North Carolina's famous coach adieu with a smile.

Yet despite the victories and the praise, some people liked to dismiss Billy Hicks, calling him on at least one occasion "Hillbilly Hicks." His thick Appalachian accent made him an easy target. He stuttered and tended to lose his train of thought when excited, and he was often excited. At times, his players didn't even understand what he was saying and they certainly didn't comprehend the hardships that their coach had overcome long ago in Harlan County, a foreign place, so close yet so far away, that most of the boys had never visited. "He makes it seem like he lived in a cave," Dakotah told his teammates once. "Like he had the hardest life—*ever*. Like he lived in a freakin' cave."

One day in the gym, upon finding a tattered relic of this mysterious past—an old team photograph, circa 1984, when Hicks was still coaching in Harlan—the Scott County boys gazed wide-eyed at the image, which was fading, wrinkled, and several years older than they were.

"He looks so young right there," Dakotah said.

"He *is* young," Austin replied.

"And he looks like he's seven feet tall," Dakotah continued.

"He's still rocking the 'stache, though," Ge'Lawn noted.

"Was he born with his 'stache?" Dakotah said. "That's what I want to know."

Together, these qualities—the folksy accent and the stuttering, the throwback mustache and the sideline antics—made Hicks a rich source of comedy among his players over the years. And so it was with this team, this year. When one of the boys was late getting on the bus, thereby holding up the entire squad, Dakotah, Ge'Lawn, or one of the other players, channeling Billy, mustered up their best mountain twang and whispered, "That's just *saw-rry*." When there was time to kill on a long bus ride to some nowhere town, the players would summon the coach's stutter and mock each other. *"Will–Will–Will,"* they would say, "you gotta get tough, honey." And when Halloween came that fall, one of the players took the joke even further: He dressed up as Billy Hicks, wearing a paste-on mustache and red sport coat, the coach's signature fashion accessory for championship games. Then, the player posed for photographs, holding his hands on his head and gesticulating wildly.

Everyone had a good laugh at that one—except Hicks, of course. If he was aware of the comedic role he played for the boys at times, he never let on. But even if he did know, Hicks probably wouldn't have cared as much as the boys feared. For starters, nothing brought the team together like making fun of their coach. Some boys' families had money and some struggled to pay their bills. Some boys were popular at school and some weren't. And some started games while others rode the bench, creating natural rifts in a locker room filled with roiling pools of young testosterone. But each of the boys had weathered a storm or two in the eye of Billy's wrath. When they had nothing else in common, when there was nothing else to talk about in the fourth hour of a half-day road trip from hell, there was always that. There was always Billy.

But there was something else, too—another reason why Hicks probably wouldn't have minded the jokes. And it was one that escaped the grasp of his young players. If there was one thing that was true about Billy Hicks, it was this: The man didn't waste his time worrying about what other people thought of him. He just wanted to coach, just wanted to win, just wanted to help his boys get better. Those who knew him best said Hicks would do anything for his players.

Once, he almost fought another coach who'd dared to curse at a Scott

County player. Hicks got in the man's face, essentially daring him to fight, if he was such a tough guy. It was summer ball, meaningless basketball, really, and the referees stood back, seemingly inclined to see if Hicks might pummel the other coach right there in front of everyone.

Cooler heads prevailed. "It's awful to do that in front of kids," Hicks said later. But still, after the game, he tried to track down the other coach to have a few words. "I wanted to break his neck," Hicks admitted, and few doubted that he had the wherewithal to do so. As assistant coach Tim Glenn pointed out whenever retelling the story later, the other coach had made a serious miscalculation about Billy Hicks that day: "He must not have known he was from Harlan."

PRACTICE WAS OVER NOW. No more drills, no more running. No more need for hollering or talking about the painful Ballard loss anymore. That was finished. As Hicks stood before the team inside the locker room, quieter now and pacing in his khakis, he asked the boys to let it go. "We can't do a thing about Ballard," he said, "except learn from that."

A new season—the rest of the season—started tomorrow. Maybe this time, they'd be ready. Maybe this time they'd remember who they were, where they lived, and what it meant to play for Billy Hicks. The opponent didn't matter. What mattered, Hicks told them now, was the name on the front of their own jerseys. "Let's get our minds focused on Scott County, guys," he implored them. "Let's get ready to go tomorrow."

"Yes, sir," Dakotah replied, answering for the team.

"Awww-right," Hicks answered. "Let's go."

He left the locker room. The boys huddled up and began to clap. Now was the time for chanting . . . *One, two, three, RUPP!* But forbidden from saying that anymore, the boys were suddenly lost. They stopped clapping and stared at each other, not sure what to say next.

There was a long, awkward silence, followed by weary, halfhearted bickering. Then, the boys turned to Dakotah, the tallest of the bunch. Surely, Dakotah Euton had the answer.

PRISONER OF THE HYPE MACHINE

THE INSULTS RAINED DOWN on the boy from the rafters, seemingly cascading off his hulking shoulders.

"Eu-ton's ug–ly!"

Clap, clap, clap–clap–clap!

"Eu-ton's ug–ly!"

Clap, clap, clap–clap–clap!

Dakotah Euton never let on that he could hear the fans taunting him. But he did. The fans were loud and often incessant, though the chants themselves were rarely creative. Dakotah was ugly, according to the masses. He was a slow, no-good white boy, which was a funny thing to say since most of the kids doing the taunting were slow and white themselves. And then, when they ran out of ways to attack Dakotah's looks or his game, they assaulted his character. They called him a failure, a reject, and worse. *"Pussy!"* one fan shouted during one game at Henry Clay High School in Lexington. But Dakotah never shouted back. He'd been raised to be tougher than that—raised to hear the shouting and let it go. On some level, he was even accustomed to it. His father, Clay, had been shouting at Dakotah on basketball courts for years, pushing to make his son better. Even Clay had called Dakotah a pussy from time to time, up in his face, hollering. *Don't play like a little pussy out there.*

That word infuriated Dakotah's mother. She often wished Clay would find a way to coach their son that didn't involve yelling or cursing. But at least Clay was rooting for Dakotah. Many others were not. By the fall of his senior year, Dakotah Euton was one of the best-known athletes in the state, in any sport, at any level, and he was one of the most reviled, too. He had let people down. He had failed University of Kentucky basketball fans, disappointing them by not being as good as the Internet scouting sites had once projected him to be. And now, instead of being a Kentucky schoolboy legend, like Rex Chapman, Richie Farmer, or other basketball stars who had come before him, Dakotah Euton was a symbol of everything wrong with the sport: kids who transferred to other schools, parents who meddled, coaches who broke the rules, and a system that placed boys on pedestals at a young age only to push them down and watch them fall.

But what did the critics know about Dakotah Euton? Did they see him now, when the rest of his teammates were still asleep, climbing out of bed at 7 A.M. and settling in behind the wheel of his dark green GMC Yukon with the wooden cross dangling from the rearview mirror? Did they hear him listening to country music as he sliced through the frozen farmland and pulled into the parking lot outside the middle school gymnasium? Most teachers weren't even at school at this hour. But here was Dakotah, bed-headed and crusty-eyed, sleepwalking into the gym through the crisp, still morning air.

Once inside, he laced up his size-14 Adidas high-tops in silence and went to work. He executed a set of one-handed bank shots from the right, then another set from the left. He did a set of hook shots from the right, then another set from the left. He backed into the basket, posting up imaginary foes, practiced turnaround jump shots from the top of the key, and then walked to the free throw line, toeing the stripe, palming the ball, bouncing it once, and letting it fly. Scott County's big man was up on his tippy-toes now, his right arm extended skyward as the ball sailed through the net.

Swish.

Again and again, he nailed his free throws. Again and again, he hit his bank shots. Then, wiping the sweat from his face with his shirt, he pulled outside, swinging around the three-point arc. Set shot—three. Set shot—three. Like bombshells raining down from the heavens, the ball kept flying and falling, its rotation perfect and its aim almost always true.

Four in a row.

Miss.

Seven in a row.

Miss.

Nine in a row.

Rattle out, miss.

Middle school kids, who'd been dropped off early by working parents to be babysat in the gym before first bell, were watching now. Over their book bags and cell phones, the children eyed Dakotah and whispered among themselves. To them, he was no boy. He was a man with chest hair, thick arms, and a beard. He was Dakotah Euton. He had it all—almost everything, anyway.

"It doesn't make a difference if someone's here shooting with him or not," noted Karen Yeager, the woman charged with babysitting the youngsters, as she peered at Dakotah over the book she was reading one morning.

"He's always here. He's a marvel."

THE BIBLE, THICK AND WHITE, could be found just inside the front door of the Euton family home, displayed for everyone to see. It was a showcase item, but it was also more. Dakotah and his parents often prayed together and attended church in a large, contemporary building atop a hill on Route 25 not far from the county line. When at the church, listening to the spirit band singing on stage—*"My shame is taken away,"* went one song. *"My pain is healed in His name. I believe. I believe . . ."*—Clay Euton would sometimes close his eyes and wave his hands in the air. In that building, he said, he could feel the Holy Spirit—a wonderful and indescribable sensation. "You can feel the Spirit move," Clay said, "and feel the Holy Ghost. You've got to feel that."

Dakotah had felt it at a young age. At ten, he was baptized in the muddy waters of the Ohio River, standing in a white T-shirt next to his father, not far from their home at the time near Ashland, 130 miles east of Scott County. The flagging steel town, population 21,000, was just across the river from Ohio and only a few miles from West Virginia. But Dakotah was pure Kentucky, fishing and hunting squirrels, praying and playing basketball—and it was clear from a young age that Dakotah was particularly good at the latter. He was barely riding a bicycle when he learned to shoot left-handed layups at the local YMCA and was soon tearing up the AAU circuit with his father coaching, yelling and, sometimes, cursing.

Clay Euton, in normal, everyday life, would sooner hit himself in the face with a hammer than utter an obscenity. But on the basketball court he forgot himself. Clay shattered clipboards in anger, argued with referees, made his players cry, got tossed from games, and on at least one occasion even physically grappled with a fellow coach on his own bench. As the two coaches wrestled on the sideline, with a third attempting to break up the fight, Dakotah and his teammates just kept playing. They had witnessed such madness before. "Scary," was the word that Austin Flannery, one of Clay's former players, used to describe his coach's antics. "It was like he was crazy, pretty much."

Once, at an AAU game in Henderson, Kentucky, referees got so tired of Clay Euton that they called the police on him. Another time, while coaching at a tournament at Disney World, Clay was kicked out of the resort's 5,000-seat arena. "I get so intense," Clay said once. "I just get tore up, man. I just gotta yell." It was his own personal Jekyll-and-Hyde act. On the one hand, he was Clay Euton, the affable Christian and loving father. On the other hand, he was Clay Euton, the maniac coach. And Dakotah, being his son, often bore the brunt of Clay's red-hot intensity for the game. "Oh my God. He would smack Dakotah," recalled Kyle Tackett, who coached beside Clay in those early years. "There were numerous times he would smack Dakotah. He would get in Dakotah's face and just call him everything you could think of."

But Dakotah never returned fire. He could take it. He loved his father. Dakotah wanted to win for Clay almost as much as he wanted to win for himself. And thanks in no small part to Clay, the boy became a child basketball star. By the seventh and eighth grades, most middle school kids were of little competition to Dakotah. So he played with the big boys, joining the team at Rose Hill Christian, a high school in Ashland, exploiting a quirk in the state rules that allows seventh- and eighth-grade boys to play with high school varsity squads.

It was no small achievement for Dakotah; NBA star O. J. Mayo had once played ball for the Rose Hill Royals. And Dakotah, even at this tender age, fit in just fine. He was already six foot three, pushing six-foot-four. The only way to beat Dakotah even then was to bully the child-athlete, push the towering thirteen-year-old around, and many teams tried to do just that. "My God, he took a beating," recalled Tim Fraley, Rose Hill's coach at the time. "I've seen kids hit him in the ribs, knock him to the floor. Especially early in games, they'd foul him as hard as they could foul him to intimidate him. Just dirty."

Still, Dakotah thrived. As an eighth grader, he nailed a three-point shot with eleven seconds left to secure a 61–60 victory against regional rival Boyd County and end Rose Hill's thirty-four-game losing streak against the hated Lions. And then came the growth spurt. By the time Dakotah had finished his freshman year, he was six foot eight, about 215 pounds, scoring over thirty points a game at times, and expected to keep getting taller. The college coaches were circling now, inquiring about the boy who played basketball like a man. Both Duke and Florida were reported to be interested in offering Dakotah a scholarship. But so was the new head basketball coach at the University of Kentucky, a forty-seven-year-old Texan hired just that April whom people in the Bluegrass liked to refer to by his full name—a rhythmic name that rolled off the tongue: Billy Clyde Gillispie.

GILLISPIE WAS A BACHELOR, childless and divorced, a man so focused on basketball that he often had no time for breakfast—a Dr Pepper would do—and no tolerance for lackadaisical play. Gillispie was so hard on his players, demanded so much, that his own mother once said that she could not play for him. But it was difficult to argue with the results of a man who coached high school basketball for nearly a decade and logged twelve years of servitude as a college assistant before landing his first head-coaching job at the University of Texas El Paso in 2002. That first season, the UTEP Miners were a putrid 6-24. But the following season, Gillispie flipped that record around. UTEP went 24-8 and made the NCAA tournament—its first in twelve years. Gillispie won conference coach of the year honors that spring and departed for Texas A&M, another basketball wasteland in Texas football country. The Aggies were coming off a 7-21 season where they had failed to win a single conference game in the Big 12. But once again, Gillispie performed a magic trick. The Aggies went 21-10 that first year under their new coach, making Gillispie the first Division I coach to boast the most improved record in consecutive seasons. He led the Aggies to the NIT that year—A&M's first postseason appearance in more than a decade—and guided them to the NCAA tournament the next two seasons, reaching the Sweet 16 in 2007 before losing by one point to Memphis. The team finished the season ranked No. 9 in the country. Gillispie's stock had never been higher. The coach, known for bristling at the media, had become something of a media darling—even *The New York Times* profiled Gillispie that spring—and now a new school was calling to inquire about his services: the University of Kentucky.

This was no rebuilding project, no hardwood wasteland. UK hadn't missed a NCAA tournament in almost two decades. The Wildcats were only nine years removed from their last NCAA championship. They were a double-overtime loss away from reaching the Final Four just two years earlier and they still had a champion in coach Tubby Smith. His career record at UK was 263-83. He had never won fewer than 22 games in a season in Lexington and he had taken home five Southeastern Conference regular season titles.

But Big Blue Nation was growing restless that winter, believing that merely competing for national championships and blue-chip recruits wasn't enough. The Cats needed to win them and, lately, they had not. UK had not reached a Final Four since 1998—that was disappointing. The school had lost four consecutive games to Vanderbilt—*Vandy?*—that was unacceptable. The Wildcats had even been snubbed in recent years by homegrown basketball stars who decided to play for out-of-state colleges—that was unheard of. And now, by 2007, fans were grousing about other matters, large and small: Smith's failure to win close games that season, the current team's lack of fundamentals and its propensity for stupid mistakes, like shot-clock violations. By the end of February, UK fans were livid. Smith's team, critics shouted, was boring, inconsistent, erratic, soft. "The number of fans may be thinning by the day," declared *Lexington Herald-Leader* sports columnist John Clay. "More and more people tell me they've quit watching the Cats."

Their record at the time was 19-9—a successful season just about anywhere else. But not here. Kentucky fans couldn't get over the fact that they had lost to Vanderbilt in Rupp Arena, the Commodores' second consecutive victory in the building. They fumed that they couldn't beat ranked opponents—not even Alabama, ranked No. 25—and they complained that the Cats themselves were unranked for much of the season. They were just another pretty good basketball team. Fans were booing—often during victories, at home—and the players had taken notice. "I would like to say it doesn't hurt at all," Kentucky guard Joe Crawford said at the time of all the booing. "But sometimes it does get to you."

UK managed to make the NCAA tournament that March, of course. But the Wildcats were a No. 8 seed—the very definition of average. And once again, the Cats made an early exit, losing in the second round to Kansas as the Jayhawks cruised to a twelve-point victory. Everyone knew Tubby Smith was in trouble now, and a few tried to save him. Even Kansas' coach Bill Self came to Smith's defense, explaining that winning 76 percent of your games over the course of a decade while playing one of the toughest schedules in the nation, as Tubby had done, was an incredible achievement to be celebrated, not denigrated. But, Self conceded, "I don't know the climate at Kentucky."

Indeed, he did not. Tubby Smith did, however. Even before his Wildcats had lost to Kansas in the tournament, fans were arguing that Tubby was the worst coach that UK had ever had and they were calling on athletic director Mitch Barnhart to fire the man who had allowed the program to "slip," as one put it, "from greatness and invincibility to mediocrity." Tubby Smith might be a nice guy, argued frustrated fan Troy Thompson, but could the nice guy recruit? Could the nice guy coach well late in a game or motivate his players to win? The answer, Thompson believed, was no.

"Barnhart needs to wake up and not let Kentucky basketball slip any further," he concluded in a blistering letter to the *Lexington Herald-Leader* that March. "It may be a politically incorrect thing to say, but it is time for the 'nice guy' to go before we finish last!"

Reporters were waiting now for word from the university about Tubby Smith's future, but it was Tubby who made the first move. Opting to control his own destiny—to jump before he was potentially pushed off the ledge—Smith announced that he was leaving Kentucky to coach the considerably less-heralded Golden Gophers at the University of Minnesota. People close to the program speculated that Smith was tired of being so successful and so criticized at the same time, so unwanted. UK fans could second-guess someone else now. Tubby Smith was gone, already off to Minneapolis, where two thousand fans stood in the Gophers' arena chanting his name—"I feel the love already," Tubby told the crowd—while back in the Bluegrass, in came Smith's replacement, the hard-working Texan, Billy Clyde Gillispie.

For Kentucky fans, it was love at first sight. Some five thousand people came out for an afternoon pep rally in Memorial Coliseum on Good Friday, two days before Easter, to welcome Gillispie to Lexington. Students skipped calculus or political science class to be there and some parents in the crowd brought young children along to witness the moment. WE LOVE YOU ALREADY, said one sign in the crowd. GREAT FRIDAY, said another, OUR SAVIOR BILLY G. As Barnhart, the school's athletic director, introduced Gillispie for the first time, the lights went out in the coliseum. Spotlights circled and the crowd roared, blue pom-poms waving, as Gillispie walked onto the stage, smiling in a sharp, blue Kentucky pullover.

He couldn't get over the size of the greeting party. "Apparently," he joked, "we don't have class today. Is that right?" People just needed to be there: to hear Gillispie call it an honor to stand before the fans or to watch him get choked up talking about what it meant to him to go from the hinterlands of Texas to the heart of the Bluegrass, "to be standing at the place," Gillispie said, "where they basically invented basketball.

"I'm a big baby," Gillispie added, placing a hand over his heart and fighting back tears. "I'll get choked up." And now, the crowd roared even louder, loving him even more, chanting his name.

"Bill-eeee!"

"Bill-eeee!"

"Bill-eeee!"

It was a full-on revival now. "Hallelujah!" shouted one fan. "Hallelujah!" Gillispie wasn't just a passionate coach, Barnhart declared, but also a tenacious recruiter who averaged eight thousand text messages a month to potential recruits. "He's got the fastest thumbs in America," the school's AD joked. And Gillispie quickly began to use them, targeting child athletes.

One on his list was a rising star in Ashland named Dakotah Euton. Dakotah had just turned sixteen that March and still had three years of high school basketball left to play, but his age didn't matter. Gillispie wanted Dakotah. One of his assistants was calling Clay Euton three or four times a week— almost daily, Clay told people—to check in on his son. Dakotah was invited that June to play in Gillispie's elite camp and soon thereafter the entire Euton family was invited to sit down with the new coach in Lexington.

Dakotah was nervous about meeting Gillispie and prayed about it. "When we meet," he asked the Lord, "please don't let me be nervous." But there was no reason for anxiety. Gillispie offered Dakotah a scholarship. And after more prayer—"God, let the Holy Spirit speak to my heart"—Dakotah accepted the offer, verbally committing to play for the Wildcats starting in the 2010–11 season, nearly three and a half years down the road. It was big news in Lexington—an indication that Gillispie was already cleaning up Tubby Smith's mess, landing local talent, and returning UK to national dominance. Dakotah had to be proof of that, many believed, and the message boards on the Internet lit up with praise for the new boy wonder destined for Wildcat blue.

"Welcome, young man."

"YESSSSS!!!!!"

"What is his height and weight?"

"He's listed at 6-8 currently. He will probably be top 25."

"Hoopsreport.com has him rated #12."

"He may be top 5 at his position by his senior year."

"Plus, he's from Kentucky."

"Go Big Blue! Billy Clyde rides again!!"

But the accolades would soon be replaced by a hot and simmering angst. With Wildcat fans poring over Dakotah's box scores the following winter and at times traveling hundreds of miles to watch him play in person, Dakotah struggled to meet expectations. In one of his first high school games as a future Wildcat that December, he turned in a weak nine-point performance in a loss. And even when he dropped twenty or thirty points that winter leading Rose Hill to victory, some UK fan, somewhere, was sure to find fault in his game. Dakotah was too slow, fans believed. "The slowest player on the court," one complained. He was no blue-chipper, fans alleged, no star. "I hate to say it, but he is not ever going to be UK material." All of Dakotah's intangibles, all of those qualities that UK fans had once praised about the boy—his work ethic, his Kentucky roots, his Christian values, and even that perfect jump shot—suddenly didn't matter anymore. Dakotah could invoke the Holy Spirit all he wanted. There was no winning over these people. "I know he is a great kid," one fan griped, "but he doesn't have the talent to play at UK."

Meanwhile, down in Lexington, 120 miles west of Ashland, the man who had accidentally anointed Dakotah a basketball messiah was only making matters worse. Billy Gillispie guided the Wildcats to a win over Central Arkansas in his UK debut that November, but the Cats lost the next game—a home game, in Rupp—to Gardner-Webb University, enrollment four thousand, from the bustling basketball hub of Boiling Springs, North Carolina. The Cats had been favored to win by 25-½ points. But instead the game went the other way. Gardner-Webb jumped out to a 14–0 lead, never allowed the Cats to draw closer than eight points in the second half, thumping UK, 84–68, in one of the most stunning losses in the history of Rupp Arena. The Kentucky players said afterward that it felt like they lost by forty. And the pounding was far from over. Before Christmas that year, the University of Alabama-Birmingham beat the Cats, and so did Houston—embarrassing losses for the program, the state, Gillispie, everyone. With the 83–69 loss to Houston, Gillispie's Wildcats had dropped to 4-5—one of the worst starts in Kentucky history. The fact that Gillispie's team managed to rally that season and slip into the NCAA tournament—as a No. 11 seed—hardly seemed to matter. The Cats had finished 18-13, failing to win twenty games for the first time since 1990. The storyline was simple: They stunk. But maybe next year would be better. Maybe the problems that season were still Tubby Smith's fault. It was Tubby's players, after all, out there on the floor. Or maybe it was injuries. Yes, injuries must explain why the Cats fell short that season. It was better to believe such things than to believe they'd hired the wrong man for the job.

But Dakotah wouldn't get any such benefit of the doubt. In fact, for him, life was about to get much harder. That February, while Gillispie was struggling to prove himself in Lexington, Dakotah's father got word that his engineering office was closing in Ashland. Clay found a new job in Lexington. The Eutons were leaving Ashland and had opted to purchase a home in a quiet subdivision in rural Scott County. They were moving from the remote reaches of Appalachia to the backyard of Big Blue Nation. Every rabid Kentucky fan would now have a chance to see Dakotah play in person, suiting up for two-time state champion Billy Hicks in the Scott County red and white.

Or would they? Dakotah had hardly settled in at Scott County High

School that April when people began asking questions about his eligibility to play next season and his sudden move to the county. Why did the Eutons move here, of all places? And why did two of Dakotah's friends, Rose Hill star Chad Jackson and AAU teammate Austin Flannery, choose to do the same thing at the very same time? In the span of one month that spring, all three sophomores enrolled at Scott County.

It was a curious coincidence and one that would not go unnoticed given Dakotah's stardom. There would need to be an investigation. There would need to be hearings. Sworn oaths would have to be given and taken. Dakotah, in effect, was on trial now. He was not just a failure anymore, but a *transfer*—a dirty word in high school athletics. True or not, the perception was out there: Dakotah Euton was a cheater.

FRANK HOWATT IS NOT A BIG MAN. If he were to play basketball, the Scott County High School principal would be lucky to be a guard. He's built like a wisp: five foot nine and 160 pounds, bespectacled with reddish-orange hair. He is a former US Marine, a left-handed sniper who was trained to kill people from a distance of 2,000 meters with a M40A1 rifle, and even now, at forty-six, he wears that orange hair nearly military-short. But Howatt, with his welcoming smile, doesn't exude a tough-guy vibe. There's no need to salute in his office, where on most days you can find Howatt sitting at his desk, his sleeves rolled up, eating a hurried lunch out of Tupperware before being summoned, with great haste, to meet with a teacher or alerted, via handheld radio, about a crisis in the halls. Many days, to be honest, Howatt doesn't even get a chance to finish his lunch, such as it is, and he certainly didn't have the time to deal with the e-mail that he found waiting for him in his inbox in early May 2008. It was from a Scott County mother, furious that Dakotah, Chad, and Austin had moved here and wishing to inform Howatt that Charles Eddie Doan, the basketball team's aging equipment manager, had recruited them.

"Over the last three days we've had two basketball players tell us about how Billy Hicks is recruiting these kids that is coming in from Rose Hill," the mother's e-mail began. "They both told us that Charles Eddie travels to do the recruiting. That Charles Eddie went to Rose Hill several times to talk to the players. That everything is handled through the booster of basketball so Billy Hicks does not get caught doing it himself."

It was a preposterous allegation; Howatt knew this. Charles Eddie loved Scott County basketball—it was true. He was like a de facto mascot, always in the gym, and always cheering with a 2007 state championship ring on his finger. He came to so many practices that Hicks finally gave him a job. The white-haired county native happily did the boys' laundry day in and day out, washing their sweaty clothes just for the privilege of being near the team. But Charles Eddie Doan was no smooth operator, no slick backroom dealmaker or shadow agent. Few people around the gym took him seriously, least of all the Rose Hill boys, who often mocked Charles Eddie to his face and openly laughed at the accusation that he had recruited them to play for Scott County.

"Can you imagine that cat rolling up to Rose Hill?" Dakotah said one day, sitting in the locker room with Charles Eddie standing right there.

"No," Chad replied.

"I wouldn't have come here," Dakotah said.

"No way," Chad agreed.

"We would have gone to Lexington Catholic. For sure."

Everyone got in on the joke, including Charles Eddie himself. "Took you to lunch, didn't I?" he'd tell Dakotah and Chad.

"Three times," Chad would reply, without missing a beat.

But as crazy as the allegation was, Frank Howatt was not laughing. He didn't need this headache. He was in the minority in Scott County in that he didn't much care about basketball. Sure, he liked a winning season as much as anyone and wanted his students to succeed in whatever they did. But Howatt, an adopted child raised in New Jersey, had never played high school sports, much less Kentucky basketball. He didn't understand the hysterics of the fans and couldn't wrap his mind around the size of the crowds that came to watch the boys play. What interested him most was education—helping kids learn—and he wondered at times if other people felt the same. Too often in recent years, he had been dragged into some debate over high school sports, not education. "You might have a kid who's just academically not getting it done, and you'll never hear from the parents," Howatt said. "But, oh my God, bench them? And they're writing the newspapers about how out of control things are."

Now, with the basketball players moving in, Howatt was about to get an education himself in what it meant to be truly "out of control." The transfers—Dakotah, Chad, and Austin—were the talk of the school that spring. Even students who didn't care about basketball knew who they were and why they were there. Jazzy Shoup—a bubbly, straight-A student whose general outlook on life would later be summed up in the high school yearbook with three simple words: *Peace. Hope. Love.*—knew who the boys were before they got there. "I thought they were, like, instantly known," Shoup recalled. "They sat with a whole bunch of people; they already knew a bunch of people. Everyone knew their names."

Cheerleaders and softball players—popular girls, mostly—befriended the new students. But many others did not. By moving in, the boys, especially Dakotah and Chad, were sure to steal someone's starting spot on the basketball team the following season. Kids who had dreamed for years of playing for Billy Hicks, toiling in obscurity on the junior varsity team, quit the squad in disgust. Instead of practicing every day now, one former player, Matt Bayer, six foot five, got a job as a host at the Ruby Tuesday near the interstate, making eight dollars an hour. At least now he had gas money, Bayer figured, trying to look on the bright side. But it was quite a fall to be showing the basketball players to their tables instead of playing with them. And some people planned to actively root against Dakotah and the other transfers, or at least not care whether they won or lost. Students said the transfers weren't "home boys." Parents accused the school of recruiting, a forbidden act in high school athletics. And people, by and large, blamed the coach. "If I was coaching today, I would not play Billy Hicks," said one retired state champion coach. "I would not play Scott County."

Hicks maintained he had done nothing wrong. And on this point, Dakotah's father defended him. Schools had indeed attempted to recruit Dakotah, Clay Euton said. Two elite basketball high schools had offered Clay a coaching job, he said, if he chose to move his son into their districts. "But not one time," Clay said, "did Billy or any of his assistants call me."

It didn't matter, though. The perception was out there. And people were angry about it. For Dakotah, Chad, and Austin, however, there were even bigger problems. The bylaws of the Kentucky High School Athletic Association bar any student from changing schools to gain an athletic advantage. And it seemed, to many, that this was exactly what Dakotah and his friends had done when they moved to Scott County. Clay Euton, perhaps not surprisingly, couldn't keep his mouth shut about it, and that only made things worse. A month before the Eutons closed on their house in Scott County, Clay talked publicly about Scott County's great gym—"We looked at the facilities," he noted—the talented teammates that Dakotah would have there, and the tough schedule that Billy Hicks's teams always played. Then, as if trying to heap more pressure on his son, he listed Dakotah's goals: becoming Kentucky's Mr. Basketball and winning a state championship. The implication, many believed, was that Dakotah would have a better chance at winning in Scott County. Thus, the family's move.

Clay Euton soon realized that he should have kept quiet. But it was too late. His quotes were making headlines across the state and KHSAA officials were reading them just like everyone else. With all the publicity surrounding the transfers, and now Clay's ill-advised comments, state officials were seemingly backed into a corner and they made their ruling: The boys were declared ineligible to play their junior seasons in the fall.

But the boys' families appealed, appearing before a hearing officer in Lexington, taking an oath before God, and then declaring that there was no collusion and no recruiting, either. The families of each boy had moved for plausible reasons: the Eutons for Clay's new job, the Flannerys to shorten the commute time for Austin's father, and the Jacksons so that Chad's older brother, Chase, might get out of Ashland, where he had run afoul of the law. Dakotah and Austin's parents had even purchased homes in the county, clearly satisfying the state's change of residence requirement. And that was more than some other transfers ever did, the boys' families argued. They believed their children were being targeted because they were talented athletes, big names. Roughly 70 percent of athletes who transferred in Kentucky won eligibility—and usually without any fuss or publicity whatsoever. Why not *their* kids? The bottom line was simple, testified Joy Berry, Chad's mother: They had not violated any rules.

"So no one at Scott County, or on behalf of Scott County, ever contacted you?" an investigator asked her under questioning.

"No, sir," Chad's mother replied. "Absolutely not."

"And you never contacted anyone there?"

"No, sir," she said again. "Absolutely not."

She and the other players' parents argued that their decision to move to Scott County was based on what they felt was best for their children, nothing more—a point that any parent can appreciate. Still, many people had their doubts—and quietly, Frank Howatt, the boys' new principal, was one of them. He was convinced that the high school had done nothing wrong. Toyota, Howatt said, hadn't paid to attract the talented players, as some opposing fans liked to allege, and school officials hadn't recruited the boys, either. But something, Howatt believed, was suspicious about the new players moving in together, given that they were teammates elsewhere and good friends. "It's just awfully highly unlikely—isn't it?—that there was no collusion ahead of time," he said privately.

At the hearings in Lexington, however, sitting next to the players and their families, Howatt made no mention of his unproven suspicions to the hearing officer considering the boys' appeals. The parents did most of the talking. This was their fight—and they prevailed. Dakotah, Chad, and Austin each earned back their eligibility to play basketball by the unanimous vote of the state Board of Control and celebrated by sending out a flurry of text messages to their friends.

"Now," said Chad, "it's time to get to work."

DAKOTAH AGREED. Even with the eligibility distractions looming over him, the boy had never stopped working. But Dakotah's junior year in Scott County played out almost exactly like his sophomore year in Ashland— only now Kentucky fans had even more reason to turn against him. He hadn't grown much since verbally committing to UK eighteen months earlier. He was still listed at six foot eight, only heavier, coming at 236 pounds, which made him appear slower. It was now clear to many that Dakotah Euton was never going to reach the athletic heights that many had projected for him. It had all been a mirage from the start. As one scout put it, Dakotah had become a prisoner of the hype machine. Built up to be something he was not, something he could maybe never be, Dakotah would have been better off if he had never been touted at all, never been courted or discovered. "If he hadn't committed to Kentucky, people would be talking about how good he is. That's the truth," said Happy Osborne, the basketball coach at Georgetown College, a small NAIA school in Scott County. But instead, it seemed, Dakotah could do nothing right anymore—and neither could the coach who recruited him.

Billy Gillispie's second season at UK was more troubled than his first. It began with a 111–103 loss, at home in Rupp, to the Virginia Military Institute, a team picked to finish seventh in its own conference. Like the loss to Gardner-Webb the year before, Kentucky's defeat at the hands of the VMI Keydets wasn't just disappointing. It was shocking—one of the worst losses in the great program's grand history. And once more, it would get worse. Conference rivals Louisiana State, South Carolina, and lowly Georgia all beat the Cats in Rupp that season. No. 1–ranked North Carolina crushed UK, exposing just how far the Cats had fallen. At one point, a freshman point guard defied Gillispie's request to reenter a game. And just when the Cats seemed to find a groove—they briefly cracked the Top 25 rankings that season—they crashed, losing six of nine down the stretch and missing the NCAA tournament for the first time since 1991.

It didn't matter that the Cats had finished with a winning record: 22-14. The frustration in Lexington was obvious. In late January that season, Gillispie snapped at an ESPN sideline reporter, Jeannine Edwards, during a halftime interview when asked what he was going to do to get a key player more involved in the game. "That's really a bad question," he replied. And two weeks later, being interviewed by the same reporter at a different game, Gillispie managed to top himself. First, he told Edwards that he hadn't heard her question. Then, looking around the arena like a man seeking a quick exit, he facetiously suggested that Edwards must be the expert on UK's game plan—not him. "You know more about it than I do, obviously."

Edwards laughed off the jabs, all charm. But Kentucky fans did not. Gillispie, many fans believed now, wasn't just a bad coach; he was a jerk, a poor ambassador for the program, a mistake. And unable to appease themselves by venting their anger at the coach himself, the fans turned on his prized recruit, Dakotah, seventeen years old now, but still just a boy. On came the ugly chants. On came the pressure. The stress was getting to everyone now. After one particularly mediocre performance by Dakotah that winter, Clay exploded, shouting at his son in their Scott County home. Dakotah had seen his father angry plenty of times, but this, he said later, was one of the worst. Before the night was over, Clay would tell Dakotah to cut his long blond hair and shave his ever-present goatee. If he was going to play like a freshman, he should look like a freshman. With the whole world seemingly piling on Dakotah, here was his father piling on, too. "I was hurt," Dakotah said later, "and a little bit scared." But he did as his father asked, allowing his mother to cut his hair and then shaving off the goatee.

Clay would repent. That night he went to Dakotah's bedroom, apologized for his outburst, and told his son it would never happen again. He prayed with Dakotah and then, for good measure, Clay shaved his own goatee. They were in this together now: a father and son, going down with Gillispie who would be fired by Kentucky just a few weeks later at the end of March. Sports commentators outside the state and fellow college coaches couldn't believe it. Gillispie's record was 40-27 in two years—not stellar, but not terrible, either. "You all need to settle down," LSU coach Trent Johnson told the Kentucky press just before Gillispie was dismissed. "This thing has become a monster."

Yet none of it mattered. Kentucky's coach was gone.

"Billy, do you think you were treated fairly?" a reporter asked Gillispie at his final press conference that week as the now ex-coach stood in the klieg lights in a light-blue golf shirt, kneading his hands and wearing a weary half-smile.

"Excuse me?" Gillispie replied.

"Do you think you were treated fairly?"

"It makes no difference," Gillispie answered. As he had pointed out in his opening remarks just a minute earlier, "I'm really looking forward to moving on."

Dakotah's verbal commitment to Kentucky now meant absolutely nothing. He had no scholarship, no guaranteed future, and little chance of playing for Gillispie's replacement, John Calipari, or almost any other big-time coach. The coaches angling to land Dakotah now were usually from less-acclaimed programs like Eastern Kentucky and Akron. And months later, shortly before his senior season began that winter, Dakotah made up his mind. He wanted out. He didn't want to play in his home state anymore. He was going to Akron.

That November, on national signing day—the first day that basketball players can officially sign letters of intent with colleges—many high schools threw parties for students who had landed scholarships. For these boys, there would be balloons and speeches, photographs and even cakes shaped like basketballs. But for Dakotah, the day passed like almost any other. He went home on his lunch break, signed the letter committing to Akron, faxed it from his church, and then came back to school. "It's no big deal," Dakotah said. "Well, it is a big deal," he added, "but everybody already knows about it." There were no balloons and no cakes. The boy, who had once been embraced by Kentucky fans, then devoured, picked clean, and tossed aside like so much trash, didn't even get recognition from some of his classmates, who had apparently never heard of this strange and exotic place called Akron.

"Where's that?" a classmate asked Dakotah one day that week in the computer lab.

Dakotah replied without even looking up.

"It's in Ohio," he said.

BUT THE SCOTT COUNTY COACHES appreciated him for what he was—not what he was not. His lack of speed frustrated Hicks at times. The coach was always hollering at Dakotah to move and execute his traps faster. "Dakotah," he said once that fall, "are you playing defense today or what?" But Hicks also knew that on this team of transfers, he needed a leader—a peer who could bring the team together when he could not—and Dakotah was his man for the job.

"Just keep setting an example," he told Dakotah. "Try to be the first one out here every day. If somebody gets down, get 'em up. If somebody starts complaining about a bad call, pick 'em up. A leader has to do these things and, boy, it's tough. You're gonna have to make sacrifices."

"Yes, sir."

"And nobody gets any layups."

"Yes, sir."

"I get on your butt some," Hicks admitted to Dakotah. "But you have thick skin and I'm just trying to make you better."

"Yes, sir."

Now, just one game into the season, Dakotah decided it was time to step up. He called a players-only meeting in the locker room that Saturday night before the Cardinals' second game against Franklin-Simpson High School. A few players were late. "Where's Chad?" Dakotah kept asking. But finally everyone showed up, took seats on a U-shaped bench, and turned to Dakotah, who was sitting on the concrete floor in front of them, unshaven in a T-shirt and sweatpants. It was cold in the locker room, but Dakotah was already sweating as he unfolded a piece of paper and began to speak from his handwritten notes.

"I don't think we did a good job against Ballard," he began. "And not just one or two people—everybody."

He called out the coaches for not scripting enough plays on offense. But the players, Dakotah said, were also at fault for failing to communicate on defense, for not passing the ball enough, and for playing like individuals, not a team. "Does anybody feel like we actually played as a team?" he asked now. "Because if you do, you're an idiot."

No one replied. Dakotah kept going.

"I can take a loss if a team is better than us," he continued. "But the reason we got beat is they wanted to win more than we did. And that cannot happen anymore. No more teams can beat us just wanting it more than us. That's just sickening. That's just sickening to have the talent, and then to get beat off pure heart—that's just ridiculous."

For once, it seemed, everyone agreed. Ge'Lawn said they needed to communicate. "Talk," he said simply—and not wait until the second quarter, he suggested, to really start playing.

"I got something to add on that," Chad said, speaking up now, too. "We just gotta come out and play hard because talent alone is not gonna win no ball games."

They were all nodding their heads now when one of the reserves, Terrence Roberts, found the courage to chime in as well. Maybe the problem, Terrence suggested, was that the boys were playing afraid. That's what it looked like to him, anyway, watching from the end of the bench in the Ballard game.

"Y'all," Terrence said, "were as cold as hell."

Terrence suggested that the boys try to relax out there and Dakotah agreed. Relax, but play harder—play hard all the time. "If we do that and we lose," Dakotah said, "then we lose."

More nodding. Then Dakotah peeled himself off the floor, folded up his notes, and called the meeting to a close.

"So," he said, "we're good."

THAT NIGHT THE BOYS climbed aboard the team bus and traveled west, slicing through the darkness to play the Franklin-Simpson Wildcats inside the Frankfort Convention Center. The boys knew hardly anything about the opposing school, including its location. The only thing they knew for sure was that if the Wildcats had traveled to play them, they must be confident. They must be good. "They must really think," said Ge'Lawn, "that they can bust our ass."

But from tip-off that night, the county boys dictated the pace of the game. They jumped all over the Wildcats, going up 10–2, with Ge'Lawn dishing to Chad at one point for an easy bucket and going the length of the court a moment later for a smooth, right-handed layup. Franklin-Simpson clawed its way back into the game and briefly took the lead, 19–18, near the end of the first quarter.

But the Wildcats would never lead again. The county boys were too good for them. Ge'Lawn had three blocked shots, four steals, and thirteen points. Chad and Dakotah each added fifteen. And just as Hicks and Dakotah had asked, the boys played hard. In one play late in the first half, Ge'Lawn dove for a loose ball and tapped it to point guard Tamron Manning who fell, tapping it back to Ge'Lawn, who recollected the ball and passed it to Austin, who threw it to Chad, scoring easily at the rim. Final score: Scott County 85, Franklin-Simpson 63.

"Man, it feels good to win," Ge'Lawn said afterward—and Hicks agreed. "Hey, guys," he said. "That's a start. And a *good* start."

Up next was Tates Creek, a Lexington city school and regional rival who, it was said, had the talent to beat Scott County this year. The two schools had developed a rivalry of late. In 2007, when Scott County ended Tates Creek's season in the regional tournament, angry words were exchanged. And just last season, the words had escalated into an unlikely confrontation between a Scott County girl and a Tates Creek cheerleader.

The kids called it a rumble, a huge deal. And Kaylie Boehm couldn't argue with the characterization. The sensational story was at least partly true.

"The cheerleaders were circling around me and talking all this crap to me—and I just punched her. I just hit her in the mouth," said Kaylie, a Scott County senior and slender blonde who took home the Miss Scott County crown the previous summer. The fight shocked just about everyone. Kaylie was a good student, a girl who more than anything wanted her classmates to view her as nice, and for the most part they did. She'd been named to the school's homecoming court that fall. But Tates Creek—and that cheerleader—had apparently awakened the fighter inside of her, and, once cornered, Kaylie raged. "I hate Tates Creek," she said.

That Tuesday night, with Kaylie and a gaggle of other girls sitting in the front row of Scott County's gym, the visiting Tates Creek fans made it known early on that the feeling was mutual, chanting insults from the rafters.

"You are inbred!"

Clap, clap, clap-clap-clap!

"You are inbred!"

Clap, clap, clap-clap-clap!

But the county kids didn't care. By late in the fourth quarter, their Cardinals were up by seventeen points. Hicks pulled his starters and the fans started chanting at the Tates Creek students filing for the exits.

"This is boring!"

Clap, clap, clap-clap-clap!

"Drive home safely!"

Clap, clap, clap-clap-clap!

The county boys were rolling now, but back in Hicks's office that night the coaches were still troubled. A home game against Tates Creek in years past might have been a sellout—or at least close to it. But tonight, the student section wasn't even filled, much less the gym, and the lack of fans hadn't escaped Billy Hicks's notice. He guessed there might have been fifty students in the house tonight.

"Where were the other two thousand?" he asked.

The assistant coaches in Hicks's office shook their heads, unable to explain the lack of support. But in the locker room, one boy knew the answer to the coach's question. Will Schu knew exactly why fans weren't coming to the games. It was at least partly because he was one of the last true, full-blooded county boys on a team full of teenaged mercenaries. He was one of the last Scott County natives wearing the beloved red and white.

"You're from here?" asked teammate Terrence Roberts, who had recently moved in from Tennessee, talking with Will one day in the gym.

"Yeah," Will replied.

"Scott County?" Terrence asked again, befuddled.

"Yeah," Will replied once more. "I'm the only one."

THE WORST TIME OF OUR LIVES

HIS BOX SCORE WAS FILLED WITH ZEROES, as usual. Zero points, zero blocks, zero steals. In the Tates Creek game, Will Schu had as many fouls as he did looks at the basket: two. And even though he had logged a personal season high in playing time against the Commodores, the six-foot-five senior had still managed to play just fifteen minutes, less than half the game. It's safe to say he wasn't looking forward to watching the Tates Creek game tape in Hicks's office the next day. Even though they had won, none of the boys wanted to watch it.

"Look at that," Hicks said, diving right into the tape the next afternoon, with the boys crammed into the cluttered darkness and the game flickering on a flat-screen television. "You guys just stand back, don't go to the boards."

Everyone, it seemed, had committed some sort of hardwood sin the night before. Chad had failed to hit a wide-open Dakotah in the low post. "Give it to him," Hicks said as he watched the play again now. "Give it to him." Near the end of the first half, Dakotah had allowed his man to score an easy bucket. "Dakotah," Hicks said, correcting him now, "that's sorry defense right there." Hicks had problems with the referees. "They called a foul on that?" he complained at one point. "Boy, that's sorry." He complained, too, about the announcements that assistant principal Joe Covington kept making now on the school's public address system. "Gosh almighty, Mr. Covington." Hicks sighed. "Get off that thing."

The bulk of the criticism on this day, however, was reserved for Ge'Lawn. The guard had finished the Tates Creek game with just nine points and four rebounds—not exactly the stat line that one expected from the No. 2–ranked player in Kentucky. Foul trouble helped explain it: Ge'Lawn picked up four fouls the night before and had to watch much of the game from the bench. But the fouls didn't explain what appeared to Hicks to be a lack of hustle. "Where's Ge'Lawn at?" the coach asked at one point, watching the game tape and criticizing the star guard's failure to crash the boards. "You're not even in the picture. The other four are rebounding. The ball's coming up the court. Where are you at?

"I'm not trying to pick on you, Ge'Lawn," Hicks added a minute later. But he couldn't help it. At least three times in twenty minutes, he pointed out moments where Ge'Lawn didn't seem to be very interested in rebounding. "You're just walking in, watching the game," Hicks said. "Walking and watching."

As Hicks spoke, Ge'Lawn sat in silence, cubic zirconium studs in both ears and ice packs on both knees. The kid feared something was wrong with his knees—tendinitis probably. Ge'Lawn felt like he had no elevation on his shot. His knees were killing him and, perhaps worst of all, he felt like the ice packs weren't helping. "See, my knees are swollen," he said that day. "See it poking out right there?" Yes, the knees had to be the root of his problems. Of this, Ge'Lawn and his father, George Guyn, were becoming convinced.

But for a few boys that day, there was praise to be had, and the unlikeliest recipient was Will Schu. Hicks made no mention of the fact that Will hadn't scored the night before. That didn't matter to him because Will was out there hustling, diving for loose balls, and rebounding. In limited time on the floor, Will had eight boards against Tates Creek—tied for most in the game—and, on one particular possession in the fourth quarter, Will had played textbook Billy Hicks basketball. As the Tates Creek point guard dribbled into the lane, Will collapsed down from the right wing to help bottle him up. Then as the guard flicked the ball to Will's man standing in the corner, wide open, Will scrambled back out there just in time to get a hand in the shooter's face. The shot missed badly.

"Good job right there," Hicks told Will in front of his teammates as they watched the play again on the game tape. "Hey, Will. That's what we're teaching right there. That's a heckuva effort play."

For Will, it was good to finally be noticed. The night before, while the others boys celebrated, he had dressed in silence in the locker room. To his right, were the underclassmen. To his left, the stars. Everyone was fired up about the win. "Yesss-sssir!" Dakotah kept hollering. "*Yesss-sssir!*" But Will, sitting in the middle of the U-shaped room, barely managed a smile.

All his life, the pasty white Scott County native had wanted this: this seat in the locker room; this jersey on his back; this gold, engraved plate secured to the wall above his head bearing his name—WILL SCHU, #44. But now that he had it, Will displayed all the joy of a funeral director presiding over a wake. Despite his location in the locker room, centered on the row of lockers, Will was often not a part of the conversations on either his left or his right. His teammates sometimes worried about passing him the ball. (Will might just throw it away.) And the coaches almost always avoided playing him in big games. (Will seemed better suited for garbage time.) The boy, with no father in his life and few defined plans for the future, sometimes wondered why he had worked so hard, for so long, to end up here: on the bench, watching a bunch of transfers play. Some people that winter didn't even seem to know that Will Schu existed.

"Is Will on the team?" one curious student asked.

"Will?" replied Ge'Lawn. "He just does his own thing."

THE BABY BOY, WITH NO FATHER, left the hospital in the winter of 1992 and came home to a trailer on the county line. The official address was Sharp Road, Stamping Ground, Kentucky. But out here, it felt like you had dropped off the map. Will's mother, Laura Schu, would find deer grazing outside and hear coyotes howling in the hills late at night. One friend refused to stay there, afraid of the wildlife. But Laura didn't worry much about it. Cows were the biggest nuisance. Every once in a while, a herd would escape from some farmer's field and be found wandering everywhere. And then there were the deer hunters. During hunting season, Laura could hear the hills echoing with gunfire.

It wasn't much, this slice of Scott County, but Laura could handle it. The Schus had a history of overcoming obstacles. Her father, Wilbur Schu, was an orphan, given up by his mother as a boy. Yet growing to be nearly six foot four, young Wilbur would become a two-sport athlete at Versailles High School one county over, impressing the locals with his athletic skills. It was said that Wilbur Schu, scrawny but tough, could punt a football clear off the high school football field and into the corn growing nearby. And on the basket-ball court, he had a sweet hook shot, kissing the ball off the glass just so. By his junior year in high school, the orphan boy was averaging almost half the team's points, and people noticed, including then U.S. Senator A. B. "Happy" Chandler, living a privileged life in downtown Versailles with his children, wife, and growing political legend.

The Chandler family, impressed with Schu, took the boy into their home when he turned eighteen and could no longer stay at the orphanage. Here, Wilbur would teach the wide-eyed Chandler boys how to play ball—"He was bigger than life," recalled Ben Chandler—and the senator's family in turn would treat Wilbur like family. The Chandlers threw Wilbur the first real birthday party he'd ever had and the senator used his connections to help the teenaged boy land a spot on Adolph Rupp's basketball team at the University of Kentucky in 1942.

Now Wilbur was a man. Now people were chanting his name: *Schu-Schu, baby!* Long after Wilbur helped lead Rupp's Wildcats to the 1946 NIT title—defeating Rhode Island at a time when the NIT title was considered the biggest in the land—Kentucky fans were still saying it: *Schu-Schu, baby.* "I don't care where we went—Lexington, Cincinnati, walking in restaurants—people always said, 'Hi, Wilbur,'" recalled longtime friend Tommy Duke Belt. "He knew everybody in the county—or they knew him. They'd call him *Schu-Schu.*"

His daughter, however, received decidedly less recognition. By her mid-thirties, Laura Schu was divorced and alone, a florist living in that trailer and spending some evenings every month with friends inside a small three-room tavern on the outskirts of Lexington. It was there, with the jukebox playing and men shooting pool in the back, that she began talking with a married man. He was a nice guy—quiet, but charming—and she fell for him, stumbling into an ill-advised affair that ended in an all too familiar way: a pregnancy, a baby, and no husband.

Some people told her to get an abortion. But Laura refused. It was her life, her choice, and her baby. She wanted the child. And when the brown-eyed boy was born, Laura named him Will after her father, the greatest man she had ever known, dead now of a heart attack for nearly twelve years.

That first night at home in the trailer, the baby cried and Laura Schu cried, too, not sure how to care for the boy, all alone out there in the coyote hills. But Laura found her way and Will grew up—a happy kid, it seemed, hanging a picture of his grandfather on his bedroom wall. There was Wilbur, in his Wildcat uniform, young and strong, before his knees went soft, his heart went bad, and the cheers of packed arenas gave way to Early Times bourbon and Lark cigarettes. Will loved that old photograph. If his grandfather could be somebody, then surely he could, too. He was Will Schu, after all—*Schu-Schu, baby*—and from a young age the boy set his mind on playing basketball for the only game in town: Scott County High.

WILL HAD A BODY for the game: long and lean, with wide shoulders and legs like stilts. By the end of middle school, he was dunking the ball one-handed, six foot two and growing. Tell him to do something on the basketball court and he'd do it—anything to improve his chances of one day playing for Billy Hicks. And many were confident that Will would do just that, given his name and his talent. "Will had tons of potential," said David Fooy, the boy's middle school coach. "It was in his genes for him to play."

Fooy figured Will would dominate in eighth grade, but that didn't exactly happen, nor did he impress the coaches at the high school. Despite his height and his knowledge of Hicks's system, Will, it seemed, was always getting pushed around. He'd grow to be one of the tallest kids on the squad—second only to Dakotah—but his teammates considered him soft and slow. Talking to Will was like talking to someone underwater. His words, rounded off at the edges, seemed to bubble up from the depths, taking their time in reaching the surface. And on the basketball court, there was simply very little menacing about Will, who had been overlooked for so long that any confidence he once had was gone. With his arms and legs churning—long and pale—Will Schu moved down the court at times like an egret trapped in a pigpen and frantic to escape.

He frustrated easily, hanging his head when he missed a shot or shouting at himself when he turned the ball over. As hard as the coaches were on him—"Tough, Will!" Hicks would holler. *"Board, board, board!"*—Will was always harder on himself, punching the air, the floor, the wall, anything. If he missed a layup, he'd holler, *"Gawwwwwd!"* And when Hicks pulled him from the game, as the coach always seemed to be doing, there would be Will, walking off the floor and shaking his head in disgust.

"If you ever come out of a game shaking your head again, I'm going to send you to the locker room and you can get dressed," Hicks said, scolding Will as the boy walked to the bench in the second quarter of the Franklin-Simpson game that season. "Don't embarrass us like that no more."

But Will couldn't help it. He was angry: angry that he didn't have a father sitting in the stands like Dakotah and the other boys; angry that his grandfather's game had passed him by and the coaches had passed him over; and, perhaps most of all, angry about all those transfers who had stolen his playing time and his dream of being a Scott County basketball star while they—not him—got all the attention from the popular girls at school.

He was a basketball player just like they were, but Will was different from his teammates in many ways. While many of them drove their own cars, Will had to borrow his mother's beige minivan whenever he wanted to go somewhere. And while many of his teammates refused to wear the $110 Adidas shoes that Hicks had purchased for the boys that fall—"Maybe because Adidas sucks," Ge'Lawn explained—Will was just happy to have new shoes. Laura's son didn't need to have padding beneath his shorts, absorbent tees beneath his jersey, or slick, white Nike shooting sleeves on his elbow—expensive accoutrements of the modern game that many of his teammates donned on the court. "All I need to play," Will said, "is socks and shoes."

To him, it was like his teammates were trying to make some sort of fashion statement while he was just trying to get on the floor and stay there. But it was a nearly impossible task to achieve—and not just because the other boys were more talented than he was.

That fall, not long before the season began, Will had sabotaged his own efforts to win playing time on this team. Out of frustration one day while scrimmaging his teammates, Will missed a layup and punched the wall beneath one of the baskets with his right hand—his shooting hand. It wasn't the first time Will had punched a wall, but this time he had really injured himself.

It felt like his hand had been struck with a hammer. It went ice cold and Will shook with pain, sure that the hand was broken, which, the next day's X-rays confirmed, it was. The doctor said he would be sidelined for at least a month. Will was now wearing a cast on his right hand—a spectator on his own team— when an assistant coach approached him two days later in the gym with a new assignment.

"Will," said Nick Napier, all smiles, "I got a job for you today."

Will shook his head no.

"What do you think I'm going to ask you?" Napier said.

"I don't care," Will replied.

"Keep the clock," Napier answered. "All you gotta do is use your left hand."

The coach walked away as Will propped his feet up on the scorer's table and began fiddling with the game clock. "They better not make me do this all season," he said. "I can't do this. It just makes me mad."

"Start it," Austin said, snapping at Will from the floor and nodding to the game clock, still not moving, up in the rafters of the gym.

Will gave him a look. "I did," he replied. "Chill out."

He shouldn't have punched that wall. This much was clear now to Will Schu. But he also felt like it was unavoidable, that he *just had* to punch the wall, that he *just had* to hit something with all his might. As Will explained to his teammates after he smashed his hand: "I just had to take some anger out."

THE ANGER IN KENTUCKY had been building for months. For the first time since 1983—when Billy Singer and other Scott County farmers watched their fields burn in that summer's withering drought—the unemployment rate in Kentucky had reached double digits. In one rural county in the eastern part of the state, unemployment had hit 22 percent. Folks, once again, were lining up outside businesses in hopes of a job, or at least an interview, and many were willing to do just about anything to get one.

At one job fair in Lexington around that time, nearly 2,600 people showed up for one hundred temporary railroad construction jobs. War veterans, unemployed roofers, and new fathers were all there. Some held their children while they waited in line for hours. Others stayed there all night long, willing to endure the darkness and the cold if it gave them a better chance at a paycheck again, and most everyone felt sick about it—physically ill even. "It's getting scary," admitted Brian Mosher, a thirty-one-year-old Scott County man who had been out of work for nearly a year and a half. "I'm worried about losing my house and my car."

Just over a year earlier, a Harvard-educated U.S. senator from Illinois had America talking about hope. And many people had bought in to that idea, sweeping Barack Obama to an historic presidential victory. But such hope was hard to find here, find now. In 2009, while Obama staffers were settling into the White House and talking about bailouts and stimulus packages, Kentucky had more people living in poverty than almost any other state in the nation, coming in third just behind Mississippi and Arkansas. The number of Kentuckians on food stamps had jumped 23 percent in two years. Many people were now relying on food banks to fill their kitchen pantries and depression, for some, had set in. According to a study published in the *American Journal of Preventive Medicine* in April 2009, Kentucky was the saddest state in the nation, a place where nearly 15 percent of adults reported feeling significant stress, depression, or emotional problems in the previous month. Kentucky, *Time* magazine noted, wasn't simply the Bluegrass State any longer. It was just blue—the heart of "the Gloom Belt." And many people could feel the sadness sitting on their shoulders. "Right now," said Beverly Roe, a sixty-seven-year-old Somerset retiree, "is the worst time of our lives."

It was a feeling that many Scott Countians had not known in a long time. As hard as life might have been for people here in the early 1980s, especially on farmers like Billy Singer, prosperity had reigned for the most part in the last two decades. For years, the growth of the Toyota factory on the edge of town had fueled the local economy, providing steady work, good-paying jobs, and buckets of tax revenue for local governmental services. Unemployment, at times, was almost nonexistent in the county, hovering around 2 percent for years. And people who lived here enjoyed other perks as well.

Toyota donated cars for local government officials to drive, agreed to make annual payments to the schools to offset the growth caused by the plant, and, in 1994, even opted to pay twenty years' worth of these payments in advance—roughly $8 million—so that the district could build a new high school, including that new gymnasium where Billy Hicks would win so many basketball games. "Without question, because of the money that has come into this community, we have the best of everything for a community this size," said county judge executive George Lusby. "I don't say that bragging," he added. "I say it for a fact."

But as Will Schu's senior year began in August 2009, few Scott Countians were bragging anymore. Unemployment in the county had nearly reached 13 percent that summer—the highest rate since the first Camry, white and shiny, rolled off the local production line more than twenty years earlier. People were struggling and a few were taking extreme measures to make sure their bills got paid. At Dan's Discount Jewelry and Pawn Shop downtown, one cash-strapped war veteran had come in recently attempting to pawn his prosthetic leg. "It was one of those things that I usually wouldn't take," said twenty-one-year-old pawn shop employee Harry Nelson. "But since he was a retired veteran, I took it. These things are pretty expensive. They're like three grand."

More than a few retail storefronts downtown sat vacant. In the months ahead, a desperate sign of the times would appear in one window. It read: RENT THIS BLDG. – FREE!! And inside the local unemployment office, with its gray linoleum floors and off-white walls, office manager Jeanne Devers heard it all: how people had no money for Christmas, how they had lost their homes, filed for bankruptcy, or were moving in with family just to survive.

Devers, a thirty-six-year-old graduate of Scott County High, tried to stay positive. "If you don't," she said, "it's a hard job." But the people who lined up for benefits were less optimistic about the future in general and Toyota in particular. Many had once worked at the plant as contractors or temporary workers. But now here they were, waiting outside the unemployment office in the dark before Devers opened the doors for the day, smoking Marlboros and drinking coffee out of Styrofoam cups. Some, like forty-seven-year-old Judy Hawkins, hadn't worked in nine months. "I was a team leader at Toyota for a contractor for fifteen years, and they laid me off," she said, adding, "I pray I get back." But now like so many others, she was just wondering if her next unemployment check would come in time for Christmas. The checks, it seemed, never arrived.

"I'll take care of you," Devers promised the people walking in the door, friendly and smiling. Yet there was only so much she could do. "Used to be, I could walk in the building and get me a job," said Denise Mason, an unemployed fifty-five-year-old administrative assistant. "But I'm in a new world now."

And so, too, was the county government. With Toyota reporting a $4.4 billion deficit, car sales in decline across the nation, and nonproduction days at the Georgetown factory increasingly common, county tax revenues were in a freefall. In just a few years, the county's general fund revenues had plummeted by more than 25 percent—and the reason wasn't hard to divine. Toyota generated roughly half of the county's general tax fund revenues, explained Lusby, the county's judge executive. And now that the carmaker was hurting, so was Scott County. "It'll be picking up," Lusby said, sitting at his desk in the courthouse one day that winter. "We hope. If it don't, we're all in trouble."

The local newspaper, the *Georgetown News-Graphic*, tried reminding people how good they still had it. Once again, editors trotted out the old headline—OH WHAT A FEELING, TOYOTA—and ran stories praising the carmaker for looking after employees. Even on idle days at the plant, people could still get paid if they were willing to come in for training or maintenance work. "I think it's incredible," said Randy Sinkhorn, one longtime Toyota worker. "I hope everyone understands the hardship on the company."

But others at the plant were no longer happy about their working conditions. They worried about taking too many sick days and possibly losing their jobs. They complained about the company cutting lucrative performance awards and bonuses. And with no union in place to fight for them, employees had no recourse but to grumble about it. John Williams, hired at the plant in 1989, figured he was making $10,000 less than he had in previous years due to all the cutbacks. He recently had to inform his three children that he could no longer afford to pay their college tuition. And what bothered him the most, he said, was he felt like Toyota had abandoned him.

"From the day that I can remember, my first day here, they always told us that they would hold back and not shower us with the same things that other auto manufacturers received—as far as pay benefits and all that stuff— because they wanted us to have a nice, level forever—even in hard times," said

Williams, wearing a pro-union T-shirt, a goatee, and glasses one day after working his shift at the car plant. "They called that the rainy day fund," he explained. "Started raining in 2008—and those son of a bitches pulled the plug on us."

B UT TOYOTA wasn't the only scapegoat for the county's problems that year. People soon began blaming one man in particular for their plight: Barack Obama, the newly elected president who had never been popular in Kentucky—or in Scott County—to begin with.

The John McCain–Sarah Palin ticket crushed Obama here in November 2008. And in the Democratic primary six months earlier, Hillary Clinton handed the future commander-in-chief an even more embarrassing defeat. At a time when Obama was closing in on the nomination and Clinton's candidacy was limping to the finish line, the former first lady more than doubled the black senator's vote totals in Kentucky, winning 65.5 percent to Obama's paltry 29.9. While Clinton celebrated her victory that night in Louisville—"I'm going to keep making our case," she said, "until we have a nominee, whoever she may be"—Obama was in Iowa. He had hardly bothered to contest Kentucky and perhaps with good reason. In exit poll interviews at the primary, more than one in five white Kentucky voters said race was an important factor in their vote.

Kentuckians bristled at the way the national media jumped on this figure, portraying them—unfairly, they said—as poor, uneducated, redneck racists. But a few conceded there was at least an element of truth in the stereotype, as unflattering as it might be. At Scott County High, for example, nearly half of the seniors said they had witnessed prejudice in the halls, with 41 percent reporting in a 2008 survey that they had experienced fighting between different races. Billy Hicks's basketball team might have been half black, half white, and harmonious. But the student body was almost entirely white. Of the 1,588 students enrolled in the high school, only 109 were black, which helps explain why senior class president John Culbertson, a leader with the Young Democrats, heard some kids dismiss the future president with racial slurs. "I feel like I'm kind of talking to a brick wall sometimes when it comes to political things,"

Culbertson said. "A lot of people are just very set in their ways. Very Republican. Very conservative."

And so, with the economy sputtering, unemployment rising, an African-American Democrat in the White House, and no end to the pain in sight, the bluegrass was fertile ground for a great American uprising. Egged on by Fox News and conservative talk radio, and fueled by a simmering rage over the state of America in the age of Obama, thousands of Kentuckians began flocking to the nascent Tea Party and rallying in city parks and on courthouse steps that year. They maintained that the events were nonpartisan, that their anger wasn't just limited to Obama, but to all Washington insiders in favor of the status quo. And while there was a kernel of truth in that claim, it wasn't exactly accurate.

At the Kentucky rallies that year, those in attendance carried signs that made quite clear for whom they reserved the most antipathy. REVOLT AGAINST SOCIALISM, said one sign. BARRACK OBORTION, said another. An elderly woman in Corbin held a sign asking, WHERE'S THE BIRTH CERTIFICATE? questioning whether President Obama was really an American citizen—a question that, while resolved for most, still bothered some Kentuckians. And in the same crowd that day, a sixteen-year-old held up a different sign. OBAMANOMICS, it said, CHAINS YOU CAN BELIEVE IN. "You've got the radical left wing in control of everything," the girl's father Jeramie Davidson complained, "and we're fed up about it."

Some came in costume—the Grim Reaper showed up at one rally—and others sold souvenirs. Anti-Obama T-shirts that read O-NO and O-CRAP were popular sales items and so were bumper stickers promoting Palin for president. SARAH 2012, they read.

"Ladies and gentlemen, it is time for the government of the United States of America to fear this!" said Leland Conway, addressing a Tea Party crowd in Lexington that April. "Say it with me, ladies and gentlemen!"

"Fear this!" the crowd yelled.

"I'm sorry if it sounds shrill," Conway continued. "But one, two, three!"

"Fear this!" the crowd yelled again.

One rally led to another. In July and again in September that year, people gathered across the state, including in Scott County, giving voice to their disillusion. And time and again, Kentuckians came back to the same question: "How's that hope and change working out for you?"

Now, into this political vacuum, came Rand Paul, an eye doctor from Bowling Green who also happened to be the son of perennial presidential candidate Ron Paul. Here was a man whom Kentuckians could support. He was antitax and antigovernment, like so many of them were. He was tired of the status quo and ready to fight back—also like so many of them were. And with his announcement that August that he was officially running for U.S. senate, Rand Paul's star was on the rise. He wasn't supposed to win the Republican primary. The nomination was surely going to Kentucky's thirty-seven-year-old secretary of state, Trey Grayson, a product of the Ivy League who had the political résumé for the job and the backing of the Republican establishment.

But within three months that fall, the Bowling Green doctor went from thirteen points down in the polls, to three points up—a swing so shocking that one of Grayson's campaign staffers nearly drove his car off the road when he heard the news. The staffer was on his way to meet Grayson in Lexington at the time, with plans for them to attend a campaign event together. But Grayson would have to go to the event alone. His staffers needed to handle this crisis.

Grayson, the presumptive frontrunner, was suddenly the overnight underdog and Tea Party supporters, emboldened by the polls, were sure that Rand Paul was going to prevail, which ultimately he did, crushing Grayson in the primary and then besting Democrat Jack Conway in a bruising, embittered general election race the following year. Rand Paul was a U.S. senator now and Scott County was at least partially responsible for his success. County voters backed the Tea Party candidate—in a landslide.

NOT THAT WILL SCHU was paying much attention to politics. Late that year, while Rand Paul was surging in the polls and Grayson's staffers were beginning to scramble, Will was just trying to improve his grades at school and bounce back from that broken hand. Even after his doctor had the cast removed, Will wasn't cleared to play.

"It's just too soon," said Dr. Timothy Wilson, a local orthopedic surgeon. "It hasn't healed."

"Yeah," Will replied, "I realize that."

"And if you fall on it . . ."

"Yeah."

"It's pretty easy to rebreak right now."

Will, sitting on Dr. Wilson's examining table, took his good hand and rubbed the wounded one. It was still swollen near his pinky finger where he had fractured the bone over a month earlier. At most, the doctor said now, Will could shoot around—nothing more than that. And Will agreed to follow his advice.

"I won't be doing any contact," he assured his doctor.

But watching his teammates practice from the sidelines was killing him—and not just because the coaches had asked him to operate the game clock. Will knew, *just knew*, that every day he sat there he was hurting his chances of getting real playing time this year—never mind cracking the starting five. The dream of being a starter was probably dead. And so, when the coaches asked Will if he wanted to practice again, he said yes—trying to forget the pain. His right hand was weak and floppy, like a half-dead appendage. But Will was going back out there. Yes, most certainly, he was going to play.

"You're sure you're ready now?" Hicks asked.

"Yeah," Will replied.

But it was clear that he wasn't. In the team scrimmage that afternoon, Will Schu struggled. He was afraid to body his man on defense and he was tentative in traffic. He dove for loose balls like an old man afraid of breaking a fragile hip and he missed layup after layup. "I would have had thirty points," Will complained, "if I could make a fuckin' layup."

His hand was throbbing now, but he refused to mention it. When the coaches inquired, he said it was fine. When they asked a second time, he said he could tough it out. "It ain't too bad," he told Hicks. But it was clearly affecting him. By the end of his first week back at practice, he was shouting at himself again, shaking his head, angry all over again. While his teammates sat together on the sidelines of the team scrimmages, he often sat alone, gnawing on his fingernails. And while his teammates huddled up after practice, Will needed prodding to join in, standing off to the side—alone, again.

"Get it in, Will," Dakotah said.

The coaches kept talking about how rusty Will looked—like he had missed more than just a month. But the problem wasn't just his hand; it was his heart. Will's was breaking. Maybe it was already broken. At many high schools in Kentucky, he would have been a starter by now—or at least competing for a starting spot. But not here. Not with the talent the county had. And that was beginning to bother him. Quietly, telling no one but his mother, Will Schu was considering quitting.

"I just feel like so much stuff has gone wrong already," he told his mom one day while waiting at the doctor's office. "I feel like every year something sets me back. And then the transfers came in and put me back a chair."

"Put you back four chairs," Laura Schu corrected him.

Will nodded. She was right. He was in a spiral now—a "downward spiral," he said, sinking ever deeper into doubt and despair. He was tired of failing, sick of never getting a chance, and not sure if he could stand another long season watching from the bench, hobbled by a broken shooting hand on top of everything else. He was fifty-fifty, he told his mother. Fifty-fifty on playing.

"It's such a hard decision," he told her. "Probably the hardest decision I've ever had to make."

Then, just before the season began, Will got some good news: the hand was healing. It wouldn't be 100 percent for a while, Dr. Wilson told him. The swelling might be there for a year. But Will could make a fist without pain, move it without much problem, and, most important, he could shoot the ball again, push off, rebound—whatever.

"You can play," Wilson told him. "Just don't hit anybody," he added. "Or, if you do, use your left hand."

"Hey," Will said, as the doctor left the room, "that was good."

For once, the boy even managed to smile. He left the doctor's office and headed straight to basketball practice. Will wasn't quitting the team, he wasn't quitting anything, if for no other reason than this: "I just don't know what I'd do," he explained, "without basketball."

.   .   .

FTER THE TATES CREEK VICTORY, it appeared Will had made the right decision. In the game tape session, Hicks wasn't just praising Will for his defense, but for the way he passed the ball to teammates slicing through the lane and crashed the boards, hustling. "I like ol' Will Schu right here," Hicks said, remote control in hand, with the boys huddled around him in his office. "Will found himself a gap."

But the praise for Will didn't last and neither did the playing time. Over the next two games—victories for the county—Will was back to playing less than ten minutes a night and averaging less than three points. In one of those games, he somehow managed to commit four turnovers, even though he was barely playing. And Will's one good game—ten points and seven rebounds against Paul Laurence Dunbar High from Lexington—came with an asterisk. Dunbar was terrible and Hicks, not wanting to run up the score, took his foot off the gas at halftime. "They've got 2,400 kids at a school in Lexington," he said, mystified, "and they can't find a better team than this?" The final was 71–43, even with the county's third-string seeing action.

The boys' last game before Christmas, however, wasn't going to be so easy. National basketball powerhouse, Norcross High School, was making a seven-hour drive from the far northern suburbs of Atlanta for the privilege of facing the Scott County Cardinals, in the Cards' home gym, a few days before Christmas. Hicks always wanted to win—every game, all the time. Even playing weak competition like Dunbar, he paced the sidelines and demanded the most from his players.

But Hicks took particular pleasure in squaring off against the best of the best, pitting his county boys against high schools with national rankings, big-name reputations, and future NBA stars on the roster. While other coaches often ducked these teams—not wanting to risk a humbling loss—Hicks courted such competition, craved it even. In perhaps his greatest moment, in February 2007, he arranged for Scott County to face the nation's No. 1 ranked team at the time from Huntington, West Virginia. The Huntington Highlanders were undefeated and led by future NBA stars O. J. Mayo and Patrick Patterson. Playing against them seemed like a bad idea. With the Mayo-Patterson tandem, Huntington was almost unbeatable—a lesson that Lexington Catholic,

Scott County's hated rival, learned the hard way that year. The Highlanders throttled Catholic, 97–64—on the road, in Kentucky.

But still, Hicks wanted the game—and he got it. Three weeks after Huntington crushed Catholic, Mayo and Patterson returned to Kentucky to face Scott County. The game wouldn't be in the county's gym, but in Lexington's Memorial Coliseum, and some 7,500 fans would be there expecting to see Mayo and Patterson put on another show. What they saw instead was a shocker.

The Scott County Cardinals—ranked No. 1 in the state at the time, but unranked nationally—never trailed that night, outplaying the heralded Highlanders from tip to buzzer. Billy's boys played stifling defense, creating twenty-five turnovers and forcing Mayo to take bad shots. He was 12-for-30 on the night and committed the biggest turnover of the game with twenty-five seconds to go, throwing a bad pass that led to yet another Scott County steal.

Ballgame. The county had won, 72–68.

"This," Hicks said afterward, "is for Kentucky."

Now, with Norcross coming to town, this season's Scott County squad had a chance to prove itself as well. The Blue Devils had won three of the last four state championships in Georgia. They hadn't lost more than four games in a season since 2003. One former player, Jodie Meeks, was currently playing in the NBA. Two more would be drafted six months later. And the Blue Devils' star *du jour*, Jeremy Lamb, was considered one of the best high school shooting guards in the nation, bound to play at the University of Connecticut next year.

None of that mattered to Hicks, though. He was confident that Norcross couldn't handle their pressure, if the boys played hard. And he laid out the game plan in the locker room just before tip-off. The Devils, Hicks said, were going to run ball screens up top for Lamb, trying to get him open looks.

"But we gotta trap that thing solid, right there," Hicks said, standing before the whiteboard. "He's six-four. He's long. He can throw over the top of you. But he's not real strong. So when we trap him, we gotta body him. Get him down low with your legs. With your hands up here, tight in front of the ball, get him down low with your legs. Don't let him split you. Trap him hard."

As Hicks spoke, Ge'Lawn sat in front of his locker, cracking his knuckles and rolling his shoulders, eyes on the whiteboard. On each foot, Ge'Lawn wore two socks—one white and one black—and a fine new pair of Nike high-tops. A coach from Western Kentucky University was going to be here tonight to watch him play and he was expecting a great game from Ge'Lawn. "The bigger the lights, the better he is," said David Boyden, the Western assistant. "I'd be shocked if he had a bad game against Norcross." And Hicks was expecting big things, too.

But Ge'Lawn was still worried about his knees. Just that afternoon, he'd gone to a physical therapist's office in town, lying on a table while therapists buzzed around him and Christmas carols were piped into the room. Fifteen minutes of heat. Five minutes on the stationary bike. Then it was back to the table for electro-stimulation therapy and some stretching.

"Does that bother you?" a therapist asked while working on him.

"A little bit," Ge'Lawn replied.

"Hurting right in there?"

"Yeah."

Now, in the locker room, just before tip-off against Norcross, Ge'Lawn kept spraying his knees with some sort of medicinal mist. Soon, the entire corner of the room reeked of menthol. But it didn't matter. To win tonight, the county would need Ge'Lawn at his best.

"You guys ain't never been beat in this house, have you?" Hicks asked the boys just before they left the locker room.

They all shook their heads no.

"Let's get after it then," Hicks growled. "This is our house. *Our house.*"

NORCROSS JUMPED OUT to an early 8–1 advantage. But the county, led by Ge'Lawn and Chad, pushed back and cut the Devils' lead to one about midway through the second quarter. By halftime, Chad had eight points and Ge'Lawn had eleven, leading all scorers. And Jeremy Lamb, just as Hicks had predicted, was a nonfactor. The touted recruit had just five points. But the Cards were still losing at the intermission, down 32–24. Dakotah was an ice-cold 1-for-7 from the field and Will had reinjured his hand.

"Will, you okay?" Hicks asked him at half. "You in pain?"

This time, Will admitted that he was, and Hicks called in the team's trainer, Dan Volpe, to examine him. "He's hurting," Hicks told him.

Will nodded, wincing, while Hicks addressed the team.

"Guys, they're just lowering their head and driving," he told the boys, unable to accept the eight-point halftime deficit. "You just gotta get position on them and make the steal. It's not like they're a great offensive team. I don't think they're that much quicker than we are. But you guys sit around like you're scared to death of them."

He begged them to play some defense and the boys, apparently, were listening. They came out of halftime on fire, taking barely a minute to tie the game and mounting a 10–0 run to take the lead.

"You see what I'm talking about?" Hicks said during the time-out that followed. Dakotah nodded. "Keep that intensity up!" the boy hollered at his teammates as they returned to the floor. "Intensity!"

The two teams were trading buckets now. It was 46–46 going into the fourth quarter. But Ge'Lawn was fading, making just one shot the entire second half. Dakotah was hardly any better; he only made two. Will, with his hand aching, played only one minute the rest of the way, and the other role players didn't contribute much, either. Only Chad was scoring consistently in the second half, dropping twenty-two on the night. But on his own, it wasn't enough. The Cards went down 64–55, a loss that Norcross punctuated in the waning seconds of the game with two monstrous, back-to-back dunks.

While Frank Howatt, the school's principal, presented a Norcross kid with the player of the game plaque—an unenviable task, to be sure—Ge'Lawn stood slumped over on the court, with his hands on those troubled knees and his jersey in his mouth. So much for never getting beaten on their home floor. So much for proving themselves against a national power.

"Our season isn't over," Hicks told his team after the game. "Our season just started." He was trying to stay positive. And there was reason for some optimism. Their defense that night was great at times—or at least really good. "We showed we can guard a team like that," Hicks said in a voice much quieter than usual. "Now we gotta get to where we can score on 'em." And then, as was his custom—win or lose—the coach led the team in prayer.

"Let's bow our heads, guys," Hicks said. "You don't win 'em all. Let's give thanks to God for allowing us to compete and let's pray to God that we can learn from this and make us even stronger."

The boys lowered their heads and sat for a spell in silence.

"*Amen.*"

But watching the game tape the next day, Hicks was all over them again: for running the wrong plays and for taking stupid shots, for allowing Norcross to drive untouched to the hoop and, of course, for not playing defense like he had taught them. "I know it's the time of peace and love and everything like that," Hicks said. "But let's get better here today."

On the practice court, however, there was little sign of improvement. Hicks was soon shouting "*Dadburnit!*" and "*Gosh almighty!*" When one player missed a shot and threw his basketball across the court in frustration, Hicks stopped everything and made him go get it. "We're waiting on you," he told the boy. And when the boys failed once more to play defense, when they failed to swarm and trap, Hicks bowed his head, shook it slowly—chin to his chest—swung his long arms in the air, and then planted his hands on both hips.

"Why?" he asked. "*Why?*"

But Hicks wasn't the only one frustrated. In the locker room that day after practice, with no coaches around, Dakotah stripped off his ankle braces and turned to his teammates with a question.

"Who's coming in and working out with me tomorrow?" he asked. "That's all I want to know."

No one answered right away. It was December 22, the winter break. For the next two days, the boys had no practice. Hicks had set them free and most of them had better plans than coming into the gym.

"You really coming in?" Austin asked Dakotah.

"*Uhhhh,* yeah," Dakotah replied.

But no one else at the moment was ready to volunteer and a silence fell upon them. The squad was 5-2—a decent record—and there were still two months of basketball left to play, plenty of time to get things right. And yet, sitting in the locker room, the boys seemed defeated, burdened by expectations they had no chance of meeting—and it was about to get harder. In four days, the day after Christmas, they were bound for Myrtle Beach, South Carolina, to play in one of the most prestigious high school basketball tournaments in the country: the Beach Ball Classic.

Every team would be like Norcross—or better. Every team would have a Jeremy Lamb—or someone better. And if Scott County played like it had the day before, those teams were going to make the boys wish that they had stayed home in Georgetown. Even Ge'Lawn, typically confident, seemed worried about the players they were about to face. "Those guys," he said, "are gonna have, like, thirty dunks apiece."

Ge'Lawn dressed in silence with the others, tiptoed out of the locker room, and headed outside, bracing himself for the cold.

SHORT, FAT GUYS RATING KIDS

JERRY MEYER WAS WATCHING. Even if the boys didn't see him sitting courtside, didn't know what he looked like, or didn't know him by name, they knew on some level that Jerry Meyer, and other scouts like him, were out there ranking them, like commodities to be bought and sold.

Not long ago, Meyer had been one of those commodities himself. He grew up a coach's son in Nashville, Tennessee, demonstrating a talent for the game at a young age. Twice in high school, in 1987 and again in 1988, Meyer was named Class AA Mr. Basketball in Tennessee. And for a while, he earned looks from big-time programs, including Kentucky, before the interest faded and he opted to play for his father, Don, at Lipscomb University, a NAIA school. He was a point guard, not especially athletic, with not much physical strength. But Meyer could see the floor as well as anyone. And when he finished his college career, playing his final season for the Minnesota-Duluth Bulldogs, Meyer earned All-American honors and made basketball history. In a 79–49 blowout that winter over Southwest State in Marshall, Minnesota, the Bulldogs' point guard flicked a pass to an open teammate, Jake Voit, on the right wing. Voit nailed a turnaround jumper. And that was that. Meyer had become college basketball's all-time leader in assists. To this day, the record still stands: 1,314 career assists in all, more than two hundred more than the NCAA's Division I all-time leader, legendary Duke University guard Bobby Hurley.

Such records mattered to Meyer then. But these days it was his job to block out such things. What records a teenaged basketball player might hold should not, on their own, dictate Meyer's opinion of the boy's skills. What colleges were recruiting him or what other scouts were saying about him needed to be absolutely meaningless, too. The only thing that matters to Jerry Meyer now is his own opinion—and it matters a great deal to other people as well. As the national basketball recruiting analyst for Rivals.com, the nation's leading Internet-based scouting service, Meyer is something of a kingmaker, a man who, by assigning simple rankings, can fulfill dreams or destroy them—and he's always in demand. If you care about high school basketball, then you have to listen to Jerry Meyer, whose Rivals 150, ranking the top 150 American high school basketball players, is read by parents and coaches as if it is the Bible itself. "That's the one all of us wait on," Ge'Lawn's father, George Guyn, said. "The others mean something—don't get me wrong. But Rivals is number one."

Ranking high school athletes is not a new idea, but the appetite for such rankings is. For decades, sports fanatics, usually men, have been ranking players based on their observations and then compiling the information in simple, stapled pamphlets usually with no frills and very few readers. Subscribers, for the most part, were college coaches and recruiters—and other sports fanatics. The information was contained and the audience limited.

But by the mid-1990s, with the Internet giving these people a virtual street corner where they could find one another and debate, for example, the minutiae of a future Kentucky Wildcat's shooting skills, the market for insight into teenaged athletes was about to explode. Shannon Terry, Meyer's college roommate and basketball teammate, was one of the first to recognize it.

Terry, a power forward with a decent outside shot, had always been a dreamer. In college, Meyer was always falling asleep at night listening to Terry talk about how he was going to make money after college. The Alabama native was never short on ideas. And now he had a good one: Web sites devoted to college sports and recruiting news about high school athletes. He cofounded AllianceSports LLC in 1996, charged fans for the content, grew the business, and then sold it to Rivals.com, a Seattle-based competitor, almost four years later at the height of the dot-com boom for roughly $3 million. Rivals was an industry giant, with plans to go public and name recognition. It had even sponsored the Hula Bowl in Hawaii. But the company relied too much on ad revenue, crashed as the Internet boom went bust, and then sold its assets at fire-sale prices back to Terry and his partner, Greg Gough, who proceeded to rebuild the busted recruiting behemoth in cyberspace.

They took the Rivals 100 and expanded it into the Rivals 150. Having more kids on the list simply made sense, but not too many more. "Who really cares," Terry said, "if a kid is 334?" They hired Jerry Meyer—the smartest basketball player Shannon Terry had ever known—to help lead Rivals's basketball recruiting content, knowing Meyer would not be influenced by other people's opinions. "He simply does not care," Terry said. And Rivals, version 2.0, quickly exploded, exceeding expectations, closing in on 50,000 subscribers just six months after the Web site's apparent collapse, and continuing to grow from there.

By 2007, in Terry's estimation, Rivals was one of the top sports Web sites in the nation, attracting 12 million unique visitors a month and 225,000 subscribers. "And all we do," Terry said at the time, "is cover college and high school sports." But they did it so well that soon Yahoo! swooped in, purchasing the Tennessee-based business for an eye-popping $98 million. The evolution of the sports fanatic's little pamphlet was now complete. Information once distributed to the few was now on the Internet for everyone to read—a profitable idea, but not necessarily a culturally enriching one. Between Rivals's rankings, ESPN's coverage of high school players' college choices, and the kids' own tweets and Facebook profiles, they are no longer just young people playing sports, but something much bigger. "Little, miniathlete gods," Terry called them with a twinge of regret. "And not just in their own communities," he added. "They used to be big men on campus and now that transcends across the United States." And there, in the middle of it all, is Jerry Meyer deciding who's No. 1, who's No. 150 and who doesn't make the Rivals list at all—an influential, but thankless task as everyone, except the boy ranked No. 1, usually ends up disappointed.

Hate mail piles up in Meyer's inbox. ("I get a barrage of e-mails every day," he said.) Phone calls or text messages from parents and coaches get screened and ignored. ("It doesn't even really affect me anymore," Meyer conceded.) And their messages asking him for a better ranking or a second look or further consideration don't last very long. ("I just hit Delete," he said.) Only he knows what he's looking for. A live body—that's what he calls it. A body with energy and bounce. A body that's going to get bigger and stronger and gain weight in the right places. A body that runs faster than the others and jumps higher than the others—with shoulders, muscular and broad. No heavy legs. No slow-moving hips. That's what he wants and he knows it when he sees it. Yet still, people attack him—in e-mails, on the phone, and to his face. Once, Meyer recalled, an elite California high school coach cursed him while standing on the sideline just before tip-off at a top Christmas tournament.

"He finally had to stop because his game was getting ready to start and he needed to coach," Meyer said. "To me, it was completely baffling. Here's a guy getting ready to coach a high school basketball game and his number-one agenda right before the game is to cuss me out because I supposedly had his player incorrectly ranked."

But Meyer has never heard from Billy Hicks—not once. Hicks doesn't care about rankings. He didn't know, for example, that Ge'Lawn had cracked the Rivals 150 that year, making it as high as No. 122, and he also didn't know that Ge'Lawn fell out of the top 150 a few months later, surpassed by other players. All Hicks knew was that these rankings were making his job more difficult. Basketball was hard enough already without players and their parents becoming obsessed with personal rankings, and Hicks begged them to ignore what people were saying about them, good and bad, on the Internet.

"Don't put any stock in that stuff," Hicks told the players' families at a team meeting in the school cafeteria just before the season began. "Because one thing I can tell you, I guarantee you, I spent a lifetime studying this game, and I know more about basketball than those guys that are rating them. And I couldn't sit down and rate our team right now and say, 'This one is better than this one and this one is better than this one.' Because basketball players bring a lot to the table in a lot of different ways. And they're just part of a team in the end. That rating stuff, that's just a bunch of little, short fat guys, sitting around, rating people, rating kids."

"Amen," Dakotah's father, Clay, shouted from a lunch table.

"And trying to make a dollar off of it," Hicks added. "This magazine, that magazine. Everybody in Kentucky now has got a magazine. They e-mail you. They want you to send rosters, information. They want to sit in their living room and do a magazine rating high school kids."

It drove him to frustration. But in Myrtle Beach for the Beach Ball Classic that December, these scouts wouldn't be confined any longer to their living rooms. They would be sitting courtside, in reserved seats. Jerry Meyer would be there, with his trusty six-by-nine-inch notepad in hand, ready to post instant updates to Rivals.com. And there would be nothing that Hicks could do to stop it.

Still, he looked forward to going. He loved playing at the Beach Ball and thrived on the format: sixteen teams, over five days after Christmas, winner take all. The tournament's list of players who had once competed here read like a NBA Hall of Fame program: Kobe Bryant and Kevin Garnett, Vince Carter and Grant Hill, Rasheed Wallace and Jason Kidd—they had all come to the Beach Ball. Only elite teams need bother applying.

All Hicks had to do, however, was place a call to Myrtle Beach's mayor and tournament organizer John Rhodes, and Scott County was in. If Hicks said he had a team that could compete, that was good enough for Rhodes. He knew Hicks wouldn't volunteer to bring a team that might get blown out. But it was one of the few places where Billy Hicks had never won and, of course, he desperately wanted to win the Beach Ball. "When he plays conference games, he'll win by double-digits," said Rhodes. "When he plays here, he'll be lucky to just win."

Y OU AIN'T MAKING BUDDIES out there," Hicks told Dakotah as the boys took the floor for their opening round game against St. Frances Academy, a juggernaut from Baltimore's Catholic League whose roster included the son of two-time NBA champion Sam Cassell. "Knock their butts off," Hicks added. "Play physical."

Dakotah nodded, but he wasn't exactly brimming with confidence. The kid he was guarding that night was six foot eight, the largest player Dakotah had faced all year. The shoot-around that afternoon inside the Myrtle Beach Convention Center had revealed dead spots in the floor where the balls would not bounce. And yet the balls themselves were extra bouncy—too hard, Dako-tah thought. Together, for an outside shooter like Dakotah, it was a terrible combination. He had a bad feeling about those basketballs and he was worried, too, about the team's offensive playbook against a squad as good as St. Frances. "They're going to figure out what we're doing," he said before the game started.

But right from the tip, Scott County showed it could hang with St. Frances.

Twice in the first half, the Cardinals went down by five; both times, they battled back. Dakotah and Austin were hitting threes. Chad and Ge'Lawn were streaking to the hoop. And by halftime, Scott County had taken the lead, 37–32.

"Good job, y'all," Dakotah said. "Good half."

"Keep it going," Chad agreed.

"We can bust 'em in the second half," Hicks told them. "I think we can crack 'em, guys. I think we can wear 'em down."

And Hicks was right. Scott County didn't trail the rest of the way. With the Cards shooting 67 percent from the floor in the second half and playing smothering defense on the other end, the boys raced out to an eighteen-point lead and never gave St. Frances even the slightest hope of a comeback. Chad was especially electric, leading all scorers with twenty-four points. Hicks almost didn't even need to holler at them, but he did, anyway. "Don't give them nothing," he shouted from the bench with the game well in hand.

Yet it was Hicks who ultimately decided to cut St. Frances a break. With ninety seconds to go in the game and the county up 75–54, he pulled his starters. St. Frances responded with a 10–0 run that helped make the final score look respectable in the newspaper the next day. But fans who had watched the game that night knew what they had seen. The county boys from Kentucky had handed their private school opponents from Baltimore a good old-fashioned drubbing—and Chad Jackson had been the best player on the floor, pulling down ten rebounds while scoring at will within five feet of the basket.

"It isn't even fair," Hicks told Chad, speaking to the whole team after the game. "You'll score every time on 'em in there. That's a 99 percent shot in there. And most times, you'll get fouled on it, too."

Always impassive, Chad simply nodded. But Hicks was as excited as ever.

"You see how we can play," he told the boys. "Look at how we can play, guys. That was a pretty good basketball team we just went out and whipped."

Next up: round two, the quarterfinals.

"What time do we play tomorrow?" Dakotah asked.

"Five thirty," replied assistant coach Chris Willhite. "Something like that."

"Wheeler, Georgia?"

"Yeah," Willhite said, nodding. "They're about like that team," he added a moment later, referring to St. Frances. "But they play harder."

WILLHITE WAS UNDERSTATING IT. He didn't want the boys getting worked up over their next opponent, but they had reason to be. The Wheeler Wildcats were the reigning state champs in Georgia with four state titles in all since 2002. *The Atlanta Journal-Constitution* had dubbed Wheeler "the boys basketball team of the decade." Their coach, Douglas Lipscomb, had more than 430 wins and owned a ridiculous .830 winning percentage in seventeen years at Wheeler. His kids routinely landed scholarships at the best basketball programs in the country and this season the Wildcats' roster included one of the most prized recruits in the nation: Jelan Kendrick, number zero in your Wildcat program and No. 8 in the Rivals 150 that fall.

Jerry Meyer and other scouts had been heaping praise on the six-foot-six swingman from Marietta, Georgia, for months. Scout.com said Kendrick had the "full package." ESPN.com reported that he had the size of a forward, but the playmaking skills of a point guard. He was smooth—scouts were always using that word when describing Kendrick. *"A smooth combo guard . . . a very smooth scorer . . . a smooth operator . . . slick."* Among small forwards in the nation's 2010 high school graduating class, Meyer would rank Kendrick No. 3, hailing the boy's "surprising burst of athleticism" and his ability to get to the basket "with the best of them, especially going right."

Elite college basketball programs, like Georgetown and Indiana, had courted Kendrick's services that year. And the University of Kentucky was reportedly interested, too. "They're trying to grow a relationship where I could come up and visit sometime," Kendrick said that November. But less than a week later, the coveted teenaged basketball player traveled to Memphis, where he convened a surprise press conference at the famous Peabody Hotel. The royal blue Memphis Tigers hoodie that he was wearing that night, along with an Atlanta Braves fitted ball cap pulled down over his ears, clearly indicated that Kendrick had chosen to play basketball for the University of Memphis next year. With flashbulbs firing and microphones in his face, Kendrick, rocking back and forth on his feet, said a few words that made it official.

"I want to announce that I'm going to Memphis to help us win a national championship and be the number one recruiting class in America," the young man told reporters. "Go Memphis," he added, raising his right fist in the air.

Kendrick went on to say that he was looking forward to playing in front of the Memphis fans ("I love the people") and that he expected to bring leadership, teamwork, and a little southern style to the game ("swag," he called it).

"Is this a verbal commitment," asked one reporter, "or did you sign the papers?"

"I signed the papers."

"So it's all official?"

"All official," Kendrick confirmed.

Memphis fans rejoiced. After Kendrick finished speaking with the media, raising his right fist in the air again and hugging loved ones, the television cameras turned their white lights on the crowd that had gathered to witness the moment. As if on cue, the people, more than two hundred of them in all, began to cheer.

"Ohhhhhhhhhh, T-I-G-E-R-S . . . TIGERS!"

Hicks, however, wasn't going to get excited over Jelan Kendrick. Nor was he going to assign one of his stars—say, Chad—to cover him in the county's quarterfinal matchup against Wheeler. The job was going instead to junior and sometime starter Tanner Shotwell, a six-foot-four wire of a boy with braces on his teeth and blond hair groomed into a tight, trim crew cut. Hicks might not have been nervous about Kendrick—"We're okay," he told the boys—but Tanner sure looked like he was. As Hicks broke down the team's game plan in the locker room before tip-off, Tanner chewed on his lower lip, cracked his knuckles, and kept blowing in his hands, as if trying to get warm. He was no star—nowhere close to the Rivals 150 and not likely to sniff that rarefied air anytime soon. "Nobody knows who I am," Tanner said that fall. But Hicks liked Tanner's chances against Kendrick. The county boy was long and quick—and hungry. "Tanner," Hicks said just before they took the floor, "you gotta make sure you know where Kendrick is at all times. Block him out."

Tanner didn't reply. Just nodded.

WHEELER SCORED FIRST, draining a three-pointer from the right wing. But for the next two minutes after that, it was all Scott County—specifically, Tanner Shotwell. He wasn't just guarding Wheeler's best player; he was scoring. When Ge'Lawn missed a three, Tanner tipped it in. When Dakotah hit him with a pass in the lane, Tanner laid it in for another easy two. And when he found himself alone behind the three-point arc, Tanner took the open shot, just as he had been taught to do, releasing the ball just over the outstretched arm of Jelan Kendrick.

Swish. All net.

Tanner bounded, almost hopping, back down the court, his shooting arm still extended skyward while the Wildcats, reeling, called a time-out. It was 9–3, Scott County. Then 18–9, the county. The Cards wouldn't trail again the entire half and Jelan Kendrick, with Tanner in his face, would struggle to score. He drove right—just as Meyer's scouting report said he liked to do—and missed. He threw up sixteen-footers in transition and missed. At one point, Wheeler's wide-hipped, six-foot-eight center set a screen to block out Tanner and free up Kendrick for a three. But Kendrick missed that, too. In all, Wheeler's star was 0-for-7 from the field in the first half until a teammate passed him the ball on a fast break with less than a minute to go. Kendrick, all alone and primed to jam the ball, bobbled the pass in mid-air and took four steps before throwing down an awkward dunk—clearly traveling. Fans howled and Billy Hicks did, too, throwing his arms in the air. But the referees didn't blow the whistle—he was Jelan Kendrick, after all—allowing him to score his one and only field goal of the first half.

"Tanner," Hicks said at halftime, "way to step up right there."

He was thrilled to be up, 33–28. "They spotted us five," Hicks said. But in the second half, the Cards came out cold. It would be nearly six minutes before the team made a basket. They were taking low-percentage shots and—it seemed to Hicks, anyway—standing around on defense while Wheeler stormed back to take the lead.

"Guys," Hicks hollered, "you can't sit and watch the game."

The coach was frustrated—and worried, it seemed, about Ge'Lawn in particular. During a time-out with 10:28 to go in the half and Wheeler up 37–34, he got down on one knee and turned to Ge'Lawn with a question.

"You okay?" he asked. "You okay now?"

Ge'Lawn nodded. His knees were on his mind, but he wasn't leaving this game. "You gotta play then," Hicks told him. "Stop watching."

Wheeler went up three; then the county tied it. Wheeler went up four; then the county tied it again. On the bench, Will Schu was cheering, standing as he clapped, while Ge'Lawn and Chad took turns scoring. Ge'Lawn from the corner for three—*YES!* Chad driving in the lane for two—*bucket!* The game was tied with less than two minutes to go when Kendrick—driving to his right again—missed a shot high off the glass with Tanner on his shoulder.

Ge'Lawn threw the ball away on the next possession, but the Wheeler kid who stole it stepped out of bounds while streaking down the sideline—a gift from the basketball gods that Ge'Lawn would not squander. With less than forty-two seconds to play and the ball in hand at midcourt, Ge'Lawn dribbled between his legs, juked left, faked right, and then found his opening, slicing into the lane with four Wheeler Wildcats closing in fast. Instead of throwing up an off-kilter shot and hoping the refs might call a foul, Ge'Lawn pushed the ball with his left hand to Tanner Shotwell, wide open under the hoop, for an easy two.

Wheeler immediately tied the game 62–62, then swiped the inbounds pass after Ge'Lawn got shoved out of position. With less than fifteen seconds to go—and no foul called on the shove—the Wildcats now had an open look at the hoop. All the Wheeler player needed to do was lay it in there. But the kid missed. Chad pulled down the ensuing rebound in traffic and got fouled.

Two shots, with 13.7 seconds to go.

Chad Jackson was not a good foul shooter. He was not a good outside shooter—period. And with the foul line fifteen feet from the backboard on any basketball court, a free throw is decidedly outside—especially for Chad. Coming into the Beach Ball, he was shooting just 58 percent from the line on the season, a problem that had less to do with his concentration and more to do with his dreadful form. The best shooters will replicate the same movements time and again, releasing the ball with ease and, at times, beauty—every millimeter measured, every movement fluid, like water rolling downhill.

That was not how Chad looked at all. Sometimes, on a jump shot, he released the ball on the way up. Other times, he sent it flying on the way down.

Sometimes, as he shot the ball, his legs crossed on the way back down—a little scissors kick. Other times, he didn't cross his legs at all. And worst of all, he had a hiccup in his approach—a little hitch in his form just before he'd shoot, which stopped everything midstream and only decreased the chances of the basketball finding the net. College coaches were scared to death of this hitch. "If you're looking for Chad to score," said one, "I think you're looking at the wrong kid." As a shooter, Chad needed to be totally rewired, broken down and built up again. Or, as ESPN's online scouts put it: Chad's shooting skills required "immediate attention."

Chad tried to block out the criticism. But of course, he heard it. He knew. Sometimes, during games, he'd pull up for an outside shot and then think better of it. "I can't be afraid to take that shot," he told himself, knowing that when he didn't shoot, people would think he couldn't shoot, which only created a sort of self-fulfilling prophecy confirming that, yes, Chad couldn't make outside shots. "Kind of killing myself, really," the boy said.

In the time-out before his critical shots against Wheeler, however, Chad tried not to think about all that. He chewed on his mouthpiece and fingered his white Nike shooting sleeve on his right arm in silence while Hicks and the boys discussed what they were going to do *after* Chad hit his shots.

"Chad's gonna put these free throws in right here," Hicks said. And then, they all needed to play defense—13.7 seconds of shutdown, in-their-face, Billy Hicks defense. Namely, they all agreed, someone needed to cover Wheeler's sharp-eyed three-point shooter, No. 14, K. K. Simmons.

"Don't leave 14," Ge'Lawn begged. "Whoever has 14, don't leave him."

"Know where 14 is at," Hicks agreed. "No three-point shots," he added. "There ain't no three-pointers on that thing."

The boys nodded. The buzzer sounded. It was time.

Chad stepped to the foul line, spun the ball once in his left hand, dribbled twice, pulled up on his tippy toes, and let it fly.

Hitch. Hiccup. *Swish.*

Scott County was up one now, 63–62. "Yeah, baby!" Dakotah hollered. "Yeah, baby!"

But Chad didn't hear his friend. He just collected the ball again, spun it once, dribbled it twice, and let it go a second time.

There was that hitch and there was that hiccup. There was the form that required immediate attention. And yet, there was the ball kissing the front of the rim and tumbling in as Chad backpedaled away from the line.

He knew it was money. And when Wheeler botched its final shot a moment later, airmailing a ten-footer that would have tied the game, it was over. Scott County was in the semifinals of the Beach Ball Classic for the first time ever.

L et's goooooooo!" Ge'Lawn hollered in the postgame celebration.

"Wheeler who?" Austin shouted. *"Wheeler who?"*

Everyone was grabbing Chad, shaking him by the shoulders, or slapping him on the back. Even Will was happy. The boy had played just seven minutes in the game, but as Wheeler's final shot missed its target, the Scott County benchwarmer jumped into the air, a wide smile on his face.

"Big-time win, baby!" Dakotah yelled. "Big-time win!" And then, when the celebration quieted down a few moments later and the boys took their seats in the locker room, Dakotah turned to Chad and just shook his head, smiling.

"Chad," he whispered, just saying his name, amazed.

Chad smiled back, but said nothing. He changed into black sweats, popped his white iPod ear buds in his ears, and sauntered to the team bus listening to Lil Wayne. There was no time for celebration. In less than twenty-four hours, the county was set to face Bishop Gorman High School, the reigning Nevada state champs who were the talk of Myrtle Beach that week. Within days, *USA Today* would have the Gaels ranked No. 15 in the nation. And at the Beach Ball, it was obvious why they merited such consideration.

Gorman was trouncing the competition, winning 79–62 in the first round and 84–44 in the quarterfinals. Billy's boys didn't stand a chance: on this, just about everyone agreed. Some were even suggesting that Gorman might be the best team to ever play here. They looked *that* good. Everything about the Gaels looked good, in fact, right down to their uniforms—shiny white, with tangerine-orange trim. But Billy Hicks wasn't buying any of it.

"They're fooling themselves, this team," he told his boys before tip-off the following night after watching Gorman warm up. "They got their headphones on. They're signing autographs. They're fooling themselves."

The first half went almost exactly as Hicks might have scripted it. The county forced Gorman into nine turnovers. The Cards led by as many as seven and never trailed by more than one, surprising just about every one of the 3,500 fans who filled the convention center expecting to see another Gorman romp. "They're not supermen," Hicks had assured his boys. And he was right. In fact, if anything, Scott County was the team that should have been doing the romping. In the first half, the Cards took thirteen more shots than the Gaels. But nothing was falling. Dakotah's aim was particularly off. He had just four points at the half, missing every which way possible: inside and outside, off the back of the rim, off the side of the rim, in and out, off both sides of the rim—just off.

It was 26–26 at the half, a tie game. But headed to the locker rooms, Dakotah lost himself. "I just blacked out," he'd explain later to Tanner. Still stewing over the three-pointer he had missed with twenty-five seconds to go in the half, he punched a heavy metal door and cursed, loud enough for everyone to hear.

Hicks, not believing what he had just heard, chased Dakotah down, cornering him inside the tunnel and scolding him in front of tournament officials, stunned Gorman players—everybody. It was a brief, but entirely public spectacle that continued a moment later in private after Hicks had managed to funnel Dakotah and his gawking teammates into the locker room.

"We're fine," Hicks declared, still not believing what he had just heard.

"C'mon, y'all!" Ge'Lawn agreed, rallying his teammates. "It's zero-zero. Let's go, man!"

"We got a sixteen-minute game right now," Hicks continued, raging in a blue blazer and gray pleated slacks. "A sixteen-minute ball game. *We're not giving up!*" the coach added, his voice raspy, ragged, growing louder by the minute, and echoing in the tiny locker room. "My *goodness*. It ain't about the *freakin' individual*. It's about the *team*."

At this point, Hicks wheeled around on his heels and slammed a fist into the whiteboard. The board rattled and shook as a silence fell upon the room. For a few moments, no one said anything. Hicks just paced. Then, gathering himself, he turned to the boys and began to say what he had intended to say in the first place. "Guys," he said, his voice softer now, no yelling necessary, "that's a great half of basketball right there, guys. I'm telling you."

Dakotah was not going to be disciplined—not now, anyway. "I'm not gonna punish this team," Hicks said, "because you didn't know how to act right there. You're gonna start the second half." But from now on, Hicks demanded, they were not going to get wrapped up in personal performances. If they were missing shots, Hicks said, they needed to make up for it on defense or hope a teammate might pick them up—they were, after all, a team. And mostly, he declared, there was no need for cursing right now. Even with the putrid shooting, Hicks was still convinced they would win the game. "If we play with the same defensive effort," he told the boys, "we'll beat 'em by ten or fifteen."

But it didn't go down that way. Scott County took sixty-one shots to Gorman's thirty-nine on the game. Yet the Gaels were on target while the Cards kept missing. Only their defense kept them in the game. With just over five minutes to go, the county was up 51–45. But then Ge'Lawn fouled out. And no matter how much he cheered on his teammates—"Let's go!" Ge'Lawn kept pleading, "Let's win this!"—it wasn't to be. With Dakotah unable to find his stroke and Ge'Lawn on the bench, Gorman rumbled past the county, going on to win 61–56.

"You have nothing be ashamed of, guys," Hicks told them afterward in the locker room. "I'm not proud of losing—I'm never proud of losing. But daggone, I'm proud of the effort."

He didn't have much more to say. They had lost. It was close. That was it. "I think we're a better team than them," he told the boys. But it didn't matter now. The Gaels were in the finals and the Cards were in the consolation game for third place. "Gosh almighty," Hicks said with a sigh. "We had that six-point lead and got some horrible calls, didn't we? But that's all right," he told the boys, trying to shake it off. "We can't do a thing about that now."

Hicks dismissed the team, but kept Dakotah behind. They needed to talk.

"What's your explanation? Give me an explanation," Hicks said after the other boys had left the room, with his blazer draped over his arm and his shirt dark with sweat. "Why would you be cussing like that—in front of *me*?"

"I dunno," Dakotah answered, sitting on a hard, wooden bench, dressed in a hoodie and black sweatpants. "Sometimes, I just . . . I dunno. Sometimes I just snap and I can't do that."

"You can't put that kind of pressure on yourself, son. You can't do that. Basketball—you gotta have fun playing it. You played with everything you had, didn't you?"

"Yes, sir."

"Okay," Hicks answered. "Sometimes that happens. There are gonna be some games where everybody on this team is gonna miss some shots, things are gonna happen. But you can't take it personally."

"Yes, sir."

"You'll destroy yourself, honey."

Hicks looked at Dakotah. Dakotah eyed the floor.

"I know you're a good kid," Hicks continued. "I know that. Shoot, I know you're not like that. I know you go to church and I know your mom and dad don't want you cussing like that. But we can't have that kind of language around the team. But even more so than that, I don't want you to treat yourself like that, honey. You didn't take a bad shot tonight. You didn't take a bad shot. Those shots were all within your range."

"Uh-huh."

"I thought every shot you took was going in."

"Yes, sir."

Mostly, Hicks told Dakotah now, he couldn't stand the idea that the boy was cursing himself.

"Don't do that, *honey*," Hicks begged. "I'm not gonna cuss you. Nobody on this team better not cuss you. Don't cuss yourself. Don't come to the shower and cuss yourself because everybody's pulling for you. Your teammates, those guys, even when I got on your tail, they was pulling for you."

"Yes, sir," Dakotah replied one last time.

He gathered up his things and headed outside, where he was greeted by a small gathering of young boys holding out pens and programs.

"Can I have your autograph?" one of them asked.

"Sure," Dakotah said.

Dakotah took the pen and began to scribble his name.

"Good game," the kid said, making awkward small talk as Dakotah handed him back his pen. "Good luck. See you tomorrow."

"Thank you," Dakotah said.

"You played hard out there," said another kid, queuing up and handing Dakotah still another pen.

"Thank you."

"You're a good shooter."

"Not tonight. But thank you."

"Good luck," the kid said.

"Thank you, buddy. Here's your pen."

The kid took his pen back and eyed Dakotah's signature, attempting to decode its secrets. With this treasure in hand, he scurried off as Dakotah turned for the door. Outside, a light rain was falling and the rest of the team was already on the bus, nodding to the beat bouncing out of their iPods and texting girls.

THE CONSOLATION GAME the next night—predictably, perhaps—was a total disaster. It was New Year's Eve. There were parties planned back in Scott County. The boys wanted to be home. And it showed on the court that night in their game for third place against Cedar Hill, a high school near Dallas, Texas. Even before the game began, everything was all wrong.

While doing the team's laundry in the hotel the night before, Charles Eddie Doan, the county's equipment manager, had lost the padding that Ge'Lawn liked to wear under his uniform. Doan was convinced that someone had stolen the pads and apologized to Ge'Lawn. "I'm sorry," he told him. "I didn't see them last night." But that didn't change the fact that the padding was missing, and Ge'Lawn, playing naked in a sense, proceeded to have a terrible game that night. He didn't make a single shot in the first half. Dakotah, meanwhile, barely shot the ball at all. And the boys kept making stupid mistakes. In the first half, Scott County had nearly as many turnovers (12) as it did points (15).

Only Chad was keeping the Cards in the game. With a few scouts still watching from courtside tables, Chad's nine points saw to it that they were only down four at halftime. And in the second half, Chad continued to impress. He scored twenty-one points and pulled down thirteen rebounds on the night while Ge'Lawn struggled to do anything at all. He was 3-for-15 from the field and 0-for-5 from three-point land—not himself, not even close. Ge'Lawn looked tired at times, broken down. At one point in the second half, he dribbled into the lane and tossed up a right-handed airball. On the very next possession, he got the ball near the foul line, dribbled once, and then threw a brick off the backboard. And both times, after missing, Ge'Lawn seemed to jog halfheartedly back down the court while Hicks's head almost exploded all over the bench.

"Hustle back!" the coach yelled.

But Ge'Lawn gutted it out. He found a way to score nine in the second half. He made a critical steal late in the game and turned it into a three-point play. And somehow, some way, it came down to the last shot: Scott County with the ball, down one, with a couple ticks on the clock. In a final time-out, Hicks drew up a play that the team had never practiced that winter, which positioned everyone along the baseline under the basket. Chad was supposed to set a pick, freeing Ge'Lawn. And then Tanner, inbounding the ball, was going to hit him with a pass, giving Ge'Lawn a chance to win it with a final shot. But when Tanner came out of the huddle to inbound the ball, the refs positioned him deep in Scott County's own back court, farther from the hoop than the coaches had anticipated.

Tanner still tried to execute the play, inbounding the ball to Ge'Lawn. But from his new spot on the court, Ge'Lawn was more than twenty-five feet from the basket and had almost no chance. As the final shot—an airball—sailed wide to the left, the buzzer sounded. Scott County had lost 47–46. The boys immediately blamed Hicks for the loss.

"He should have called a time-out," Ge'Lawn said.

"Lord have mercy," Dakotah replied.

"What was that play right there?" Ge'Lawn said.

"We couldn't have done nothing," Chad replied.

"Exactly," said Ge'Lawn.

The Cards had finished fourth in the Beach Ball Classic—and they should have felt good about it. But hardly anyone did. Hicks was embarrassed by the team's first half performance—just fifteen points?—and disappointed by his own play-calling at the end. "That's coaching," he admitted to the boys. And the boys themselves were down. After the team prayer, they didn't stand to rally up like usual. Hicks needed to prod them into it. "Guys," he said, "somebody rally the team up right there. Don't sit on your butts. Get your hands together there."

Outside, darkness had fallen on Myrtle Beach: on burger joints and T-shirt shacks, on giant fiberglass sharks and towering crabs, on Dollar Stores and surf shops, go-kart tracks and pawn shops, on miniature golf courses where no one was playing and restaurants where few were eating. At one diner, two blocks from the ocean, the marquee outside read in large block letters: AMERI- CAN OWNED. COME IN AND EAT OR WE'LL BOTH STARVE.

The championship game was still to be played that night, an all-tournament team was still to be named, and awards were to be handed out. But Scott County wasn't hanging around for any of it. The boys would be on the bus that night when they got word that Gorman had won the tournament. They would be on the bus when they learned that they had earned the Team Hustle Award and that Chad had been named the tournament's best defensive player—a great honor. And they would be on that bus to ring in the New Year.

Just before midnight, assistant coach Tim Glenn stood up in the aisle to give a toast. He asked the boys to make a solemn vow. With everyone holding cups of sparkling cider in the air, Glenn asked them to vow right now not to lose the rest of the way.

"We're gonna work hard enough where referees don't matter," he said. "Certain nights—it don't matter. Certain teams—it don't matter. Where we play—it don't matter. *We're gonna win.*"

"Yessssir!" Dakotah hollered.

And then they counted it down.

"Ten, nine, eight, seven . . ."

Somewhere outside of Spartanburg, South Carolina, fifteen boys were yelling now, plastic cups held aloft in the night, cider spilling onto the floor- boards. It was a brand-new year and they were young enough to believe that such a thing might matter. With their dreams laid out before them, they sank back into their seats as the bus pushed north toward home in the moonlight.

Soon, they were laughing. Soon, they were joking. Soon, it was like they had forgotten all about Myrtle Beach. It was three hundred miles behind them. And yet, something had changed there, something significant perhaps.

This was Chad Jackson's team now.

Part II

MAYBE GOD IS AGAINST US

THE SON LIKED TO VISIT his father. Not every day or even every week. But every so often, at least every month or so, Chad felt the urge to go see him. Mark Jackson was easy enough to find. He was just across the county line, on the outskirts of Versailles, not far from where Will Schu's grandfather had once become a high school basketball star. Once Chad hit downtown Versailles, he almost knew the way by heart. Right turn off Main Street. Left turn off the state highway. One more mile now, down on the right, in the shadow of the town's light bulb manufacturing plant, Chad would find his father. With the heating units of the nearby plant whirring in the distance, there was very little tranquility here. But that didn't matter much to Chad. He just stepped out into the cold, shoved his hands into the pockets of his jeans, and walked the rest of the way, his feet leaving size-13 footprints in the snow and his eyes scanning the tombstones, looking for the one bearing his father's name. IN LOVING MEMORY OF OUR SON, BROTHER AND FATHER, the epitaph reads at Mark Jackson's grave. OCTOBER 3, 1967–APRIL 27, 2007.

Those who had seen both men—the father and the son—play basketball marveled at their similarities: that same bright smile, that same easygoing gait, that same build—lean and muscular and perfect for basketball. Mark was six foot three and 185 pounds. Chad was six foot four and 185 pounds. Neither the father nor the son tended to get worked up over anything. With the Jackson boys, there was often no raging fire, just slow-burning embers, which at times people could mistake for laziness. But within a few feet of the hoop, neither the father nor the son could be denied, soaring to the rim with a ferocity that belied their listless demeanor. There they were, two people, divided by two decades, playing a similar game. They even wore their hair in similar styles. As a senior at Woodford County High School, Mark had two lines shaved into the left side of his head, giving him a sort of streamlined appearance. And recently, Chad, unknowingly echoing his father's style, had done the same, getting two lines shaved behind one of his ears. "It's almost scary," said Bob Gibson, one of Mark's former teammates. Even Chad's grandfather, Fred Jackson, got confused at times. He often mistakenly turned to his grandson, Chad, and called him by his dead son's name: Mark.

But on the court and off, the father and son weren't exactly the same. Mark had terrible hands and clumsy feet while Chad, even at his height, could play point guard, smooth with the ball. Chad was more physical than his father, more talented, and more intelligent, too. He wasn't going to end up like Mark Jackson: in prison, on drugs, dead at age thirty-nine, and laid to rest in this cemetery near the lightbulb factory. And Chad was also not going to end up like his older brother, Chase, who, at age twenty, had already been in and out of jail and in and out of trouble. One night that fall, a month before the basketball season began, Georgetown police responded to a call that a tall black man was walking naked in the Walmart parking lot. When the police arrived ten minutes later to investigate, Chase Jackson, six foot ten, was wearing his clothes and informed the officers that his twin brother was the man police were looking for. Then Chase walked away from the police, became violent, punched a handicapped sign, ran, and had to be subdued with a Taser.

"It's put a lot of stress on my mom," Chad said that fall of Chase's problems, which he rarely discussed with his friends and teammates. "And that's why I get on my brother a whole lot," he added. "I just tell him it's not right." Chad was worried that Chase was headed down the same path that his father had once traveled. But Chad was on a different road. He had scored well on the ACT standardized test on his first try—far higher than his teammates. He wasn't just a talented athlete, he was bright—quiet, yes, but mature—and he was determined to leave Scott County even if it meant going to a small school, like James Madison University, which was one of the few colleges recruiting Chad when he returned home from Myrtle Beach. James Madison was no elite program. But still, it wasn't Georgetown—and for Chad, that was a start.

"I gotta get outta this place," he told friend Bree Saunders one day while the two lounged in the gym. "The day I graduate, I'm gone."

"Where's James Madison?" Bree asked him.

"Virginia," he said.

"Virginia?" she replied. "You're going to leave me?"

"Yeah," Chad said again. "I'm gone."

I T WAS JUST middle school basketball. But even now, almost three decades later, people who witnessed the moment still can't shake what they saw in the gym that day. Mark Jackson, an eighth grader at Woodford County Middle, got the ball in the low post, head-faked to his left, drop-stepped to his right, and then threw down a dunk over Scott County Middle School's monstrous center.

It wasn't the stuff of NBA highlight reels. The ball rattled around the rim before falling in. Still, it was a dunk, and people who witnessed it were stunned, including, apparently, Mark, who promptly tripped and fell, as he rumbled back down the court—a moment that seemed to capture everything about the young basketball player all at once. He was clumsy, but strong, awkward, but athletic, a raw talent with the potential for greatness. "We laughed and rode him," said former teammate Jeff Moffett, recalling Mark's awkward fall. "But you couldn't laugh too much because he was an eighth grader and he had dunked it."

Jackson didn't play much his freshman year at Woodford County High. But as a sophomore, he contributed. And by his junior year, he was a starter and something of a star. He was the team's second-leading rebounder, averaging nine points a game, but head coach Gene Kirk grew frustrated with Mark at times. He had to get on him about his grades and his work ethic. He could be unfocused—both on and off the court—and sometimes just plain goofy. The boy had a tendency to break into a wide, sheepish grin right in the middle of a coach's tirade. And then there were his dreadful hands, which were about as reliable for catching a basketball as a pair of bricks. Kirk would whip basketballs at Mark in practice, trying to teach the boy the art of catching, which helped, but couldn't cure the problem. "It was like he had butter on his hands," said longtime friend and former teammate Robert Greenlee, Woodford County's five-foot-ten flash of a point guard.

Coming into his senior year, however, there was reason for hope. Mark

Jackson was among four seniors returning for the 1985–86 season. Kirk believed they would compete and he was right. The Yellow Jackets buzzed out to a 9-0 record, their best start in school history, finished the regular season 18-5, and then won districts, earning a trip to the eleventh region tournament and a shot at Rupp. A really, really long shot, anyway.

Woodford County had never made the state tournament, not once. It hadn't even made it to an eleventh region final game. The road to Rupp in this region almost always ran through Lexington, through the city schools. Since 1970, a Lexington school had represented the region at state in every year but one. "All my life," Moffett mourned that season, "Woodford County has been in the shadow of Lexington." And that trend wasn't likely to change this year, not with Henry Clay High School looming in the regional tournament bracket.

The Blue Devils entered postseason play ranked No. 6 in Kentucky, just three years removed from their latest state title. Their point guard was Sean Sutton, the son of then UK head basketball coach Eddie Sutton. They weren't just favorites to win the region; they were contenders to win it all. And the Devils had absolutely owned Mark Jackson and his teammates that season. Henry Clay had beaten Woodford County twice, both times by double digits.

But when the Yellow Jackets won their first game of the regional tournament, advancing to play the Devils in the semifinals, Gene Kirk unveiled a new game plan for his boys: slow it down, hold the ball.

In effect, stall.

What happened that night in early March 1986 in the civic center in Frankfort remains, to this day, a topic of conversation in Woodford County. The hometown Yellow Jackets matched the big-city Blue Devils blow by blow. They were only down two at halftime. Only down three at the end of the third quarter. And then they slipped into the lead, up four with under two minutes to play and two thousand Woodford County fans on their feet. In the end, the game would be decided by free throws and referees and one borderline foul call—with three seconds left—that went in Woodford County's favor. But the play that the Woodford County boys would remember most happened well before all that.

It was earlier in the game. Woodford County had missed a shot and the ball clanged off the back of the rim, ricocheting almost straight up into the air. No fewer than five players were bunched up near the basket at the time, waiting on the rebound, including Mark Jackson, who was standing flat-footed in the paint almost directly beneath the hoop.

Mark had almost no shot at the rebound. Already now, the ball was sailing away from him, inching toward midcourt. Two Henry Clay players were in much better position to pull it in. But it was Mark who jumped first and jumped higher, leaning back, reaching out with his right arm fully extended, finding the ball with an outstretched hand just above the lip of the rim, and slamming it home in one fluid, violent motion.

The rim quivered, the backboard lurched forward and sprung back, and Mark bounded away, almost skipping on his long legs, while his teammates punched the air with their fists. There would be no tripping after this dunk, no clumsiness whatsoever. For once, Mark Jackson, the boy with bricks for hands, was absolutely perfect. And his teammates could feel it now: Maybe they could win. Mark had given them reason to believe. "When he looked at me, when we made eye contact on the other end of the court, he had this gleam in his eye," Moffett said, recalling the play nearly twenty-five years later. "I think we all saw it."

Woodford County didn't just beat Henry Clay, 39–38, that night. It won the regional finals the next night, too—this time, in a walk. Mark Jackson and his teammates were headed for Rupp and the entire county rallied around them. It hardly mattered that the Yellow Jackets would be eliminated in their first game in the state tournament. What counted was that they had made it there at all. As the boys prepared to leave for Lexington the day of the Sweet 16, they gave speeches at a pep rally in the gym and then boarded a yellow school bus waiting outside. Stepping on board, Mark Jackson, cool and calm as usual, said nothing as he pulled the hood of his windbreaker over his head. But the crowd outside was decidedly more animated, surging around the bus, thankful to be close to history, and chanting.

"*Rupp Arena!* . . . *Rupp-Rupp Areee-na!*

"*Rupp Arena!* . . . *Rupp-Rupp Areee-na!*"

. . . .

THE FATHER AND THE SON never talked much about Mark's play-ing days. Mark Jackson didn't tell tales about the pep rally in the gym before the Sweet 16: how he had stood before the fans on the gym floor wear-ing a dress shirt and tie; how he had acknowledged the fans as they cheered for him, pointing his fingers in the air; or how, finally, he had taken his turn at the microphone, raising a hand to hush the crowd.

"Hold on, hold on, hold on," he said. "Wait a minute. Wait a minute." And then Mark Jackson began to speak. "I'd just like to say thank y'all for all the support y'all gave me for all the four years I've been up here."

"*Shhhhhhh!*" someone said from the stands.

"I knew all the time that we could take y'all to the Sweet 16."

Mark couldn't have been more thrilled about it at the time. Teammate Mike Moraja remembers Mark being even more excited than most of the boys. The week of the game at Rupp, there was Mark in line for tickets at the high school early one morning, hoping to score a few of the allotted eight hundred seats before they sold out in thirty-five minutes flat. And there he was, three nights later in the locker room before the game at Rupp, getting a chance to meet former U.S. senator, two-time Kentucky governor, and proud Woodford County resident A. B. "Happy" Chandler, who visited with the boys, shook their hands, and told them how much he loved them with tears in his eyes. "I'll tell you what," an emotional Chandler said after taking his seat at midcourt that day, "they broke me down. I could tell they had accomplished a dream."

But the dream for Mark Jackson would not last. After graduation, he had hoped to play basketball somewhere—maybe Sheridan Junior College in Wyoming—and then catch on at a Division I school. But instead, he began working for his father's lawn service. He met a woman in Lexington, got mar-ried and had two sons with her. But within a year of their marriage, the two had separated. Mark admitted to drinking, smoking marijuana, and using crack cocaine. And by the fall of 1992, Joy Jackson was reporting to police a series of violent assaults, which, that December, turned especially brutal when Mark broke into Joy's house through a window in the middle of the night and assaulted her in the presence of their two sons. He had been drinking again, but Joy ultimately escaped, flagging down a police officer outside.

The district attorney, who had failed to prosecute Mark in the previous incidents, could not ignore the problem any longer, handing down serious criminal charges, which led to Mark Jackson's arrest and, finally, a guilty plea. With Mark staring down prison time now, people began writing letters to the judge, asking for mercy and describing him as a gentle man who had lost his way. He was loving and caring. A Christian. A sincere young man. A proud father. His former coaches, including Kirk, wrote letters saying he had sacrificed his own goals for the good of the basketball team. Probation was what he deserved, everyone agreed, including Joy, who told the judge she wanted Mark to be there for his boys, and, of course, Mark wanted that, too. He felt lonely, depressed, and worried. "I am truly scared," he told the judge in a letter penned in perfect cursive handwriting. "I have two little boys who really need me . . . I was raised up in Versailles, Kentucky, and anyone there will tell you I am not a violence person."

Psychologists, however, disagreed. One called Mark Jackson dangerous and another said that he acknowledged little wrongdoing. And finally, in early June 1993, with Chad closing in on his second birthday, a judge sided with the psychologists, sentencing the former basketball player to seven years in prison. Mark served four years, got out, and then got in trouble again. There was a cocaine charge, and more prison time, and then, finally, in 2004, freedom. But his old teammates were worried about him now. "It was like the drugs had took over," said Greenlee, who had known Mark since third grade. "He didn't care about nothing no more." And he was grappling with other issues, too. Mark had a history of heart attacks, hypertension, and cardiac arrhythmia—problems that had worsened during his time in prison and could be exacerbated by further drug use. And so, when he died in April 2007, succumbing to complications of an enlarged and weakened heart due to chronic substance abuse, Greenlee was heartbroken if not exactly surprised. Upon getting the news, Mark's old friend dropped the telephone and began to cry. "It was like I had lost a brother," said Greenlee, who would serve as a pallbearer at the funeral, carrying Mark's casket to the cemetery near the lightbulb factory. "He was my best friend, but also a brother."

Chad Jackson, Mark's youngest son, was crying now, too. At his father's funeral in Versailles, Chad, just fifteen years old at the time, was unable to finish the poem he was supposed to read without sobbing. "It was just hard to know," Chad said, "that he was gone." But Mark Jackson's former teammates had at least one fond, recent memory to which they could cling.

A few of them had seen Mark about a year before his death in the winter of 2006. Woodford County High School had invited members of the 1986 basketball team back to the gym for a reception to mark the twentieth anniversary of the school's one and only trip to the state tournament. Moffett, the team's leading scorer, was there. Greenlee, the little point guard, was there, too. Even Coach Kirk came out for the night—and then in walked Mark Jackson.

He looked tired, his old teammates thought, hollowed out, not well. But Mark was happy to be there, smiling and hugging everyone. "Mark," Moffett recalled, "probably hugged me twenty-five times." And when the night was over, Moffett said he could almost feel his old teammate not wanting the moment to end, not wanting to leave the gym and go home. Mark Jackson wanted to keep talking. He wanted to talk about his boys—Chad in particular. "Man," he told Moffett with that gleam in his eye once again, "let me tell you about my son."

CHAD JACKSON SLEPT most of the way home from Myrtle Beach, laying down across two seats on the bus, with his long legs draped across the aisle. Just after dawn, when the bus rolled up outside Scott County High School, Chad walked to his car and went home. It was New Year's Day, no practice. But the next day, the boys were back at it, returning to the gym for their first game of the new year against a tiny religious school named Lexington Christian Academy.

The game was a perfectly scheduled easy win, sandwiched between the Beach Ball and the start of the county's tough district schedule against Henry Clay and other Lexington schools. Lexington Christian had about four hundred students—one-fifth that of Scott County. The Eagles were small; their starting point guard was about five foot eight. And the good Christian boys from Lexington, dressed in their blue uniforms with white trim, had never beaten Scott County anywhere, much less inside the Cards' home gym.

Dakotah felt good about their chances—and about the team in general. Even with the ugly ending in Myrtle Beach, Dakotah felt better about the team this year than he had at this time the previous season. And Chad felt good, too, quietly dribbling a ball between his legs in the locker room before the game. With the award he had won at the Beach Ball and other accolades—he'd been named to the all-tournament team, too—Chad figured it was only a matter of time before top colleges started calling. "I could be a different man," he said.

And Hicks seemed to agree. In his locker room speech before the Lexington Christian game, he kept singling out his quietest player, praising him for his play at the Beach Ball and telling the other boys to find Chad on the floor tonight, to get the ball to Chad. Hicks had even written it on the whiteboard in the locker room, summarizing the offensive game plan against the Eagles' zone defense in three simple words:

"Look for Chad."

Ge'Lawn may have been the No. 2 ranked player in the state when the season had begun, but now it felt like he wasn't even the best player on his own team. Ge'Lawn wasn't playing tonight. It was the knees, the tendinitis, the pain. The right knee was particularly swollen, but they both ached. "They hurt too bad," Ge'Lawn complained. And so, when the county's public address announcer introduced the starters—"And at guard, six-foot-four-inch senior, number one, *Chaaaaaaaaaad Jackson!*"—Ge'Lawn was on the bench. The only way he was playing, Hicks informed the team, was if someone got hurt or got in foul trouble.

"We'll see how it goes," he told Ge'Lawn.

T HE COUNTY BOYS looked flat from the tip. Austin mishandled a pass, leading to three points for Lexington Christian on the other end. And Chad bungled the next pass, leading to an Eagles fast break. The boys amassed twelve turnovers in the first half in all, just as they had in their half-dead performance against Cedar Hill two nights earlier, looking careless at times and hapless at others. The Eagles, meanwhile, were pressing on defense and patient on offense, seemingly pulling a page from Woodford County's old playbook: waiting for the right shot, working the ball around, holding it for up to a minute at times.

In effect, stalling.

And it was working. Hicks couldn't believe it. What was supposed to be an easy game—a low-stress night in the gym—had suddenly become a throbbing headache for the coaches and a nuisance for the boys, still tired from the long trip back home. Like pesky gnats buzzing in the ears of giants, the smaller boys from Lexington Christian wouldn't go away and couldn't be swatted and killed. The last minute of the first half said it all.

With the Cardinals up 25–23, the Eagles' diminutive point guard—a full foot shorter than Dakotah—stepped in and swiped the ball from Scott County's big man. The little guard pushed the ball up the court, where the Eagles worked the ball around for an open jumper on the left baseline. The shot was short, but the kid who missed it, knowing it was off, darted around Dakotah for the rebound, the put-back, and the tie. Hicks was so upset that he dispatched Tanner to take Dakotah out of the game. But the half would end before Tanner got that chance when Scott County had one shot blocked, and then missed a second shot, before the buzzer.

It was halftime, a tie game, basketball Armageddon in the county.

"How you feeling?" Hicks asked Ge'Lawn before the players had even taken their seats in the locker room. "You ready to go this half?"

Ge'Lawn nodded.

"Get a ball and get warmed up," Hicks instructed him. "You've gotta get ready to go this half."

It was one thing to struggle at the Beach Ball Classic, playing some of the top teams in the country. It was another thing to struggle here: against *Lexington Christian*, on Scott County's *home floor*. Hicks was so steamed up over it that he ripped off his sport coat and paced in only his shirt and tie. And he was so angry that he could barely speak. As Ge'Lawn left to shoot around on the court in preparation for the second half, the coach turned to the rest of the team, stammering and shouting, sputtering and sighing.

"Shoot, we can't guard . . . we couldn't guard . . . we couldn't guard a daggone little league team with that bunch we got out there right now. *Gosh almighty!* We've got to be some of the *sorriest* defensive players who have ever walked on this earth. Some of you guys just stand out there under the goal and don't even move. Just stand there and watch the ball move around."

There was a long pause as Hicks just glared at the boys. Then . . .

"Gosh almighty!" he said again. "How on earth did we let those guys out-hustle us like that, guys? How many turnovers have we made with them outhustling you? Just *stupid* turnovers, just getting the ball and giving it to them, not catching the ball or not being tough with the ball. Tough? *Gosh almighty!* Some of you guys act like you're basketball players—you're *too soft* to play basketball."

There was another long pause. More glaring. And then . . .

"Any little team, like that," Hicks continued, "that wants to come out there and be harder and tougher, they just come out there and knock us around, *steal the ball, outhustle us,* right on our home court."

Home court. Hicks kept coming back to that idea. The coach from Harlan County may not have built this gym—not with his own hands—but he might as well have. The two state championship banners in the rafters, the two Mr. Basketball winners who had graduated, the seven trips to Rupp Arena, and the three hundred season tickets that the athletic department sold for basketball games, generating $25,000 for the boys and girls basketball teams—all these things could be traced back, directly or indirectly, to Billy Hicks. People could criticize him all they wanted. They could call him a cheater and a whiner. They could mock him for the way he talked or the way he dressed or the way he stomped up and down the sidelines, his arms flailing and his mustache twitching. They could call him overrated or past his prime. But they couldn't call him a poser. Hicks lived in this gym, for this gym. "I thank God," he said once, "every day I step on that court." But these boys, these transfers from elsewhere sitting in the locker room before him now—who really knew about them?

"I don't know," Hicks said, "if some of you guys even got a home court."

"Gosh almighty!" he added. "I've never been so aggravated in my life with a basketball team."

And then, a moment later, Hicks just sighed—a long, pained wheeze of a sigh emanating from a dark place deep inside of him.

"Pheeeeeee-eeeeew."

ET'S GO, GEE! Shut 'em down, Gee!"

The fans sitting behind the Cardinals bench were thrilled to see Ge'Lawn Guyn back on the floor to start the second half. But Ge'Lawn looked about as lost as his coach. The first thing he did was pick up a technical foul for trying to intervene as a Lexington Christian player elbowed Will Schu in the back in a scrum for a loose ball. He missed a three-pointer, then a layup, one jumper, and then another. Even his best plays seemed to backfire. When Ge'Lawn collected a long rebound from one of his own misses, backing into the lane and making a no-look bounce pass to Tamron Manning in the low post, Tamron missed the easy shot.

The only people cheering in the gym now were the smattering of Lexington Christian fans, watching as the Eagles went up and stayed up. Chad got in foul trouble and Ge'Lawn did, too, and the game seemed lost with thirty-four seconds to go and the county down five, 67–62.

But then came the rally.

On the next possession, Tamron missed a shot, but Chad tipped it in. Down three with 24.9 seconds to go. The Eagles got fouled and drained one free throw at the other end. But Dakotah countered with an NBA-range three-pointer—his first three of the game. All net. And now the county was only down one, with 16.4 to go.

The plan now, Hicks told the boys in the ensuing time-out, was to foul—foul on the inbounds pass and put the Eagles on the line, which Tanner promptly did. The Lexington Christian boy—10 for 14 from the line on the night, but under pressure now—missed both shots. The county got the rebound and here came Ge'Lawn with the ball, passing it to Tamron, who whipped it to Dakotah, who tossed it back to Ge'Lawn outside the three-point arc, about twenty-five feet from the hoop.

The Eagles' little point guard was guarding Ge'Lawn now as the Scott County star cut to his left and spun near the foul line, striding into the paint before letting it go. With his height advantage, Ge'Lawn had a clear look at the basket and the shot was right there, on target. It kissed the front of the rim, rolled to the back, and then tap-danced back to the front—before falling out.

Game over. Lexington Christian 68, Scott County 67. A shocker. One of the most embarrassing losses in Scott County in the last fifteen years, maybe longer. An all-time low.

IN THE WEEKS AHEAD, Eagles head coach Tommy Huston would watch Scott County play and ask himself a question: "How did we ever beat that team?" But Hicks knew the answer before he even hit the locker room. His boys didn't play hard. "It just doesn't come natural to this team," Hicks told them after the loss. And maybe, they weren't that good in the first place. "Right now," he said in his brief, weary postgame speech, "we're just an average team."

He was confused and Ge'Lawn's father, George Guyn, was angry. For months, George, who was a sanitation worker in Lexington, had suggested he might take his proverbial ball and go home. Months before the season began, he briefly considered transferring his son to another Kentucky high school. The other school, George claimed, really wanted Ge'Lawn. "They was ready to get me a house down there and a job down there," he said, "making twenty dollars an hour in garbage." The family didn't go, but the threats that fall continued. Ge'Lawn could go play for a prep school somewhere, George suggested. Ge'Lawn could leave Scott County, just quit. And now, in the aftermath of yet another loss and another rough night for his son, George was saying it might be time for Ge'Lawn to stop playing. "Ge'Lawn," he declared, "doesn't have to play another game."

He believed the coaches didn't care about Ge'Lawn's knees and were running him into the ground. He was upset that the team's equipment manager, Charles Eddie Doan, had lost Ge'Lawn's padding in Myrtle Beach. "How did his padding get stole?" George asked. "Something like this don't make sense to me." And the whole thing—Ge'Lawn, his knees, his father, and the case of the misplaced padding—had become fodder for jokes in the locker room. The boys took every opportunity to needle Charles Eddie for allegedly wronging Ge'Lawn—at least when Ge'Lawn wasn't in the locker room to hear it.

"I tell you what, Charles Eddie," Dakotah said that day before the game, "you lose one more thing . . ."

"I'll just quit then," Doan replied.

"Oh, here we go," Dakotah said. "A pity party for Charles Eddie."

"Somebody stole it out of the wash!"

"Ain't no big deal, Charles Eddie. Just cough up a hundred dollars."

But for the coaches, Ge'Lawn's troubles and his father's concerns weren't funny at all. Sitting in Hicks's office after the game, they were convinced that Ge'Lawn could play through the tendinitis in his knees. Many basketball players suffer from the problem at one point or another and most endure it—treating it with ice and heat, but still competing. In the middle of a season, there is often little other choice.

The real problem, Hicks said, was that George Guyn couldn't get over the idea that Chad had won that award in Myrtle Beach or that Chad, not Ge'Lawn, was leading the team in scoring. Even coaches at other schools suspected that the rise of Chad, combined with the struggles of Ge'Lawn, was causing problems in Hicks's locker room. Or at least they hoped it was. Either way, one thing was clear: Ge'Lawn was falling short in his senior year. The dream, for the boy, was slipping away, and the father couldn't bear to watch it happen. "I know he's hurting," George said. "I can see the pain on his face."

The coaches usually waited until the next day to watch the game tape. Win or lose, it was good to have a little distance. But tonight, Hicks couldn't wait. With his assistant coaches, he had to see it right away, almost to prove to himself that, yes, Scott County had just lost to Lexington Christian. Yes, Scott County was 7-5 on the season, barely .500, mediocre.

"Where's that camera?" Hicks said. "I'd like to see this thing."

He found the video camera amid the clutter of his office, hooked it up to the television, and then settled into his desk chair for the next hour to watch the game, playing back the loss—fast forward, rewind, slow motion, repeat—while yelping at the TV as if the boys could hear him.

"Get up on your man and get ready to play him."

"You gotta push it up. Gotta take it to the hole."

And then came Ge'Lawn's shot to end the game.

"There's time left," Hicks said, hopefully. "Sixteen seconds."

But of course, Ge'Lawn missed the shot on tape, just as he had earlier that evening. And the coaches, once again, couldn't believe it.

"Gosh almighty," Hicks said. "I swear, guys. *Man*."

Billy Hicks, one of the most successful coaches in Kentucky basketball history, closing in on the No. 2 spot in the record books for all-time coaching victories in the state, had been reduced to a stuttering, muttering mess in his own gym, on his *home court*. Even the light of a new day didn't seem to clear his head. Sitting in his office the next afternoon, reviewing the Lexington Christian game tape for the third time in less than twenty-four hours, Billy Hicks came up with a new theory to help explain the team's problems.

"Maybe," he suggested, "God's not on our side."

He was just joking. God had more important things to worry about than high school basketball—even Scott County basketball. But maybe Hicks was onto something. Maybe there was a sliver of truth in his offhand remark.

Maybe the Lord had indeed turned on the county.

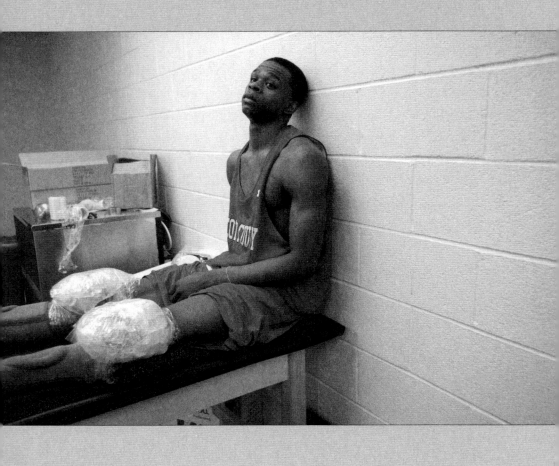

MORAL PEOPLE, MORAL FIBER

THE NIGHT OF THE VOTE the county courthouse was crawling with people, weary of fighting a war that had been raging between them for years. On one side were the preachers, the Bible-thumping teetotalers, the doctors, mothers, and true Scott Countians whose people had lived here for generations and could not accept change—almost any change at all. On the other side were the businessmen, the land-hungry developers, the chain-restaurant executives, outsiders, and native heathens who, apparently, cared more about getting blind-drunk on Main Street than keeping Scott County safe.

The issue dividing them was simple: Should restaurants in Georgetown be allowed to serve alcohol—yes or no? But the question cut far deeper, dividing husbands against wives and churches against businesses. For nearly sixty years, Scott County had been dry—no alcohol sales allowed. To change that now, to go wet now, meant more than just allowing people to enjoy a beer with dinner. It meant that after years of infiltrating the county, taking jobs at Toyota, and sending their children to Scott County High School, the outsiders had won.

It was November 7, 2000—Election Day. Across the nation that evening, voters sat rapt before their televisions, watching late into the night to find out who'd won the presidential election: Al Gore or George W. Bush. But in Scott County the wet-dry vote—the county's third such vote in four years—loomed larger than national politics. The issue was so divisive that most local politicians refused to take a position; to do so would only upset half the electorate. Better to stay silent and let the masses do the fighting—and fight they did, marching and praying, invoking the Bible and stealing each other's campaign signs.

The battle was not unexpected. With the dawn of the new millennium, dry counties across Kentucky were considering going wet for the first time in decades, interested in reaping more tax revenue. And the fight in Scott County was especially inevitable. People here lived close to Lexington, where alcohol could be purchased with ease, and many Scott Countians often drove south on Route 25 to do just that. But that's where many people wanted their liquor: across the county line. And so, when a white-haired attorney named John Cornett publicly invited these purveyors of sin to sell beer, wine, and whiskey in the shadows of Scott County's church steeples, people turned on him with righteous anger.

They didn't want his alcohol and they didn't appreciate his morals. They asked him to be quiet and begged him to go away. It didn't matter to them that alcohol sales might bring in new chain restaurants. This was *their* county, *their* home. They would decide. Just as they couldn't cheer for a basketball team overrun by transfers, they couldn't support an issue favored by so many transplants. Scott Countians didn't want the outsiders to win.

"What does Cornett not understand about the people of Georgetown not wanting seedy liquor stores sprouting up around a town long known for its decency, cleanliness, and standard of Christian moral values?" wrote Sally Wilson in a letter to the local newspaper amid the fight over alcohol. "Please, Mr. Cornett," she added, "leave us alone."

HE TOILED BY DAY in his law office beneath a portrait of John Wayne. But growing up riding horses bareback on a swath of rugged land just west of Georgetown, John Cornett had sometimes fancied himself the Indian, not the cowboy. He was the antihero, alone and under attack, but not afraid. Few kids, he liked to boast, could ride a fast horse like he could.

He was a bureaucrat's son, born in Washington, D.C., before moving to Kentucky. But there was little bureaucratic about him. Cornett was prone to wearing jeans to work and fond of punctuating his points with obscenities. He liked to enjoy a drink at times—fine, he'd admit it. It was nice to have a cold can of Stroh's after a long day defending petty criminals—drunk drivers, mostly. And he was different from his neighbors in other ways, too. Cornett wouldn't be found in church on Sunday mornings, listening to some preacher's sermon and worshiping the Lord. "Organized religion," he said, "is probably the biggest scourge on the face of the Earth"—fighting words in Scott County, if there were any.

But the wet-dry issue for Cornett wasn't about religion and it wasn't nec-essarily about drinking, either. It was about choice. Maybe, Cornett hoped, li-quor licenses would lure a few nice restaurants to town, sophisticated eateries where a guy like him could enjoy a glass of red wine with his meal. It didn't seem like too much to ask. "How about a white tablecloth?" he said. "Instead of just something plastic that you wipe off with a rag, how about a tablecloth?"

In the fall of 1996, the thirty-seven-year-old, prematurely gray criminal defense attorney first informed his wife Barbara about his plans to challenge the county law forbidding the sale of alcohol. Barbara, a minister's daughter, was not pleased. The last time anyone had dared to challenge Scott County on this matter was the summer of 1946—three years after the county went dry—and it had not gone well. In the buildup to the referendum that year, people opposed to the sale of alcohol organized, forming the Scott County Dry Forces. They held mass meetings at churches and invited so-called booze bust-ers to speak from the pulpit. They staged temperance dramas—one was called *Temptation on Main Street*—and asked people to observe days of prayer. The goal, organizers said, was "to call upon Almighty God for the curtailment of the liquor traffic in America." And the Dry Forces didn't stop there. They also filled the newspapers with ads portraying alcohol as evil. In one such ad, an artist rendered a scene of a barnyard with a mother hen looking over her chicks. The hen represented the liquor trade and the nine chicks represented her vile off-spring: immorality, insanity, poverty, waste, accidents, crime, and ill-health—specifically, "T.B." and "V.D."

"Let's keep Scott County dry," the ad concluded. And that's exactly what the voters decided to do, rejecting alcohol by a 62-to-38 percent margin. The people had spoken and for more than fifty years most were satisfied with the result. But now, here came John Cornett, collecting signatures to put the issue back on the ballot. And at least one prominent organization was backing him: Applebee's. With the approval of liquor sales, Applebee's owners declared, they could move into Scott County, and they bought full-page ads saying as much. "America's favorite neighbor," Applebee's said, "wants to be your neighbor in Georgetown."

But once again, local religious leaders whipped up opposition and the dry forces formed anew, under a different name, but with arguments so similar it was as if they had been pulled from the past. If Applebee's wanted to be such a good neighbor, they argued, the chain restaurant could open without alcohol. They weren't going to let some corporate entity dictate their behavior. And they weren't going to suffer Cornett in silence, either.

In the weeks before the vote in January 1997, Cornett received a phone call at his house one night from a man threatening to burn crosses in his yard if he didn't stop this madness. Cornett didn't take it seriously. But his wife did. Worried about the safety of her young son, just two years old at the time, Barbara told her husband that maybe it was time to end this argument. "You don't know what people will do," she said. "You don't know what people are capable of." But there was no convincing her husband.

"I'll be God-damned if I'm stopping now," John said.

It was bold and defiant. But all the defiance in the world could not alter the outcome. Cornett's wet measure failed by the exact same margin as it had five decades earlier: Sixty-two percent of the county came down against it.

THE DRY FORCES celebrated that night. No champagne necessary. But three years after his first measure failed, Cornett was back, intent on putting the wet-dry issue up to a second vote. And this time he had money. Backed by developers who owned land near the interstate, Cornett's group was able to hire a political consultant, send pamphlets to registered voters, launch a Web site, and better target people sympathetic to their cause.

Yet still, it was a difficult sell. In the run-up to Scott County's second wet-dry battle, a woman canvassing a nearby county to gauge support for alcohol sales was informed that she was going to hell for merely asking the question. (The woman marked that voter down as a no.) And wet measures in other counties had failed, much to the relief of Christian voters. As it became clear that the dry vote was going to carry the day in Mercer County in September 1999, people gathered on the courthouse lawn, holding hands and singing, thanking Jesus in the night. "Oh, victory in Jesus," they crooned, "my savior, forever . . ."

But dry supporters in Scott County weren't content to simply invoke the Lord's name and quote from the Bible, although they often did both in the weeks before the second vote in April 2000. Many were angry now and making their feelings known in a torrent of letters to the *Georgetown News-Graphic*. They mocked Cornett with sarcasm. "Let the liquor flow freely," wrote Jim Sanders, "and maybe John Cornett will give us jobs in his liquor emporiums!" They painted doomsday scenarios, arguing that alcohol would attract unsavory characters, like homosexuals. "Look at the counties that are wet," Loretta Tackett wrote, "and who have adult businesses. How many so-called 'Gay Bars' occupy their streets?" And they imagined what the county might look like if Cornett got his way, arguing that downtown would be stained with neon bars.

One bar might be called Spanky's, wrote Kevin Reber, a Georgetown man. Another might be The Redneck Lounge, he suggested, and still another might be The Electric Cowboy, where men could ride an electric bull, revel in their "macho drunkenness," and then be "thrown off onto their numbed rear ends to the roaring cheers of the crowd." "Won't it be neat," Reber concluded, "to have all these great bars downtown replacing those quaint eyesore antique shops?"

Cornett's wet measure failed—again. And although the margin of victory was slimmer—just a 53-47 margin—the Scott County dry forces hoped the question had been answered once and for all. But within weeks of the vote, state lawmakers passed a loophole into law. No longer would places have to decide if they were going to be wet or dry, all in or completely out. Under the new statute, which was slipped into a legislative housekeeping bill, counties and cities could now choose an in-between place where bars and liquor stores were still illegal, but certain restaurants could serve beer, wine, margaritas, whatever.

Scott Countians in favor of staying dry didn't know what to do. They challenged the new statute on constitutional grounds—but lost. They held rallies and supporters attended as usual—but they were also beaten down. It just didn't seem right that they had to vote on the measure for a third time. "It has been decided twice already," said county resident Janet Riley, unable to grasp the turn of events. "How many times do we have to go dry before the 'wets' let it rest?"

It was getting ugly now. Campaign signs were being stolen and more crank calls were being made. By Election Day 2000, people were exhausted and just wanted to get on with life, no matter the outcome. And so, when Sheriff Bobby Hammons stood up in the courthouse to read the returns that night, a hush fell upon the crowd. The results were in.

Wet: 3,509.

Dry: 2,925

THE NEWCOMERS had won. The dry forces had lost. Applebee's was coming and some people would boycott the restaurant for years to come. Yet the doomsday scenarios didn't exactly come to pass—statistically, anyway. Convictions for driving under the influence of alcohol in Scott County fell 38 percent over the course of the decade. And high school seniors reported in surveys that it was now harder to get their hands on liquor—not easier.

Still, they found ways. Drinking and smoking marijuana were common among some students. And harder drugs were available at times, too—ferried into school on at least one occasion by a star Scott County basketball player. In 2007, six months removed from Billy Hicks's second state title, Bud Mackey, one of the state's best players with a basketball scholarship waiting for him at Indiana University, showed up at school smelling of pot.

"He just reeked of marijuana," recalled assistant principal Dwayne Ellison, who confronted Mackey in the foyer of the school that day and then ushered him into the principal's office for a standard pat-down. At first, checking Mackey's pockets, Ellison found nothing. But then, moving to the boy's socks, Ellison noted the distinctive feel of cellophane and tried to remove the tiny package from its hiding place, thinking Mackey was carrying marijuana.

"He kind of reacts and kind of fights me for it," recalled Ellison, a former high school quarterback. "Not fighting, but kind of wanting to keep me away from it. So we kind of jostle with our hands a little bit. And it kind of gets in my hands and breaks open. And I've got all this crack cocaine in my hand. It's like a daggone rattlesnake in my hand. I throw it onto the table. I'm like, 'What are you doing?' I just fuss at him. 'What are you doing?' I was just amazed, just shocked. I think we all were. And to be honest, at that time, he was so high he just put his head down. He just put his head down on the table."

The Bud Mackey story—including the arrest, conviction, and jail time

that followed—was just another sign of what some locals called a general ero-
sion of values. And the latest example of that was easy enough to find. Nine
months before Dakotah and Ge'Lawn's senior season began that fall, the
Georgetown City Council considered expanding the sale of alcohol yet again.
Local proprietors wanted to sell it on Sundays over opposition from several
people, including a short, sixty-three-year-old woman named Angie Tedder
who enjoyed playing golf and tennis.

Tedder, a devout Christian who read the Bible daily, tried to sway a few
votes by playing to council members' morals. "I know you're moral people," she
said. "I know you have moral fiber." And the moral thing to do, she believed,
was to vote no—no to alcohol sales on Sunday. "It is the Lord's day," she reminded the council. "I'm asking you, I'm begging you, think about it."

But city council members, craving more tax revenue in a time of budget
shortfalls, didn't listen. One of them didn't even pronounce Tedder's name cor-
rectly, calling her Ms. *TEE*-der. They voted 7–1 in favor of Sunday sales and
Tedder left that night warning that there would be ramifications—a prediction
that played out in a prescient and very personal way.

On a Sunday night that September, six months removed from the council's vote, Tedder was at the wheel of her gray Hyundai Accent, headed home
from church, when a white Ford pickup truck headed in the other direction
drifted across the double-yellow line in the dark, sideswiped an SUV, and then
smashed into her little import car. At the time of the crash, another motorist
was on the phone with a 911 dispatcher, trying to get a police officer to stop the
truck, which was swerving all over the road. It appeared that the man driving
the pickup, Kenneth L. Carter Jr., was impaired—and police determined that
indeed he was.

Investigators received an anonymous tip that Carter had patronized that
Sunday two Georgetown establishments that sold alcohol, and they also found
some firsthand evidence of possible wrongdoing: an open bottle of Jim Beam
whiskey right inside the truck. His blood alcohol content registered at .089, just
over the legal limit, and the collision was so violent that it ripped one wheel right
off the pickup truck, shearing it away from the axle. Carter died of his injuries.

Tedder got lucky. She suffered two snapped femurs, a crushed ankle, and a broken elbow in the crash, forcing her to use a wheelchair and then a walker to get around. There would be no more tennis or golf for a while. But she was alive, a shattered woman held together by pins and screws.

"This is my right femur—that's all metal," Tedder said months after the accident, pulling out cloudy X-rays of her surgically repaired limbs and laying the images on the table before her.

"This is my right ankle," she continued. "They did three surgeries on it. And then this is my left elbow. This one right here. I can't make a fist yet. But I'm doing a whole lot better than I was."

She couldn't remember the accident and she didn't hate anyone for causing it: not the driver of the pickup, nor the politicians who voted for Sunday alcohol sales. But that January, just days after Scott County lost to Lexington Christian, Tedder mustered up the strength to go back before Georgetown City Council, hoisting herself out of her wheelchair, and then using a walker to inch over to the podium erected for public comments.

"The devil," she told the council, "wanted to kill me that night." But the Lord had saved her, Tedder explained, perhaps for this very moment right now, so that she could stand before the city's elected officials and show them that there were consequences to their decisions.

"You failed me," she said. "You failed me."

Then she hobbled back home to her house near the eighth green of a golf course in a subdivision not far from downtown. The development was a desirable place to live, with quiet streets named after golf's greatest courses and tournaments: Valhalla Place, St. Andrews Way, the Masters. But lately, Angie Tedder had begun to lose her faith in Scott County.

"Actually," she said, "I want to move."

BILLY HICKS WAS TRYING to stay optimistic. In the locker room the day after the boys' stunning loss to Lexington Christian, he went out of his way to list five positive things about the team: Chad's play in the low post, for example, Dakotah's leadership, or Ge'Lawn's ball pressure. Sure, they had lost—a loss that never, ever should have happened. But there were plausible explanations for it. The boys were tired from all the travel—Hicks conceded that now. And there was still time to atone for their mistakes. "Our goals," he said, "are still ahead of us." The next night, as if to prove they were okay, Scott County went out and beat Henry Clay, outgunning the Blue Devils on the road in Lexington, 61–48. The county's brief, but alarming three-game losing skid was over. But if the boys were going to keep winning, Ge'Lawn needed to get healthy. His bothersome knees were suddenly the number one topic of conversation in the gym.

"How you feeling?" Hicks asked Ge'Lawn again and again that week.

"Sore," Ge'Lawn replied on one of those occasions.

"Same? Worse? A little better?"

"Same."

The choice, for Ge'Lawn, was simple. He could play through the tendinitis, Hicks told him, continuing with physical therapy and getting additional treatment from the school trainer. Or, the coach offered, Ge'Lawn could take a couple weeks off and hope the rest helped.

"What would you rather do?" Hicks asked Ge'Lawn one day that week while he sat in the trainer's room getting his knees worked over with a concoction of gel, ice, and electrical impulse therapy.

Ge'Lawn gazed down at his knees. He and his father were worried about the future, worried that if he kept playing now his knees would be shot by the postseason—or worse. They wanted an MRI, assurances that there were no structural problems, peace of mind. And the man handling Ge'Lawn's recruiting calls and correspondence with Rivals.com was worried, too. Thomas Muhammad, a round, soft-spoken man, was kin to Ge'Lawn. Muhammad said his great uncle was cousins with Ge'Lawn's mother's father, which would make him and Ge'Lawn distant cousins of some variation. But Ge'Lawn called Muhammad his uncle. The man was in the gym almost as much as Ge'Lawn's father. And now he, too, wanted Ge'Lawn to sit. "I wish he would sit down and rest. Just not play," Muhammad said. "You're making yourself look bad."

But Ge'Lawn knew that if he sat, it could take him weeks to get back into playing shape, and he didn't have that kind of time. There were two months of high school basketball left to play, two months for Ge'Lawn to show college coaches what he could do. He wanted to play. He *lived* to play. And beyond that, he didn't want people whispering about him, like they already were. The Lexington Christian game was hardly over before a fan stated on a popular basketball Internet message board, erroneously, that Ge'Lawn hadn't played in the first half for disciplinary reasons.

"Somebody actually said that?" Ge'Lawn asked the next day when a former Scott County player, Richie Phares, told him about the comment.

"It was in the paper, my dad said."

"Dang," Ge'Lawn replied.

There were benefits to playing for Scott County: praise and notoriety, attention and girls—jersey chasers, the boys called them at times. It was, Ge'Lawn said once, something like fame—"so-called fame." But with it came expectations. Not just from Internet scouts and college coaches, but from teachers and classmates. Not just from strangers, but from friends. "Ge'Lawn's gonna go somewhere with his life," said Megan Fint, who sat next to Ge'Lawn in Spanish class. "I know it," she added with great certainty. "I just know it." And so, when Hicks asked Ge'Lawn whether he wanted to rest his knees or play through the pain, the boy barely paused before offering up his answer.

"Play through it," he said.

Hicks nodded and made a plan. For the rest of the week, he would pick up Ge'Lawn in the morning and personally drive him to physical therapy. Ge'Lawn might miss first-hour gym class to do it, but that didn't matter. Ge'Lawn didn't need gym class. He needed basketball. Everyone understood that, including the gym teacher, Amanda Wands, who agreed to the temporary arrangement. "Use first-hour class," Wands told Hicks, "to do what you need to do."

IT SNOWED ALL WEEK, canceling school on Thursday and Friday and the winter formal on Saturday night. Even practice was canceled one day, freeing the boys up to go sledding on the frozen hills of the county on plastic toboggans and rubber tubes.

"Get a tube," Will said, "I'm telling you."

"You think the one we have at my house would work?" Dakotah asked.

"You mean the one we use for water?" Austin replied.

"Yeah."

"I don't see why not," Austin said.

But the basketball game that Saturday night was still on. Scott County was facing Male High School at a showcase in Lexington. Thomas Muhammad was going to have a courtside seat at a table reserved for scouts and coaches. The game was going to be televised and Ge'Lawn was going to play.

"Get on home before them roads start freezing over," Hicks told the boys the night before the game. He was worried about the combination of ice, cars, and teenaged drivers. "Y'all need to be careful, guys. And listen, tap that brake. Don't slam that brake." But Hicks wasn't worried about the game or about his star.

"Ge'Lawn," Hicks said before tip-off in Lexington, "it all starts with you."

"Yes, sir," Ge'Lawn replied.

The Cards scored first against Male, but then missed their next shot, traveled, turned the ball over, missed two three-pointers in a row, then missed again, turnover, turnover, miss—until, mercifully, there was a television time-out late in the first quarter. The score: Male 14, Scott County 2—the makings of a blowout.

"We could go down by forty points," Hicks hollered in the sideline huddle. "Or we could go out there and get back in this game." Which, he asked them now, did they want it to be?

The boys opted for the latter. With Ge'Lawn shouting—"Let's go, y'all! Pick it up!"—and Austin Flannery coming off the bench to score nine points in limited minutes, the county clawed back into the contest, finally tying the game, 26–26, with under four minutes to go in the half. A three-pointer by Austin—his second of the half, fired at the basket a moment later—put the Cards ahead. And that's the way it stayed heading into the locker room at halftime. A twelve-point deficit had become a three-point lead. The county was up 33–30 and Hicks was about to make a change.

For weeks, he hadn't been able to decide on a fifth starter, shifting boys in and out of the lineup like a man trying on different pairs of shoes to see which one fit best. It was Austin Flannery at the start of the season, but he was too slow. Then Tanner Shotwell in Myrtle Beach, but he was too inexperienced. And now, tonight, sophomore Isaiah Ivey was starting. But not anymore.

"Austin," Hicks said as the team left the locker room at halftime, "you're starting off the second half."

The boy—part Kentuckian, part Korean—responded by playing his best game in two years. He swatted away passes, leading to easy steals. He got the ball to his teammates, leading to easy buckets. And he scored plenty himself, dropping twenty-three on the night, including a flurry of points at the end of the fourth quarter to lock up the win for the county, 69–54.

Ge'Lawn had scored fourteen, but the praise went to the boy who had started the game on the bench. Austin was named player of the game. He even got a trophy. "Don't drop it and break it," he told his teammates who wanted to hold it afterward. Reporters wanted to talk to Austin now. And so did the high school girls, who closed in around him after the game, wearing tight jeans ripped asunder at the knees and smiles painted on with red lipstick.

Austin was partial to one of the girls in particular: Kaylie Boehm, the county beauty queen who had once tangled with the Tates Creek cheerleader. The young couple had been seeing each other for weeks—*talking*, the kids called it—giving Austin's teammates plenty of ammunition for jokes at his expense.

"I want to know the average length of your dates," Dakotah said once. "It's gotta be over five hours."

"It's gotta be over six," Tanner corrected him.

"It really probably is," Austin conceded.

Even Chad got in on it, teasing Austin for showering Kaylie with gifts and attention.

"You sent her *flowers*," Chad groaned.

"What's wrong with sending a girl flowers?" Austin replied.

"You don't do that at eighteen years old," Chad informed him because doing that—sending a girl flowers—could only mean one thing: Austin was whipped.

"I'm just different than you all are," Austin explained.

"Yeah," Chad said. "You're whipped."

But as Kaylie approached Austin now in the afterglow of his big game against Male, Austin's teammates said nothing, backing away to give the couple a moment outside the gym.

"So . . . uh," Austin said, self-conscious and bashful.

"So . . . uh," Kaylie replied, mocking him and smiling.

He blushed. She giggled. By morning, it was official: Austin was the county's fifth starter, and his father went out to scoop up extra copies of the Lexington newspaper, which included a story on the game. But one father's joy was another's disgust. While Ron Flannery congratulated Austin after the game, kissing his son on his head with love as if he were still a little boy, George Guyn paced outside the gym, frustrated and desperate, it seemed, for a way out.

It didn't matter that the county had won. And it also didn't matter that Ge'Lawn had played well. The boy hadn't played well enough. It was those knees—George Guyn was convinced of it, even if the coaches weren't. Late in the Male game, Ge'Lawn turned to the sideline and asked for a breather, but he didn't get one. And that was it. The Guyns were making the call. They were giving notice now. Ge'Lawn wasn't going to be playing for a while. Ge'Lawn was going to be taking a break, sitting down, and resting those knees.

"Gee, they hurt?" Dakotah asked at practice the next day.

Ge'Lawn nodded.

"They sore?" Dakotah asked again.

Ge'Lawn just looked at his teammate now.

"I'm out," he said.

THE STREETS GO ON FOREVER

GE'LAWN'S DADDY was built like a bowling ball: he was bald, round in the middle, and difficult to reason with once he got rolling over basketball matters large and small. *Ge'Lawn's teammates weren't passing him the ball.* "We can go back and look at this year, at games—game film," George said. "And you'll see it. You'll see it." *Billy Hicks didn't know how to coach.* "I think he might need to hang up the basketball," George said. "Because he's done lost the concept of it." *Or some scout, somewhere, had improperly ranked Ge'Lawn, thereby devaluing his basketball stock and potentially affecting his son's future in very real ways.* "I don't think Ge'Lawn should be number one in every poll," George said once. "But to put him at number five?"

The man led with his chin, quite literally. He suffered from a severe underbite and periodontal disease. One by one, George Guyn, just forty-three years old, was losing his teeth. And he was acutely aware of how the whole thing made him look. Even the layout of the basketball team's annual program became fodder for George's suspicions that he and his family did not matter.

On the cover, in a picture of the team's five seniors, there was Dakotah standing front and center with a ball in his hand while Ge'Lawn stood out to the side, on the end, on the margins. And inside the program, George pointed out, his two younger sons, who served as team managers, were pictured last, after the two white managers whose parents, he said, had better jobs. "But maybe I'm just seeing it that way because George is dumb, he's broke. So he don't know a damn thing, he don't see that," George Guyn complained one day as he guided his hulking garbage truck down the streets of Lexington. "C'mon, man," he said. "I see that."

Some people thought him crazy—and George knew it. At basketball games, he often sat far away from the other parents. But few thought George

Guyn would make good on his threat to sit his son during his senior season, to essentially put Ge'Lawn on the bench with six weeks of basketball left to play.

"Ge'Lawn told me, 'Coach, I want to play,'" Hicks informed trainer Dan Volpe the day after the Male game and the Guyns' decision to sit Ge'Lawn down.

"But we're stuck," Volpe replied.

"It's George. It's all George," Hicks protested. "Crazy George."

Men who had coached Ge'Lawn in the past raved about the boy. Ge'Lawn was polite and respectful, talented and high-energy. He had that quality that scouts wanted to see: *a live body.* And he possessed another intangible, too: he always wanted to win. One college coach called Ge'Lawn a bulldog. Take something from him and the boy was going to come and get it back.

But with the boy came the father—a package deal that didn't always work out, as the coaches at Henry Clay High School in Lexington learned. Ge'Lawn's high school career had begun there. And by most accounts, it was a good beginning. As a freshman, he started twenty-three of thirty games, averaging nearly eight points a night while taking the third most shots on the team. Yet it wasn't enough to keep Ge'Lawn in a Blue Devil uniform. Before his sophomore season, Ge'Lawn left Henry Clay and transferred to Scott County—a blow to Henry Clay's program, but one that coaches there met with a certain sense of relief. They missed Ge'Lawn's talent on the court. But they didn't miss what Henry Clay's head coach Daniel Brown described as "outside distractions."

Even former coaches who liked George Guyn conceded that the man was difficult to work with at times, questioning the referees, the coaches, or anyone who appeared to be standing in the way of Ge'Lawn's success. But it was a brand of craziness that Weldon Cunningham, one of Ge'Lawn's former AAU coaches, understood to some degree—especially now, with Ge'Lawn struggling in his senior season. Unlike other players whose parents could afford to send their children to college without an athletic scholarship, the Guyns had no Plan B. They hoped that one day Ge'Lawn might make money playing basketball, either overseas or in the NBA. But short of that, they just wanted him to get a college education and have a better life than the one they had. And to do that, to go to college and get that life, Ge'Lawn likely needed to play basketball—and play it well. Even if it meant coming home to a house with hardly any living room furniture. And even if it meant going to practice on an empty stomach. "This is really his ticket out of the 'hood," Cunningham said. "This is like the type of stuff you see on TV. This is what he's playing for. It's almost like life or death."

And so, yes, George was crazy, all right—obsessed at times perhaps, but only because he wanted a better life for his son; possessed at times, it seemed, but only because it mattered so much, because it was everything. At times, George conceded, it was like an addiction for him. Ge'Lawn absolutely needed to succeed. But like any addiction, this one took its toll. If Ge'Lawn was the bulldog, George Guyn was often the hound, the old, battered stray with darting eyes, wary of everyone and liable to bite strangers, even those trying to help him.

"I don't know where this season is headed," George Guyn said in a moment of calm the week after the Male game. But he knew where he had come from. It was a neighborhood where it paid to distrust others, a drug-infested housing project once described as the scariest place in Lexington, where Ge'Lawn's father had a dark and secret past.

The place was called Charlotte Court.

THE BLACK COMMUNITY didn't like the name. Months before Charlotte Court opened in 1941, the Negro Civic League of Lexington asked housing officials to change it. There simply had to be someone more deserving of the honor than Aunt Charlotte, a freed slave who was most famous for buying at auction a white vagrant who became a hero for digging graves during a cholera outbreak. But city officials ignored the request. Charlotte Court was the name, like it or not. And even if black people didn't appreciate the decision, they still wanted to live there.

Lexington's first housing projects had opened with great fanfare just three years earlier. Some seven thousand people—far more than the development could ever accommodate—toured the facilities when they were first unveiled, admiring the yards, new refrigerators, and general location on two oval drives east of downtown. One oval, named Bluegrass Park, was for white families.

The other, called Aspendale, was for black. The dividing line was not subtle: a barbed-wire fence kept races from intermingling. And yet, the segregated project was deemed a great success. Soon, not a single room was available in Bluegrass-Aspendale. For roughly $17.75 a month, a family could rent a two-bedroom apartment, live on those oval courts and live well. But poor people living elsewhere in the city had a different story to tell.

A survey of Lexington dwellings in the mid-1930s reported that many were "distinctly substandard." Some lacked bathtubs or indoor toilets. More than half of them were considered too crowded to really be a home. And nearly eight hundred dwellings in Lexington were classified as "wholly unfit for human habitation." Officials wrote, "These unhealthful, insanitary settlements are a menace to health, morals, and safety."

The word of the day was slum. And the antidote was what officials called slum removal. By building behemoth projects, the city could mow down dilapidated houses, replace them with squat brick encampments, and transform entire neighborhoods. The new units at Bluegrass-Aspendale were just the beginning. Even in 1940, plenty of parts of town still needed help. In neighborhoods bearing names like Davis Bottom and Irishtown, people weren't living in homes, but rather in flimsy shacks, hardly capable of keeping out the wind and the rain. Life in such homes wasn't just unsanitary; it was often damp. But Charlotte Court, a project designed specifically for black people, was going to help change all that.

"The best in modern living conditions," boasted one newspaper account. "Model homes that will rent at nominal sums," said another. The bulldozers rumbled into to Lexington's West End, a historically black neighborhood, leveling the crooked, ramshackle buildings that people had once called home, so that large concrete foundations could be poured for a great American development. Charlotte Court was coming. Once more, the apartments went fast. And in time, the project, which was not far from Interstate 75, on the way to Scott County, became an actual community filled with bricklayers and cooks, clerks and porters—working people clawing their way to the middle-class.

Residents knew each other and, often, looked out for each other. When a child fell ill with cancer, residents banded together to help. When summer came, children played basketball together, learning the fundamentals on nearby courts where league organizers religiously replaced the nets. And when someone blew up the black-owned pharmacy near the project in September 1968, Charlotte Court residents banded together once more, rushing into the ruins of the detonated building to rescue Zirl Palmer, his wife, and their four-year-old daughter, who was trapped and bleeding, but alive, amid the debris. The rudimentary time bomb, which looked like a cheap alarm clock, may have flattened Palmer's drugstore and injured his family, yet people here still took pride in the neighborhood. No hateful blast was going to destroy that.

THIS IS MY HOME, read the manual that the city distributed to Charlotte Court residents, describing a place that sounded like an urban utopia. And for many years that was at least somewhat true. But by the 1980s, the dream was beginning to ebb. Charlotte Court, though desegregated years earlier, remained almost entirely black—one of the most segregated housing projects in the state. White people didn't want to live there. And many black people didn't want to, either. The development, once populated with gas station attendants and farm laborers, was now littered with dope dealers and stoop-sitters, the unemployed and the uninterested. Charlotte Court was no longer a way station to someplace better; it was becoming, according to Austin Simms, the city's housing director, a "hellhole."

And there, amid the decay, stood a man whom police detectives would come to know well. He was about six feet tall, 180 pounds, and getting thinner by the day. But he was perhaps easiest to identify by one detail in particular: his initials were engraved into his gold front teeth, plain for everyone to see.

G.G.

THE MURDER, BACK IN CINCINNATI, should have been a sign that the drug trade was not for George Guyn. Just after midnight on a Friday in March 1990, a group of his associates, armed with guns, barged into a house and began to beat a fifty-six-year-old man who owed them $4,500. They then dragged the man to a station wagon waiting outside, warning those at the house not to call the cops. "If you call the police," one associate threatened, "we'll be back."

The group, which sold cocaine on the streets of Cincinnati, intended to scare Donald Hill, a man with needle tracks on his arms, for taking money from them. But after driving Hill to an overgrown vacant lot sandwiched in between a cemetery and the interstate, and walking Hill to the bottom of a secluded slope, the plan somehow changed. With Hill on the ground and pleading for his life—"I'm going to get the money," he said, according to one account, "all I need is a chance"—most of the group returned to the car.

But two men remained with Hill. One of them pumped three bullets into his back, piercing his heart, lungs, liver, and kidney. And although they ran, eluding the police for a while, the law ultimately caught up with them. Patrick Coffey was sentenced to life in prison. Tyrone Ballew, one of George Guyn's oldest friends, got the death penalty. Guyn got off altogether; he had done nothing wrong. He wasn't even with them. But he could have been.

Guyn was good at selling cocaine. On the streets of Cincinnati, Ballew recalled, some customers would ask for George specifically. "Where's George at?" Ballew said. "Always asking for George." He was personable, a dealer who could relate to his clients. And the murder, despite the consequences, wasn't going to end George Guyn's drug-dealing career. There was too much money in it. And so, with his friend headed for death row, Guyn returned to Lexington, setting up in the shadow of Charlotte Court, not far from where he had been raised as a boy and where, now as a man, he would sell a potent product: crack cocaine.

Lexington Police first noted the drug's presence on city streets in 1992—a discovery that concerned them, but didn't exactly surprise anyone. Crack had saturated major American inner-cities years earlier. In Los Angeles, rock houses, where crack could be purchased for as little as ten dollars, dotted the landscape. In New York City, traffic choked streets in some neighborhoods due to the glut of dealers and buyers, both rich and poor, black and white. Crack rings consumed entire apartment buildings, forcing law-abiding citizens to move out. Crime spiked and addicts limped into overwhelmed drug treatment centers. And still the dealers continued, unmolested. "They are so open," complained Sister James David, a nun at a New York elementary school, "you'd think they were selling newspapers." Meanwhile, in South Florida, one four-day stretch before Christmas 1986 laid bare, in micro, the problems of an entire nation.

Dec. 20. Dateline: Fort Lauderdale. A thirty-four-year-old man, working as a driver for a temp service, repeatedly stabs his supervisor in the face with an awl, a tool shaped like an ice pick used for punching holes in leather. The supervisor loses an eye and his attacker, who has no prior criminal record, cooperates with police officers, greeting them when they arrive. "Lock me up," the man tells them. "I stabbed him, I stabbed my boss. I'm addicted to crack. I just went berserk."

Dec. 21. Dateline: Opa-Locka. A forty-five-year-old man driving a brown Cadillac parks his car in an area known for crack dealing. The man says he just wants to buy beer at a nearby store. But before he can get out of his car, a man brandishing a submachine gun approaches. "I say move," the gunman tells him. "This is my turf." The man inside the Cadillac does as he is told. It is 7:30 P.M.

Dec. 23. Dateline: Lake Worth. A Boca Raton woman, who once worked as a fortune-teller, stops traffic on a bridge for more than ninety minutes while she stands on the edge and considers jumping into the boat channel down below. She's here to commit suicide. She feels like she wants to die. She says crack cocaine has ruined her life.

And now, finally, the drug had come to the heartland, to small-town America. Crack had come to Lexington and, specifically, Charlotte Court, where the quaint sense of community had been replaced by an overriding feeling of fear. The grass, which the tenant manual had asked people to be mindful of, was gone, worn down to the dirt. Streetlights had burned out, shrouding the neighborhood in darkness at night and giving criminals plenty of places to conceal their drug deals and dice games. And summers, by far, were the worst as people living without air-conditioning turned on each other. "They shoot out here almost every night," eleven-year-old Anthony Williams said at the time. "You've got to watch your back all the time."

Riots, starting in August 1991, became an almost annual ritual at the project. Residents attacked each other, then the police, firing guns and throwing bottles. Skirmishes raged all night at times, fueled by crack, alcohol, anger, and disillusionment. Black leaders called for more church involvement, increased recreational opportunities for young people, or rules prohibiting short skirts, slouching pants, bandanas, and earrings.

But little changed. Dealers, like George Guyn, kept selling, and children, like Ge'Lawn, kept falling asleep to the sound of sirens wailing outside. By 1996, Charlotte Court accounted for roughly one-fourth of all crack violations in Lexington. And the police were closing in now, launching raids and targeting troublemakers. The biggest problem, they declared, were the street-level dealers. In other words, detectives were coming for George Guyn.

His wife, soon to be pregnant with Ge'Lawn's youngest brother, asked him to stop—and George knew she was right. But he couldn't. He wasn't just hooked on the money anymore; he was hooked on the product, smoking crack at night while Ge'Lawn and the other children slept. And perhaps that's why George didn't catch on to the sting. Perhaps that's why he didn't sniff out the police informant, wearing a wire, who began to buy crack from him in late October 1996. At one point, he eyed the undercover police vehicle monitoring the purchases nearby, suspecting that it might be the "feds." But his suspicions didn't stop him from selling. In six monitored deals over the course of a month, Guyn sold roughly 3.5 grams of crack to the informant for $340. And there was no doubt, according to investigators, about the identity of the dealer. The man had two gold front teeth with his initials engraved upon them: *G. G.*

WANTED signs were printed with George Guyn's name and picture. TO ALL PEACE OFFICERS IN THE COMMONWEALTH OF KENTUCKY, read the warrant. YOU ARE HEREBY COMMANDED TO ARREST THE ABOVE NAMED DEFENDANT AND BRING HIM FORTHWITH TO THE CIRCUIT COURT. And ultimately, that's what happened. George Guyn was now facing as much as thirty years in prison for six counts of first-degree drug trafficking. Wisely, he struck a deal pleading to two counts. Yet serious prison time still loomed. The recommended sentence was ten years. In the end, though, it was up to Judge Thomas L. Clark, a bearded man with glasses perched on the end of his nose.

"Now, Mr. Guyn," Judge Clark said in April 1997, looking down at Ge'Lawn's father from the bench, "before I set forth the terms, I want you to understand one thing, sir. I have gone back and forth in my mind all week over your case."

"Yes, sir," George replied, standing in shackles, flip-flops, and a stained, green, inmate jumpsuit.

"I ought to be sending you to prison."

"Yes, sir."

"My gut reaction tells me I ought to be sending you to prison."

"Yes, sir."

"It's probably where you need to go, probably where you should go."

Pause. The judge looked at him.

"But I'm going to give you one shot in this community with some specific terms and conditions. And if you so much as spit on the sidewalk, do anything to violate your probation, you're outta here. You understand?"

"Yes, sir," George replied. "Yes, sir. Thank you."

He began to quiver. He began to weep.

"Good luck, Mr. Guyn," the judge said a moment later.

But this time, George said nothing. The bailiff was already leading him away—a man in shackles, but not for long.

Ge'Lawn's daddy was free—and he would stay clean, avoid trouble. Anything for his family. Anything for Ge'Lawn. He vowed to be there for the boy and his other children. He'd attend their games, cheer them on. They were going to know their father, even if he wasn't perfect. And George Guyn was going to provide for them, too, as best as he could. No more drug deals. No more crime. He was going to drive a garbage truck—a decent-paying job that he felt no one respected. "They stand in the window and drink coffee and look at you get their stuff," George said one morning while navigating his truck through traffic. "You *better* get their stuff." And so he did, every day, leaving home before 5 A.M., alone in the dark, a man with his thoughts and other people's trash, up Lily Drive and down Sandra Court, up Fallon Road and down Newmarket Way, up and down streets. "Feels like the streets go on forever," he said once. "Don't it?"

GE'LAWN SAT in the trainer's room all week, a star in exile, getting treatment and taking grief from his teammates for his alleged aches and pains. When word began to circulate in the locker room that Ge'Lawn might need to get an injection to soothe his tendinitis—a cortisone shot, perhaps, to help his knees—Dakotah, in particular, pounced on the idea, telling his ailing teammate that the needle used in this procedure was unusually large.

"It's huge," Dakotah said. "It is. I'm telling you."

"There's no way," Ge'Lawn replied.

"Ain't that needle they're going to stick in Ge'Lawn's knee about six inches long?" Dakotah said, turning to assistant coach Nick Napier

Napier nodded. "It's not the length, it's the width," Napier clarified, playing along with Dakotah's game. "It's about as wide as a nail."

Ge'Lawn, sufficiently worried, left the locker room to ask Hicks if the story was true. Hicks told him no. No, the injection, if he got one, would surely come from a regular-sized needle. Still, Dakotah kept after him.

"Ge'Lawn," he said, holding two fingers several inches apart in front of his face. "I ain't playing. It's *that* long."

But Ge'Lawn had other, more pressing concerns on his mind. Part of him still couldn't believe that he wasn't going to play in the Cardinals' next game on Friday night—a key district showdown against Bryan Station, a Lexington city school with an almost entirely African-American roster, two imposing six-foot-six big men, and a six-foot-eleven giant waiting on the bench to relieve them.

"Coach said I can play," Ge'Lawn told the trainer, joking at one point.

"Without practicing?" Volpe replied.

"Don't need to."

"What are you? *Special?*"

Everyone knew the rules. To play at Scott County, you had to practice. And one thing was obvious: Ge'Lawn, sitting in the trainer's room with a cross dangling from a chain around his neck, was not practicing this week. While his teammates ran drills on the court outside, Ge'Lawn sat with his arms crossed, staring at the cinder-block walls. While Chad Jackson took center stage—*"Look for Chad,"* Hicks hollered during practice that week, *"look for Chad!"*—Ge'Lawn was moving ever closer to the margins. "George knows he's got us over a barrel," Hicks conceded. But the coach was intent on playing with the team he had, working them hard in grueling practices every night that week and singling out any player whom he believed was not giving his all.

"If you can't do that," he shouted one day in the gym, "maybe you should be playing for a junior varsity team somewhere."

Pause. Silence in the gym.

"You gotta play with intensity."

Pause. More silence.

"If it don't mean nothing to you, get outta here."

But no one left, not even Ge'Lawn. He was there every day that week, emerging from the trainer's room at times with ice on his knees to watch practice from a chair, sitting amid the benchwarmers and underclassmen—the worst kind of torture. "Feel my knees," he said. "They're, like, below zero."

Still, the night before the Bryan Station game, Ge'Lawn was hoping he might play. And George Guyn was hoping for the same thing, too. He had only wanted a respite for his son, he explained, a break to help ease the pain in his son's knees. And now that Ge'Lawn had rested, not practicing all week, George expected him to play. But the coaches, predictably, decided against it.

"If he plays tomorrow night," assistant coach Chris Willhite said, "there are a few guys in there who'd probably quit."

"You can't do that," Hicks agreed. "You can't play him."

"Win or lose," Willhite said.

Again, Hicks agreed. "We're fine," he said, nodding. "I'm excited about tomorrow night." But it was like he was trying to convince himself of the idea. The Cards hadn't been able to beat humble Lexington Christian without Ge'Lawn on the floor. So stopping Bryan Station wasn't going to come easy. No one knew what was going to happen. Yet after six days of stewing over Ge'Lawn's status, the boys seemed eager just to get back on the court and move past the distractions. Some newly scrawled graffiti on the basketball schedule taped to the wall outside the gym, seemed to sum up the feeling best. The vandal, using a pencil, was direct and to the point. One word said it all:

"Drama."

"YOU PLAYING OR NOT TONIGHT?"

Ge'Lawn had hardly stepped inside the Scott County gymnasium Friday evening when people began asking him questions about his status for the game. The star glided past, wearing white Nike high-tops, faded jeans, earrings in each earlobe, and a shirt with the word "Royalty" stitched on the left breast. But over his shoulder, Ge'Lawn tossed out an answer to those inquiring about his availability.

"No," he said, "probably not for the next couple of weeks."

He was the first varsity player to arrive, but soon the others joined him in the locker room, where the mood was relaxed. Will Schu seemed happier than usual, sipping blue Gatorade, all smiles, and Chad appeared more focused. In a rare show of pregame emotion, he clapped his hands and furrowed his brow. It was a Friday night in mid-January—cold and dark. "A great night for basketball," Hicks said. Even the school marching band was there, with sousaphones swaying in the upper deck. And though the student section was half empty—as usual—the kids who were there took pleasure in taunting the Defenders from Bryan Station during warm-ups.

"You're terrible!"

"Go home!"

"Where's the varsity? Did the varsity come?"

And then, finally, this gem: "Bryan Station players, after the game, stay in your seats, Scott County will be signing autographs."

But the Defenders, led by veteran coach Champ Ligon, paid the fans no mind. Ligon, a slight man with boyish blond hair, was a winner, with 353 career victories before the season began. He had turned around Bryan Station, a proud program that had just two wins in 2002, the season before he was hired. In each of the previous two seasons, the Defenders had been ranked in the state's top ten; including a No. 1 ranking in 2008. That season, Ligon was named coach of the year. And perhaps even more important than the accolades and the records was the success that Ligon's teams had often enjoyed against Billy Hicks. Translation: Bryan Station often beat Scott County—and sometimes badly.

"Stay together," Ligon told his boys in the locker room before the game. "Have fun and take it to those guys. *Take it to those guys*. We match up physically. If this was a weight-lifting contest or a track meet, we win. So let's play good basketball and let's win on the basketball court, all right? You got nothing to fear. Take it to them."

Then the Defenders rallied up.

"One, two, three . . . *STATE!*"

On the court, before tip-off, Ge'Lawn hardly knew what to do with himself. He sat on the bench at first. Then, when the team ran out of room, he retreated to a seat in the stands, sitting down behind the bench. His younger brothers, the team managers, were both on the floor with the rest of the team to greet the starters with high fives as they were announced. But Ge'Lawn wasn't. Not sure where he was supposed to be or what he was supposed to do, he just sat there, cell phone in hand, watching as the Defenders swiped the ball from Chad on the second possession of the game and streaked down the court for an easy bucket, jumping out to an early 2–0 lead.

The battle was on. For much of the first quarter, the game was everything fans had come to expect from a Bryan Station–Scott County contest. The Defenders scored, then the Cards. The Cards scored, then the Defenders. Bryan Station, long and quick, was beating Scott County on the boards. But the county boys looked sharp from the get-go, making crisp passes that led to open looks. Chad scored and scored again, flying to the rim and blocking shots. Austin drained an off-balance three-pointer from the right wing, then Dakotah dropped one from long range. And even Will was scoring. With Ge'Lawn out, he got more minutes than usual, scoring six points in the early goings—double his season average. The boys were on, and they were communicating, too. When Dakotah failed at one point to block out the Defenders' six-foot-eleven center, he turned to his teammates and blamed himself. "That's my fault," he said, tapping himself in the chest. And within minutes, the rout was on.

Scott County went up seven, then sixteen, then twenty-one, and beyond. At halftime, the score was 47–23, a thorough beat-down that no one had seen coming: not Ge'Lawn, not his father, not the Scott County staff nor the Bryan Station coaches, who, in the locker room at half, were furious that the Defenders weren't just being outplayed, but embarrassed.

"Did I not tell you that they were going to give you their *best shot*?" Ligon hollered. The only good news, he offered a moment later, was that they weren't going to get Scott County's best shot the next time. "Because," Ligon said, "they're not gonna respect you the rest of the year unless you do something in the second half. And if I was them, I wouldn't respect you, either. You don't play. You don't play together. You don't play defense. You don't play hard. You don't do *anything*."

The Bryan Station coaches begged their boys not to go down like this. "I don't want to go down," Ligon said, "getting outplayed." But in the second half, Scott County only extended its lead, going up thirty-one by the end of the third quarter and forty-one by the fourth.

"Daggone it," Hicks said as the game got out of hand, still coaching, "let's see if we can get better."

But ultimately, Hicks pulled his starters, showing mercy on Ligon, whom he liked. The county fans roared. One ten-year-old boy even came out of the stands to find Will Schu on the bench and ask him for an autograph. And from the rows of red plastic seats, Ge'Lawn watched it all, popping Starbursts in his mouth while girls congregated around him, spilling into the aisle and sitting literally at his feet, until the game was over, the girls dispersed, and Ge'Lawn joined his teammates in the locker room for the postgame celebration.

"Gosh," Hicks told the team once the whooping and hollering died down, "there's nothing I can say that can take away the way you're feeling right now."

As he spoke, Ge'Lawn rubbed his knees with the palms of his hands. *He should have been out there.* He wanted to be out there. "Man, it was a packed house," Ge'Lawn would say later. "TV stations there, everybody there." Outside, reporters were waiting. Two television stations wanted to interview Dakotah who had scored twenty-two points on the night and, after a few minutes, he finally emerged from the locker room to give them the sound bites they needed.

Reporter: "Did you expect this one to be this lopsided?"

Dakotah: "We had a great week in practice. We practiced extremely well."

Reporter: "You're a lot better than your record would indicate, aren't you?"

Dakotah: "I think we're getting there. I don't think we're there yet. Tonight was a huge step."

Reporter: "Soooo . . . do you think about March?"

Dakotah: "Right now, we're just trying to worry about the task at hand."

Reporter: "Is March on your mind, though?"

Dakotah: "Honestly, it's definitely on your mind. I'm definitely thinking about it—the tournament, everything—and trying to get my team ready."

Reporter: "Can you talk about playing without Ge'Lawn?"

Dakotah: "Hopefully, he'll be back soon."

Reporter: "Good luck to you."

Dakotah: "Thank you, I appreciate it."

But it was Champ Ligon who needed luck at this point.

"It's just simple," the Bryan Station coach told his boys in the visitor's locker room after the game. "We rolled over. We didn't play."

Within three weeks, the forty-seven-year-old coach would announce that he was resigning, stepping down after eight seasons. He wasn't opposed to coaching again. "I think I've got at least ten more years in me," he told the press at the time. But clearly, if he did, it was going to be elsewhere. Not here. Not with a team that apparently didn't understand what it meant to be a Defender.

"Y'all quit before the second quarter," one assistant told the team now.

"Before the first quarter," interrupted a second assistant.

"That shit's crazy, man," the first assistant answered.

"Two o'clock tomorrow, gentlemen," Ligon told the team by way of conclusion.

"And be sure that you got somebody there to pick you up," another assistant said, chiming in. "Because there will be no rides home. Okay? Nobody's taking anybody. Y'all haven't earned shit."

In the gym that evening, just before the game, George Guyn had told people to expect the unexpected, implying that Scott County would struggle without Ge'Lawn in the line-up. But that didn't happen. Not even close. The Cardinals had played as well as they had all season.

The final score: Scott County 89, Bryan Station 55.

THAT NIGHT, in a secluded cul-de-sac across the interstate, six miles northeast of Georgetown, about a hundred Scott County students, including several basketball players, gathered in the dark to watch the bravest, or the stupidest, among them fight each other in the headlights of their cars.

The cul-de-sac, at the end of Endeavor Drive, was part of the Lane's Run Business Park, four hundred acres of rolling land that the city had purchased several years earlier with financial help from Toyota. The park had opened in 2003 with great expectations. According to one study, the development had the potential to create 5,400 jobs, generate as much as $24 million in city taxes annually, and diversify the local economy, which for the most part revolved around making Japanese cars. Everette Varney, the Scott County High School basketball coach in the 1980s and now the mayor, believed that Lane's Run could change everything. "This is going to be the future of our city" the genial, white-haired mayor said at the time.

But almost seven years later, there was very little business happening in the business park and very few people endeavoring on Endeavor Drive. Only a few tenants had moved in, making the desolate business park the perfect place for kids to gather in large numbers and throw punches in the dark.

Fight Night, the kids called it—and many loved it. It was something to do in a place where they felt like there was nothing to do, excitement in a place where they felt like there was none. Sometimes, it took place in barns. Other times, it went down in someone's garage. Once, the kids recalled, they held Fight Night behind the Burger King on Broadway until the police busted it, so now they were cagey about their plans, spreading the word about its location via text messages and cell-phone calls at the last minute. Josh Woolums, a Scott County senior with fists the size of coffee cans, said it had to be that way.

Tattooed, five foot nine, and thicker than a wall, Woolums took special pleasure in organizing Fight Nights. They always used gloves—fourteen-ouncers, he said—except when the resentment between two fighters ran deep. "If people really hate each other," he said, "we'll fight with four-ounce MMA gloves." And sometimes it got ugly. Woolums himself had been bruised and bloodied at Fight Night, he said, and on at least one occasion a fighter had been knocked out. The fights, however, weren't always about settling a beef. Often, it was just something to do, a way for bored teenagers to pass another weekend night in Scott County.

"The guys are trying to look good in front of the girls," explained Woolums, who would be voted Most Likely to Survive the Apocalypse by his classmates. "The guys are trying to prove to each other who's bigger, who's badder, who's the badder guy. You're out late—like eleven o'clock, twelve. You're away from the cops and you're doing something you know will get you in trouble because, I guess, they're anal about that.

"I don't know," Woolums added. "It's kind of like the feeling of freedom."

The basketball players had been talking about Fight Night for days: Should they go? Would they fight? What if someone called them out? Dakotah, for one, was against going—and definitely against fighting.

"You for real think I'm gonna fight?" Dakotah asked.

"When someone comes up to you and chooses you, you will," Ge'Lawn replied.

"We got state coming up," Dakotah answered. "No way."

But after the Bryan Station win that night, sitting over plates of scrambled eggs at the Waffle House near the high school, they opted to go and found their way to the undeveloped cul-de-sac, parking their cars on the street and walking the last hundred yards in the dark. The boys were not going to fight anyone. There was too much to lose. But they wanted to be there all the same.

"What are you going to do if someone calls you out?" Dakotah asked Chad, crafting contingency plans as the boys stood together on the fringes of the crowd.

"Leave," Chad replied, simply.

On the cul-de-sac now, at the end of Endeavor Drive, the basketball players watched as Woolums stepped into the headlights of the parked cars. He checked the gloves on the two boys who were prepared to fight next and then backed away to watch the show.

The boys began to swing, rarely landing their punches, but raging nonetheless while the other kids, both black and white, formed a circle around them, surging in and out as the young, awkward gladiators stumbled across the pavement in their sneakers, lunging at one another.

"Keep your hands up!" kids yelled. "Keep your hands up!"

"Oh-oh-ohhhhhhh! Let's go!"

"Don't get hit!"

In the distance, through the clearing in the trees and just down the hill, the kids could see the Toyota factory spewing steam into the night and, beyond that, the traffic on the interstate, rumbling north and south, bound for somewhere else. Next came the cow pastures, awash in yellow light. And then, somewhere out there in the darkness, maybe only another mile or so to the west, stood the high school gymnasium, where Scott County fans had lingered that night long after the big win over Bryan Station.

Everyone was happy—everyone, it seemed, but George Guyn. After the game, he told people on the basketball court not to expect to see Ge'Lawn anytime soon. "He was gonna play tonight. But they said no," George told one Bryan Station parent after the game. "So we're going on ahead and letting him rest the whole three weeks. Why not?"

The message was clear: If Scott County wanted to play without Ge'Lawn, then go ahead and do it. Go ahead and try. But Billy Hicks was unconcerned about the threat. He knew Ge'Lawn wanted to play and he also knew that it had to hurt watching the team win—and win big—without him.

"Reckon that'll help Ge'Lawn's knees?" he said in his office after the game.

The assistant coaches chuckled. But Hicks wasn't joking. At the team's next practice, Ge'Lawn was back on the floor, a ball in his hand.

Scott County's star was ready to play.

WITH GE'LAWN BACK IN THE FOLD, Scott County began reeling off a string of victories, one more impressive than the next. The Monday after whipping Bryan Station, the county boys traveled nearly three hours to face McCreary Central, just north of Pine Knot, about six miles from the Tennessee border. The Raiders hadn't gone to the state tournament since 1983. But this year they were ranked No. 14 in Kentucky. They had a legitimate star in Aaron Watts, a senior closing in on three thousand points for his career. And they had been dominant at times—at least against other rural schools— blowing out Garrard County three weeks earlier, 92–36, after building an implausible 60–8 halftime lead. But the Raiders' goateed coach, Robert Jones, knew that Scott County was no Garrard.

"Guyn playing?" Jones asked Billy Hicks after the team bus arrived.

Hicks nodded. McCreary Central's air raid siren rang out, echoing in the gym. "You want to compete?" Jones asked his boys before the tip. Now, was their chance.

But there would be no upset tonight. Even with Watts scoring twenty-six points. Even with the hometown Raiders going to the foul line nearly twice as many times as the visiting Cardinals. And even with Ge'Lawn scoring just five points in limited minutes. Chad and Dakotah were simply too much for the Raiders to handle, guiding the Cards to a hard-fought, double-digit road win broadcast statewide on cable television.

"You look at it," Jones told his boys after the game, trying to find hope in the loss. "They've done a lot of teams a lot worse than that."

"How much did they beat us by?" one player asked.

"Fifteen, sixteen," replied Jones. "But it was right there. Right there."

Hicks was pleased about the win, sitting in the front seat of the bus for the long ride home in the cold, January darkness. Beating McCreary, he told the boys, might have been an even bigger statement than crushing Bryan Station. "I hope you all realize," Hicks told them after the 65–49 victory, "how hard it is to come over here and beat them in this gym." But sitting several rows behind him, alone in a seat on the passenger side of the bus, Will Schu was decidedly less excited about the win.

His stat line that night was filled with zeroes—yet again. Zero shots, zero points, and zero rebounds in less than six minutes played. In any game that mattered, it seemed, there was Will on the bench, biding his time. And he was pretty sure that's where the coaches wanted him to stay.

But in his office, out of sight, Hicks was advocating for Will, working to get him into school somewhere—namely, Berea College, enrollment 1,496, about an hour south of Georgetown. Berea wasn't the big time; it was NAIA Division II, about as small-time as it got. But it was something—more than Will had, anyway. And when Berea's head basketball coach John Mills called Hicks that winter informing him that he was coming out to watch Will play, Hicks was thrilled, almost shouting into the telephone.

"Oh, great," he said. "I'll have Will ready to see you."

The night Mills came to watch, Will impressed the Berea coach with his ability to run the floor and his grasp of the game's fundamentals. At six foot five, Will figured to do well at the next level. And after the game, Hicks tracked down Mills in the gym to talk up Will a little more.

"Down the road," Hicks said, "he's gonna make a heckuva player."

"Yeah," Mills replied. "But he's raw."

It was true, Hicks agreed. Will was "raw-boned," he conceded. But the Scott County coach kept selling him. "He's a good kid, John." Sure, he made mistakes and got down on himself too much. But he had potential and a nice shot. With hard work—and three meals a day—Will could really blossom, Hicks said—and, Hicks added, Will needed this. "Ol' Will wants to go to college and needs to. He's a poor kid. He needs a college education. Gosh, let's stay on this and get him in," Hicks told Mills. "I'll eat my words if he don't. But I think he'll make a heckuva player one day. I think he'll be a dandy."

"I do, too," Mills said finally. "I really like him."

The problem was, Will was pretty sure he didn't have the grades to get in. And maybe worse, he wasn't sure that he cared about playing anymore. "I really don't know," he said after Mills's visit, "if I can play another four years of basketball." Then again, he wanted to leave Georgetown—"a boring old town," he called it. "I've lived here my whole life," he said, "and I'd really like to get out of here." And maybe Berea was his best shot. Maybe it was his only shot.

It was one of those times when Will wished he had a father. His mother was on him to apply to Berea, saying all the right things about how a college degree from a four-year school could change everything for him. But it might have been different hearing it from someone like Dakotah's dad or even Ge'Lawn's—a man, someone like him, someone who could rebound for him while he heaved up shots all night long in the gym.

Will thought about it all the time. "Like every day," he said, "I think about it." How he had no relationship with his father outside the child-support payments. And how, if his father had had more of a place in his life, maybe he would be a better person, a stronger person. Sometimes, Will pictured what it would be like if he bumped into his father somewhere, how he would curse him, and what he might say. *Why did you leave? Why did you abandon me and Mom?* Or maybe, Will wouldn't say anything at all. Maybe it was best, he said, to walk right past. "If he never wanted to meet me," Will explained, "why would I want to meet him?"

And so, while his teammates were dreaming about playing basketball at college and beyond, Will Schu was setting different, longer-term goals for himself. "I'm gonna be," he said, "the best father in the world." And yet, Will couldn't let go of basketball entirely, he couldn't stop caring entirely. On the long ride home from McCreary, sitting alone on the bus with the windows fogging up around him, he took his finger and traced a message on the glass, leaving his mark in the mist as if to prove that he was there.

"Schu," he wrote, "number forty-four."

Then, as quickly as he had written it, the boy wiped it away.

THE NEXT GAME, for Will, didn't change anything. The Ballou Knights had driven all day from Washington, D.C., to face the Cardinals in the first game of the county's signature late-January tournament, the Toyota Classic. The Classic combined everything that was right and good about the county: building cars and playing hoops. And it didn't hurt that the four-day tournament was a massive fundraiser for the athletic department, generating some $100,000 through sponsorships, gate receipts, concessions, and a silent auction. Even after accounting for expenses, that left some $60,000 left over for Scott County athletics—a financial windfall almost unheard of in a time of teacher layoffs. And yet few officials, if anyone, complained about the allotment of resources. As associate athletic director Sonny Denniston put it: "They'd be hard-pressed to ask for that money."

Thanks in part to the Classic, the athletic department was almost entirely self-sustaining. "We pay our bills," Denniston said. And then some. A Camry giveaway during the finals of the Toyota Classic even helped raise money for other schools' athletic departments, distributing funds to any school that opted to sell raffle tickets. People wanted that Camry—some 43,000 tickets were in circulation—and they wanted to be here for the games. "It's what everybody's waiting for," said Bill Moore, a fifty-three-year-old Scott County fan and diabetic with a Cardinals sticker plastered to the prosthetic leg where his right leg used to be before it had to be amputated. "There's good weather tonight. Ain't no snow, ain't no ice. People are looking forward to this, big-time."

The county boys rarely lost on this stage, but they almost did against Ballou after staking the Knights to an early 15–5 lead that left Hicks hollering on the sidelines. "If we just throw it around out there," he shouted, "they're going to score one hundred points on us!" Everyone was off-kilter from the start. Chad had been late and a few boys, killing time, had chosen an odd pregame snack: concession stand nachos, dripping with yellow cheese.

"Are we just gonna wing it today?" a befuddled Dakotah asked.

"What do we usually do?" Tanner replied.

But early in the second quarter, the county scraped its way back into the contest—and the lead—when Ge'Lawn nailed a timely three-pointer from the top of the arc, backpedaling down the court, money. And though Ballou would challenge the county until the final moments, tying the game with less than a minute to play, Dakotah drained two free throws to make it 80–78, en route to a four-point victory. Round one was theirs. And round two would go to the county boys as well, setting up a Saturday night championship game against Butler High School from Louisville.

At halftime, with the Cards leading 31–23, it seemed the only thing that was going to be given away that night was the raffled-off Camry. But in the second half, Scott County squandered its lead, allowing the undersized Butler Bears back into the game. With seven minutes to go, the Bears cut the lead to one, 48–47, scoring in transition after the Cards bricked a three-pointer off the back of the rim. Ge'Lawn tried to answer, but missed. Two Butler post players seemed positioned to wrap up the rebound. But a county boy, boxing out, reeled it in instead, scoring the put-back as the announcer hollered his name.

"Will . . . Shhhhhooooooooooo!"

Butler countered with a bucket of its own, but Will countered back, getting the ball in the low post on the next possession with Butler's six-foot-six center on his back. One dribble, head fake. Up and in, off the glass—good. Another basket from Will. Another three-point lead—and this time the county would not relinquish it. The bench was on its feet now, cheering on the unlikeliest of heroes—*Schu-Schu, baby!*—who for one critical stretch in the second half scored six points and pulled down six rebounds, even collecting one as the ball skittered into the corner, calling time-out as he fell out of bounds.

At the scorer's table after the county's 73–62 victory, there was little discussion about it. The defensive player of the game award was going to Will Schu, who grabbed his head with his hands as he heard his name announced over the loud speakers.

"Oh my God," he said.

The team had done more than just win its seventh consecutive Toyota Classic. It was coming together. In the locker room, after the game, Hicks praised Will for his play that night. And everyone cheered for him: the starters and the scrubs, the stars and the no-name nobodies, shouting for Will, slapping his legs, and rubbing the mop of brown hair on his head.

"Will," Hicks said, "we're really proud of you tonight."

And then, seizing the moment, sensing the happiness spilling forth, filling the room and lapping at the cinder-block walls, Hicks made a surprise announcement.

"Y'all are sitting down, aren't you?"

The boys looked at him.

"We're gonna give you the day off tomorrow."

At first, the boys said nothing, not knowing how to respond to the news. *A day off?* They hadn't had one in weeks. But then, turning to each other, with mouths agape and eyes wide, they began to cheer, shaking each other with excitement.

No practice, for once. No worries, for now.

A basketball was passed around the locker room for everyone to sign, to be held perhaps in some trophy case, somewhere, recognizing this year's Toyota Classic champions in perpetuity. And the boys jockeyed for position, itching to sign the ball, and mocking Dakotah for penning his signature, in bold, as if he were John Hancock himself.

"You took up the whole section," Ge'Lawn told him.

"Look at how much is left," Dakotah argued.

"But you took up the whole thing," Chad agreed.

Everyone was laughing, especially Will, who was sitting in front of his locker, cradling his plaque, and waiting for his turn to sign the ball. "Let me just make this ball worth millions, right quick," Will said, finally taking the black marker in hand. "Should I sign 'Will the Thrill'?"

There was still more laughter—and Hicks didn't care. The boys could laugh all they liked tonight and sign whatever they wanted. But he was serious about them resting the next day, resting their legs. He was thinking about the stretch run. Eight games until districts. And he was already thinking about their next opponent: Clark County, a place where basketball mattered so much that the school board finally decided to intervene.

THE SCHOOL BOARD CHAIRWOMAN had heard the rumors weeks before she got official word of the problem: Some parents, whose sons played middle school basketball, wanted to hold their boys back and have them repeat a grade, so that the boys might become better athletes, the rumormon-

gers alleged, better basketball players, bigger, stronger, and more likely to succeed somewhere down the road.

Judy Hicks (no relation to Billy) was stunned by the thought of it. In her
four years on the school board in Clark County, Hicks, a fifty-six-year-old retired schoolteacher and mother of two, had been asked to weigh in on countless
educational and fiscal matters. But nothing quite like this issue, which the superintendent, Robert E. Lee, brought to Hicks's attention officially at last in
June 2005.

The school system, Lee told her, was staring down a situation—a potential
situation—describing it like this: Two sets of parents, whose sons were good
students, had approached the principal at Conkwright Middle School, asking
that their sons repeat seventh grade. The principal was opposed to granting the
request, based on the fact that she could not find academic cause for it. Lee, in
turn, had met with the parents. And although they had not mentioned sports,
or basketball specifically, as motivation for keeping their boys back a year, Lee's
gut told him that athletics was playing at least some role in their plans. "What
role? How much role?" he asked. "I don't know."

What worried the superintendent was precedent: Lee, who had logged
four decades in the school system, didn't want to have a district where they were
essentially recycling students to develop their athletic programs, making line-
backers bigger, point guards faster, and trips to Rupp Arena more likely. A policy needed to be drafted, he told Hicks, making it clear that such things would
not be tolerated in Clark County—and Judy Hicks agreed.

She was a Virginia native, raised in the mountains not far from the Kentucky state line, but far enough away that she would not become a rabid basketball fan—even after moving to Kentucky in the 1960s to attend college
and teach high school at George Rogers Clark, home of the Clark County
Cardinals.

Over the years, Hicks often attended basketball games in the school's
steep-walled, solid-brick gymnasium named for Letcher Norton, the coach who
had led Clark County to its last state basketball title in 1951. But unlike many
fans, Hicks refused to boo, hiss, or taunt during games. As a rule, Hicks said,
she applauded both teams at all times, cheering when anyone scored, no matter

if it was the visiting team and no matter if the hometown fans, sitting near her, looked at her askance. She wanted Clark County to win, sure. But mostly, she wanted all the kids to do well. They were, after all, just kids. And it was, after all, just basketball. "This," she said, "is only a game."

It was a quaint notion. But Hicks knew that not everyone shared it, and the fact that the school board was now having to debate whether or not children could repeat a grade for athletic purposes—essentially redshirting—seemed to make that clear all over again.

Historically, use of the term *redshirting* has been limited to college athletics. A talented quarterback or power forward straight out of high school could choose, with the blessing of his college coaches, to redshirt his freshman year, attending classes and working out, but not playing. The purpose is maintaining a year of athletic eligibility while a player overcomes an injury, bides his time to become a starter, or grows stronger, faster, and more prepared to face the opposition the following season.

Lately, however, the idea of redshirting has trickled all the way down to kindergarten, where every year thousands of American children are held back—not because they have late birthdays or poor social skills, but because parents want their kids, typically boys, to be the oldest, the biggest, and the strongest of their peers, thereby improving their chances of outsmarting their classmates in school and dwarfing them on the playing field—or so they hope. The buzzword is maturity; parents want their boys to be mature. And many are, at least physically. Scouts watching high school seniors play basketball these days aren't just watching seventeen- and eighteen-year-old boys, but, at times, nineteen-year-old men. That's how it was in Scott County, where Ge'Lawn turned nineteen before the season even began and Dakotah would turn nineteen before the season was over. And that's all Jay and Ann Stenzel in Clark County said they wanted for their son, Robbie, when they informed school officials in 2005 that they wanted him to repeat seventh grade. They just wanted another year for their son to mature.

Robbie, wire-thin and quiet with long arms and tender eyes, had basketball in his genes. His father, Jay, wasn't just tall, coming in at six foot six; he was a former NAIA All-American at Berea College, the school that was now interested in Will Schu. In 1988, his senior year, Jay Stenzel, playing forward, led the conference in scoring, averaging more than twenty-eight points a game, and even broke the school's all-time scoring record, logging 2,323 points in all. He married Ann, a Berea cheerleader, and together, just before Christmas 1991, they welcomed Robbie, their second child and first son, into the world.

Before the boy was even out of diapers, he was playing basketball on a Michael Jordan hoop in the living room, a pacifier in his mouth and a ball in his hand. Robbie, shooting with his father, would break that hoop over time. And there would be other casualties in the living room. They broke a few lamps, too. "But it was worth it," Jay Stenzel said, realizing while Robbie was still young that the boy didn't just have a love for the game, but a talent for it.

By middle school, however, it was clear that the playing field wasn't exactly level. Other players in Robbie's grade were much older than he was. Ge'Lawn, for example, was a full thirteen months older. The Stenzels began to consider holding back Robbie. They believed it to be a personal decision and a private matter. If they thought it best for their son to repeat seventh grade—for whatever reason whatsoever—it was their decision to make. Robbie was their son. They knew what was best; not some school official, principal, or bureaucrat.

But the school board was asking questions now—of the Stenzels and the other parents interested in retaining their son in seventh grade, debating a private matter in a very public forum. It was clear to Judy Hicks that athletics was a factor in the Stenzels' decision—even if they didn't say it out loud. Why else, she asked at one of the school board meetings, would the family choose to make this request in seventh grade?

"Because if they make that request in eighth grade," Judy Hicks said, answering her own question, "it will cost them a year of high school eligibility."

"That's their prerogative," countered board member Rick Perry.

"But is it?" returned Hicks.

Robbie Stenzel was enrolled in a public school. Clark County taxpayers, in essence, would be paying for him, or any other student, to repeat a grade. And then there were issues of accountability to consider. If Robbie were retained, it would appear in statistics that the school hadn't done its job and that might reflect poorly on the school system as a whole. "Is this going to count against the district?" Hicks asked. "Is this going to count against the school?"

The parents themselves were protesting now. While one father threatened legal action—"We have, as you can expect, consulted with legal counsel"—Jay Stenzel asked Hicks and the other board members to try to see it from his perspective. He was Robbie's father. And together, with Ann, they had given a lot of thought to the decision. "Mostly importantly," Jay added, "it's one we feel as parents is in the best interests of our son at this time in his life."

The school board listened, but disagreed, voting 4–1 against redshirting. And Hicks believed the matter was settled: Robbie and the other boy, she figured, would be moving on to eighth grade with their classmates, on schedule, as planned. But without Judy Hicks's knowledge, the superintendent made a different decision. Believing that there was at least some academic reason for the requests and that it wasn't fair to enforce a new policy on parents who had come forward weeks earlier, Lee allowed Robbie to repeat seventh grade, though Robbie would do it at the other middle school in the county.

Hicks was annoyed and somewhat disappointed. The administration was expected to implement policy passed by the board. "And that," she said, "didn't happen here." But by the time she learned about it, it was too late to fight it. Robbie was already well into his second seventh-grade year. He would have that extra year to mature, that extra year to grow. And by eighth grade, a year later, he was a star for George Rogers Clark—still quiet, but likeable, and playing up with the high school boys, like Dakotah once had done. "If you can't get along with Robbie," GRC's head coach Scott Humphrey said, "you can't get along with anybody." The coach bragged to the media that Jay and Ann Stenzel's boy was "the most poised kid in our program." And he trusted Robbie so much that Humphrey turned to him in the biggest game of the season that March.

It was the regional semifinal. GRC's two senior leaders, and best players, had fouled out. There were twenty-two seconds to go and Humphrey scripted the play for Robbie, the fifteen-year-old eighth-grader, asking him to take it to the hole. Robbie did as he was told, got fouled on the way, and then knocked down both free throws to secure a 53–52 win en route to GRC's first trip to

Rupp Arena in seventeen years. "He doesn't play to his age," Humphrey told reporters, "I'll tell you that."

But amid the newspaper accolades, there were pockets of anger in Winchester, population 16,700, the Clark County seat. During middle school games against his old school, people had booed Robbie. He was called a cheater and a traitor. "Just hurtful stuff," Robbie recalled. And even now, it followed him. Even now, as a junior in high school, he heard the opposing fans taunting him for doing publicly what other athletes had done privately: repeat a grade. In a game that winter, a few weeks before GRC's showdown with Scott County, students at Madison Central held up an oversized, poster-board driver's license bearing Robbie Stenzel's name and photograph.

Birth date: "12/20/1964?"

Expiration date: "Tonight."

"How old are you?" the fans asked.

But Robbie just laughed it off. He had heard it all before.

"I'm the chosen one," he said, "who cheated."

THE SCOTT COUNTY BOYS should have felt good coming into the game against George Rogers Clark. They had won seven in a row, including that emotional Toyota Classic championship. Their record was now 14-5 and the basketball pollsters, impressed by what they were seeing, had recently returned the boys to their proper place in the state rankings.

"Do you know we're ranked number one?" Chad asked Austin that week during psychology class while sitting at computers in the library.

"We are?" Austin asked. "In what ranking?"

"*The Herald-Leader*," Chad replied.

Getting the nod from the *Lexington Herald-Leader* should have been cause for confidence, if not exactly celebration. Ever since the drubbing that the Cards had handed Bryan Station, people were talking about the county again, speculating that Billy's boys were getting ready for yet another title run. Even opposing coaches were discussing it.

"You gonna thank me for that number-one ranking?" Bryan Station coach Champ Ligon asked Billy Hicks when the two coaches bumped into each other while scouting opponents in late January at a basketball game in Lexington.

"No," Hicks replied with a smile.

A number one ranking, in Scott County, would have been big news fifteen years earlier when Hicks first rumbled across the county line, slicing north through the hills in his beat-up Subaru. But not anymore. The Cards, under Hicks, were routinely ranked among the top five teams in the state, making number-one rankings almost routine, a birthright of sorts that came with wearing Cardinal red. And as such, many people—not just the fans, but the players, too—seemed to take it for granted. Of course Scott County was number one. But now that these boys, now that this team, had been bestowed with that title, they weren't sure that they wanted it or deserved it. As Chad informed Austin of the news—*Scott County was number one*—Austin just looked at him, perplexed.

"Why?" Austin said. "We suck."

Thirty miles away in Clark County, the feeling couldn't have been any different. Like Scott County, George Rogers Clark was on a winning streak: eight games and counting. Like Scott County, GRC had blown out the competition at times, laying a forty-one-point loss on the Ashland Tomcats just that week. And like Scott County, GRC was now ranked among the top teams in the state: number three, according to the *Herald-Leader*, a powerhouse to be feared and respected.

The difference was, the people in Clark County wanted to believe. It had been almost sixty years since the county's last state basketball championship and many hoped that the drought would end this year, with junior Robbie Stenzel leading the way. Few in Clark County dared to boo him anymore for his alleged transgressions of the past. Not with George Rogers Clark a favorite to win the region and return to Rupp Arena. And not with Scott County scheduled to play in Norton Gymnasium on Saturday night. Vinny Zollo, one of Stenzel's teammates, a six-foot-eight, 220-pound center who had transferred from Ohio, could feel the love. "You're seen as gods around here," Zollo said. And nothing was going to stop these gods from playing Scott County—not even a winter storm that dumped snow across Kentucky the night before the big game.

Ten to fifteen inches in the mountains, four to six inches in the Bluegrass. Freezing temperatures moving in and ice licking the roads. Church services would be canceled. But the high school basketball game, Cards versus Cards, number one versus number three; would go on—pushed back from Saturday night to Sunday afternoon, yet still drawing a crowd. It didn't matter when they played this game; Clark County fans were coming. Even Judy Hicks, the school board chairwoman, would be there to watch. This was their moment, right now, this was their time, with the cars parked fender-to-snowdrift outside. With some two thousand people, cold but getting warmer, taking seats in the gym. And with AC/DC's "Thunderstruck" wailing from the speakers over the court.

THUNDER!

Heads bopped.

THUNDER!

Kids rocked.

Clark County needed this.

"Bad," said senior Logan Johnson.

"Unbelievably bad," agreed senior Logan Bennett.

"More than life itself," nodded senior Parker Puckett.

"This," concluded senior Josh Wells, "is the biggest game in the state."

Already, in the huddle on the Scott County bench, the boys were having trouble hearing the coaches. But they knew the game plan, which started with Chad winning the opening tip, just as he had done in almost every single game this year.

"I don't have to bother going over that, do I?" Billy Hicks asked.

"Naw," Chad answered, dismissing the thought.

And so it was settled.

"Chad's gonna win this tip," Hicks shouted. "Don't worry about it."

CHAD LOST THE TIP, out-leaping GRC's six-foot-five, 250-pound center, but flipping the ball into open space, where Robbie Stenzel gathered it in, moving faster than Ge'Lawn, anticipating the ball. Two dribbles and Robbie was streaking to the hoop. But he missed the open layup as the crowd sighed.

It was ugly all around from the get-go. Scott County started off 1-for-7 from the field, missing inside and out, and GRC wasn't much better, leading to still more sighs from the fans. When Robbie Stenzel fired up a shot just inside the three-point line a few minutes into the game—an off-balance hook that missed badly—some fans were grousing before the ball even clanged off the backboard. "Pass the ball!" one moaned from the upper-deck. *"Jeeee-sus Christ!"*

But soon both teams settled into a groove. Scott County went up six and GRC tied it. Scott County went up eight and GRC cut the lead to three. Ge'Lawn was hurting, banged up after nearly crashing into the wall while trying to haul in an errant, overthrown pass on a fast break.

"Where you hurting at?" Hicks asked him during a time-out.

"My knee buckled," Ge'Lawn replied.

"You need a rest?"

"Yeah."

"Austin," Hicks said, calling for the substitution, "get Ge'Lawn."

But Chad, as usual, filled the void, scoring eighteen in the first half and pushing Scott County out to a 35–31 lead. "Sixteen minutes to go," Hicks told his boys. "And now they're spotting us four." No one was panicking, however, in the Clark County locker room on the other side of the gym, where Humphrey was telling his boys to settle down and stop playing in such a hurry. This, he said, was still their game. They would win the second half. "You'll guard them," Humphrey said, "and we'll knock their ass out."

Initially, he was wrong about that. In the third quarter, Scott County only increased its lead, going up 46–38 on a three-pointer that found the bottom of the net. But just as it looked like Scott County might pull away, the boys from George Rogers Clark climbed back into it with back-to-back three-point plays of their own, knotting up the score at 48–48 with less than a minute to go in the quarter.

Clark County fans were on their feet now, hooting and whistling while Tamron Manning dribbled the ball near midcourt, killing thirty seconds and waiting for the last shot of the third quarter. The bleachers began to quake. The noise continued to rise. On the floor, GRC's center, Vinny Zollo, would later say it was so loud that it felt like someone was actually "pushing on your head."

And before Scott County could get off a shot, Tamron threw it away. Dakotah had to foul to stop GRC from making an easy layup at the other end. And, just like that, Scott County was losing, going into the fourth quarter down 49–48.

"We're okay," Hicks assured his boys. "The game ain't over. Yeah, they got the crowd in the game, hollering and all that—that's fine. We're gonna play this fourth quarter. We got eight minutes to play. *We're gonna play.*"

Chad nodded. The GRC students screamed.

"White!"

"RED!"

"White!"

"RED!"

It was the moment that Robbie Stenzel had been picturing for days as he lay in bed at night, unable to fall sleep, or sat in class at school, struggling to focus. "What if you guys lose?" kids had wanted to know all week—a thought that Robbie didn't want to consider, both then and now, as he drove into the lane, pulled up for a six-footer, nailed it, got fouled, and then hit his free throw.

Three-point play, Stenzel. Four-point lead, GRC; 4:49 to go.

But here came Scott County with a three of its own, and then a bucket, and then the lead. Ge'Lawn put the county up one, driving for a basket—his biggest of the season—with 1:23 left in the game. And then Dakotah had a chance to extend the lead, stepping to the foul line for two shots with 53.4 seconds to play.

With an entire county cheering against him now—*"Miss it!"* the GRC students yelled. *"Miss it!"*—Dakotah took his time at the stripe, palming the ball in his left hand, and taking a series of breaths, deep and slow, his chest rising and falling with each beat.

One . . .

Two . . .

Three . . .

Dakotah put the ball on the floor. One bounce and let it fly.

Swish.

There was no rattling Scott County's center, who would hit his second free throw as well. The county boys were now up, 65–62. But GRC came back with a bucket, cut the lead to one, and fouled Ge'Lawn who would miss the front end of a 1-and-1. Clark now had the ball with twenty seconds to go, down one, with a chance to win it. And here came Robbie Stenzel dribbling up the far sideline in front of the hometown fans, who once again were on their feet.

"Shoot it!" one yelled.

But Robbie wouldn't get that chance. He dribbled the ball off his foot as he closed in on the hoop. It skittered out of bounds. And GRC's efforts to steal the ball—or foul Scott County and stop the clock—on the subsequent inbounds pass failed. Dakotah flung it seventy feet down court to Tanner, who flicked it to Ge'Lawn, who swung it to Tamron, who found Chad, all alone in the low post.

Up 65–64, there was no need for Chad to score. But he couldn't resist the wide-open look, throwing down a two-handed jam right in front of the GRC student section as the buzzer sounded. The quiet Scott County star was screaming now, flexing his muscles and stepping toward the GRC students, who surged toward him. A fight was in the offing, especially with Chase Jackson, Chad's towering brother, striding into the fray. "If Chase started swinging," Dakotah's father, Clay Euton, said the next day, "somebody was going to jail." But police, parents, and coaches intervened in time to stop it.

"I had to do it," Chad told his mother after the game.

He was almost apologizing for the dunk and the outburst that followed. "I kind of got a little scared," he admitted. "I don't know why." But there was no need for apologies. Chad had scored twenty-seven points while pulling in seven rebounds—possibly the best game of his life, which, within twenty-four hours, would earn him Player of the Week honors from LEX18, the NBC affiliate in Lexington. "They got my name on there and everything," Chad said as he eyed the engraved trophy that came with the award. "That's beautiful."

But for Robbie Stenzel there would be no trophies or awards—just comments penned by anonymous critics on popular Internet message boards, like Bluegrasspreps.com. The junior guard had led GRC with twenty-one points, playing every single minute of the game, and he had added nine rebounds on the night, second most on the team. But Robbie had also committed nine turnovers, including five in the fourth quarter, three in the last ninety seconds, and the one where he dribbled the ball right off his own foot.

"Hard to make up for that!" wrote one critic.

"His three turnovers really hurt GRC."

"He took a lot of questionable shots."

"But we need to remember that these are mostly underclassmen . . . JUNIORS!" wrote one person in defense of the GRC boys.

"I agree that they are all juniors," came one reply, "but few if any of them are 'true juniors.'"

In all, Robbie figured, he must have heard about it for a good month: how he was selfish, how he had lost the game, how Clark County had failed. And of course, as usual, it was all his fault.

SETTING THEM UP TO FAIL

THE MORNING AFTER beating George Rogers Clark, a few Scott County basketball players didn't bother showing up for school. Their reasons for calling in sick that Monday were entirely plausible. They were nursing sinus infections and sore throats. They were injured, beat up, and exhausted. For days, at least one player had been taking medication to get better and another had been hacking up sticky globs of yellow phlegm in the locker room. The cold winter—combined with the long basketball season—was beginning to take its toll.

But Monday afternoon, while most Scott County kids were piling into school buses and heading home for the day, the basketball players—every single one of them, sick or not, tired or not—strolled into the school, a few for the first time that day, pulling on their red mesh practice jerseys and lacing up their high-top shoes in the gym. In Scott County, you didn't miss basketball practice—not for almost anything. School, at times, was another matter.

By Kentucky testing standards, Scott County High School was a slightly below average place to get an education. In the 2009–10 school year, students obtained proficient or distinguished scores in reading, math, science, social studies, and writing—the five categories measured by the state—at rates just lower than their statewide counterparts. Scott County's attendance rate of 91.6 percent was slightly below average and its graduation rate—83.2 percent—was almost exactly average.

Scott County juniors, however, consistently scored about a point higher than their peers across the state when taking the ACT standardized test, a college entrance exam mandated for all juniors in Kentucky. Opportunities abounded in the halls of the high school for those interested enough to take them. Spanish was offered, as was Japanese and even Japanese choir. Scott County's marching band boasted more than two hundred members, making it one of the largest in the state. And for the brightest kids, there were even more opportunities. In recent years, enrollment in advanced placement classes at the high school had nearly tripled.

Some AP students showed up at school an hour early every day for the privilege of taking an extra class. And being smart didn't necessarily make you unpopular. That fall, Scott County students elected Cori Biggers as their homecoming queen—she of the AP class load and perfect 4.0 GPA with friends in the band, not on the basketball team. "I felt really proud and happy to be homecoming queen—because that's a big title," Biggers said later. "People were saying, 'Yeah! Finally, a normal person.' Like I'm a normal person, I guess."

Actually, exceptional was the word people used to describe motivated students like Biggers. Yet, on occasion, Scott County teachers also found ways to reach the other students, the ones who were far from achieving "proficient" or "distinguished" status. Lynn Fiechter, a third-year English teacher at the high school, recalled one recent assignment where she asked her students to choose a poem to read aloud and discuss it before the class. Not unexpectedly, some students took the easy way out, reading the likes of "Casey at the Bat." But one boy, Fiechter said, chose to read "Funeral Blues," an elegy written by W. H. Auden, a gay poet, about the death of a male companion—a bold choice that essentially outed the student as a homosexual to his classmates. "He told everyone," Fiechter recalled. "And it was lovely."

But not every day went so well for Fiechter and the other teachers trying to reach the general population of students, many of whom didn't see the point in studying. Of the previous year's graduating class, only 54 percent of students planned to enroll in college, with the rest headed off to vocational school, a full-time job, or military service. Teachers complained of laziness and apathy, and students at times copped to it. WE DON'T NEED NO EDUCATION, declared a headline above a two-page story in that year's yearbook, detailing the students' favorite way to pass the day: texting one another on their cell phones. Teachers still tried to lecture, pushing on with lessons plans, but some shied away from assigning homework at the end of class for a simple reason. "What's the point?" explained math teacher Ivon Mucio, with twenty-two years in the high school. "They won't do it."

Reading a book seemed like an especially difficult thing to ask of them. When Fiechter assigned a book report that fall—calling for students to write a five-paragraph essay about the book of their choice—many turned in shoddy work or no work at all. "It was a book report," complained Fiechter, who was just twenty-eight years old and was generally well liked by her students. "It was thirty points. It was five paragraphs. They're sixteen and seventeen years old. There's literally nothing more I can do." And perhaps that explains why some English teachers no longer asked students to read many books at home. Shakespeare's *Macbeth* or Fitzgerald's *The Great Gatsby*, works once considered basic reading for American high school students, were now apparently so hard to digest that teachers chose to read the books aloud, in class, hoping the students were listening. Yet, of course, many weren't.

"How many people know who the first vice president of the United States was?" U.S. government teacher Rush Sullivan asked one day during his fifth-hour class while talking about the three branches of government.

"Dick Cheney?" answered one student.

"Why would we know that?" said another.

"Why would you know?" Sullivan replied. "You only live here."

But later Sullivan admitted that he was not surprised that his students couldn't answer the question. "It would have surprised me," he said, "if they would have known it."

The problem, teachers said, was getting students to engage with the material. And the solution for some, it seemed, was supplementing lessons plans with Hollywood movies. That fall, one parent, Nancy Curtis, criticized the use of *Slumdog Millionaire*, an R-rated Oscar-winning film, which had been shown in her daughter's world civilization class. Teachers should not be using valuable class time, Curtis argued, to play movies filled with violence and profanity, which students could watch on cable, she said, if their parents allowed it. "I believe this generation," said Curtis, who served on the school's Site Based Decision Making Council, "is a victim of our own low expectations."

But R-rated movies represented only a small slice of the feature presentations shown inside Scott County classrooms. In English: *A Knight's Tale*, starring Heath Ledger. In forensic science: *Sleepy Hollow*, starring Johnny Depp.

Social studies teachers got in on the game. At least one teacher had students watch the insightful Kevin Costner vehicle, *Swing Vote*, about a know-nothing constituent whose vote would determine the presidential election. And in one senior-level math class, where the teacher was out due to an illness in the family, students complained that they had been forced to watch the astronaut drama *Apollo 13* not once—but twice.

"We have not done math in, like, a month," Allie Wilburn said.

"We watched a movie," agreed Courtney Hisel. "And then another movie."

"I'm fine with watching a movie in class," added fellow student Courtney Ritchie, getting in on the conversation. "But I don't want to watch the same movie over and over again."

The movie issue troubled administrators. But in the months ahead, instead of doing away with movies, the high school essentially codified them, creating a list of more than hundred films that might be shown in the classroom. The approved movies, posted on the school's Web site, included classics such as *Schindler's List, Gandhi,* and *All the President's Men*—films, which when properly presented, might move students in ways that a book or a lecture could not. But the list also included the animated movie *Ratatouille* (rationale: it helps students understand "the influence of French foods on the culinary world"); the summer blockbuster *Jurassic Park* (rationale: it helps students understand "geologic time"); and the football tale *Remember the Titans* (rationale: "miscellaneous as needed").

Fiechter, for one, wasn't keen on showing movies. "If it doesn't line up with my content," she said, "they're never going to come in here and watch a movie." But after only three years in the classroom, the journalist-turned-English-teacher seemed beaten down. "I'm tired," Fiechter said one day, sitting at her desk at an auxiliary trailer behind the high school. "Yeah," she added, a moment later, a little more convinced of the idea this time. "I'm tired." She wanted to be making a difference, but it was hard to know if she was.

"On the days when I have a good day, it's real nice to come home and tell my husband, 'I had the best day.' They *got it* and they were talking and they loved the book or whatever," Fiechter said. "But then there are some days when I come home and say, 'My lesson just failed.' Does that mean that they don't get it? Is it me? Is it them? It's a lot. I dream about my students. It's a lot of stress."

English instructor Erin Wilson said teachers found themselves grappling with a catch 22: Ask them to read *The Great Gatsby,* for example, and many would not do it, rendering lesson plans worthless. "I'd have no class," Wilson explained. But by not assigning homework, teachers might be doing the students a disservice, failing to prepare them for life after high school. "I think in a lot of ways," Wilson conceded, "they're shocked when they go to college." Her colleague and fellow English teacher, Lucinda Ward, put it this way one day while standing outside her classroom between third and fourth hours: "You almost feel like you're setting them up to fail."

THAT NOVEMBER IN SCOTT COUNTY, the debate over academic expectations came to the fore when Gene Norris, a parent of twin teen-aged boys, suggested that the school raise the GPA required to play sports.

Norris was a supporter of Scott County athletics—and of basketball, in particular. "You won't find anybody," Norris said, "who loves it more than me." At almost every home game, he could be found sitting near the scorer's table, cheering on Dakotah, Chad, Ge'Lawn, and the rest of the team. Norris was fifty-three, a lean, articulate Toyota plant employee who, like Nancy Curtis, served on the high school's Site Based Decision Making Council, crafting school policy. But he also knew what it was like to be young, black, and great at sports. More than three decades earlier, Norris had starred on the basketball team at Cumberland County High School, where, he admitted now in hindsight, he had skated by at times on the jersey he wore. "If you were the superstar," he said, "you really didn't have to do a lot of the things that other kids had to do."

Norris had no hard evidence that such things were happening in Scott County. But the 1.6 GPA that was required to play ball troubled him. At that level, students were somewhere between a C and a D average—passing, yes, but not by much. And what worried him was the future: A boy pulling down, say, a 1.8 GPA might be able to play basketball or football now, he said, but later that boy might realize that such scores weren't enough to get him into college—even with an athletic scholarship—rendering his high school sports career meaningless, even if it had been stellar. Norris argued that a 2.0 GPA—a solid C average—wasn't too much to ask. In fact, he believed young people, especially athletes, tend to work toward expectations. Ask for more, he argued, and the school would get more—simple as that.

"If it's still okay to perform at a 1.6, if it's still okay to perform there, I may just want to perform there," said Norris, stating his case at an SBDM council meeting in the high school library that November. "And there's nothing you have put in place to cause me, or force me, to do any better."

He wanted to raise the required GPA as soon as possible—January, perhaps. But administrators and other SBDM council members didn't share his point of view. For one thing, assistant principal Joe Covington said, the athletes' grades were decent. The best performing teams—girls tennis, girls soccer, girls basketball, and girls golf—all had GPAs of 3.5 or higher. And even the lowest scoring teams—boys football and boys basketball—did better than a 2.45. In short, most athletes were already doing far better than a 1.6.

For those students who struggled, however, sports was often a lifeline, administrators argued, the one thing that kept them coming to school. Frank Howatt, the school's principal, said administrators saw it all the time. As soon as a sports season ends, Howatt said, students' disciplinary problems often spike. "Their absenteeism goes up," he added, "and their grades go down." It was best, he argued, not to raise the GPA requirement immediately, but to roll out that spring a pilot program, where athletes struggling to maintain a 2.0 could get extra tutoring.

"I gotta tell you, I think it's a winner," Howatt said, trying to wrap up the debate and forge some consensus. "I think it's a winner."

But Norris was unconvinced. "I don't think it is," he replied. "I think it's despicable."

The pilot program, he believed, was just a delaying tactic. "Delay, delay, delay," he said later. And although Norris might have been wrong about the alleged motivation, he was somewhat prophetic about the end result. The pilot program that spring involved just eight students participating in baseball, softball, and chorus. Three of them, with mentoring, were able to bring their grades above a 2.0. But it would be many more months before any formal policy took hold at the school—and even then, Howatt admitted, he wasn't sure how many athletes were getting the extra guidance they needed.

The problem, Howatt explained, was partly money. The high school didn't have cash for new textbooks, much less extra tutoring. With county tax revenues falling, spending per Scott County student had declined more than six percent district-wide in the last three years. And the future didn't look much better. Per-student spending was projected to continue declining for at least another year. Meantime, enrollment was up 20 percent in the last four years while staffing was down, forcing Frank Howatt to cram the students, 1,588 and counting, into increasingly crowded classrooms, hoping for the best.

"It's now not uncommon for some classrooms to have thirty-four, thirty-five students," Howatt said shortly after basketball season that year, explaining that some rooms were too full to fit another body inside. "We have to count on students being absent," he added, "just so we can have a little bit of space."

And so, in an odd way, it was something of a blessing when a few basketball players didn't attend school. At least then, the rest of the students would have a little more room. But even when everyone was there, it was hard to take school seriously, especially with the basketball postseason growing closer by the day. One afternoon that winter, with their math teacher out for the day, Dakotah, Chad, and Ge'Lawn spent part of sixth hour talking about hoops and all the layups that Chad had missed in a recent game.

"I missed layups?" Chad said.

"Chad, omigod," Dakotah replied, "you missed at least five."

"Chad," Ge'Lawn added, "you missed, like, seven layups."

"You all writing?" asked a teacher covering the class for the hour, as she interrupted the boys' basketball reverie.

"We're talking about the game," Chad replied, sarcastic but straight-faced. "That," he said, "is more important."

IT WAS THE WAY GE'LAWN WALKED. This was the new theory the week after beating George Rogers Clark. Ge'Lawn's gait—up on his tippy-toes—had to be exacerbating his knee pain, which was slowing him down, which was jeopardizing everything, not only for him, but for the team. Maybe, Hicks suggested, Ge'Lawn just needed to stop walking on his tippy toes.

"That ain't normal," Hicks said, pulling Ge'Lawn out of a shooting drill at practice one day that week and calling over the team trainer, Dan Volpe, to weigh in on the matter. "It would have to be stressful on your legs."

"Have you ever noticed that before?" Volpe asked Ge'Lawn.

"You're walking up on your toes," Hicks explained.

"You're on your toes," Volpe confirmed, peering down at Ge'Lawn's feet. "You're on your toes right now, just standing there."

"Huh?" the boy replied.

"Ge'Lawn, I'm a shooter," Hicks continued, "and I don't see how you can shoot like that. Because that throws your balance off."

"You feel like you're on your toes right now?" Volpe asked Ge'Lawn. "You're on your toes right now."

"Yeah, I know," Ge'Lawn replied.

"Just standing there," Volpe continued, "you're on your toes."

"Yeah." Hicks nodded. "And that can't be good for the front of your legs."

Ge'Lawn, standing near center court, eyed his coach and his trainer as if they were door-to-door vacuum salesmen, trying to talk their way into his living room. Maybe, Ge'Lawn suggested after a moment, the problem was the arch supports that he often wore inside his shoes.

"Well," Volpe said, "I'll have to take a look at those."

"Yeah, because that ain't right," Hicks added, "the way he's on his toes."

There was more discussion, then more staring at Ge'Lawn's feet.

"You're leaning forward right now," Volpe said.

"That might be what's causing it," Hicks replied.

"Do you even feel that?" Volpe said.

"Huh?" Ge'Lawn said again.

"Do you even feel that?" Volpe said.

"Feel what?"

"You're leaning forward right now."

"Yeah, I know."

They asked him to walk a few feet across the floor. "*Normally,*" Hicks instructed him as he and Volpe stood back and watched. "See, his heels never touch." Then, they asked him to walk again, this time putting his heels down first. "Bend your legs, bend your knees," Hicks said. "Walk normal, walk normal.

Put your heels down. See, that's a normal walk right there. All right, come on back now—heel first, heel first. See, right there's a normal walk. That feels different, I bet, don't it?"

Ge'Lawn didn't reply. He just stood there, knowing where he was headed next. It was back to the trainer's room for further examination.

"Stand for me for a second," Volpe said.

"On my heels?"

"No."

"Regularly?"

"Yeah."

"Dan," Ge'Lawn asked, "you think that could be some of the problem?"

"Could be," Volpe replied.

Volpe wasn't sure—and neither was Ge'Lawn. The boy didn't seem to be sure about anything anymore. That winter, in Ge'Lawn's psychology class, the students had been asked to keep a dream journal—an easy enough task. There was just one problem: Ge'Lawn wasn't having any dreams, at least not many that he could remember in the morning. There was only one that stayed with him, he said, only one that he could recall with any clarity. In the dream, Ge'Lawn was falling, falling, falling.

"I hurt," he said now, "in everything I do."

But the team kept winning. The Cards thumped Bryan Station again—this time on the road, in Lexington, by twenty points. They nipped Henry Clay at home three nights later, squandering a thirteen-point lead with two minutes to play in the game, yet holding on for an ugly 67–63 victory. And then, the next night, it was back to Lexington to face Sayre School, enrollment 610, a private school that had no business playing in Scott County's district, but did due to simple geography.

No one really wanted to play the game, least of all the Sayre boys. "The only positive way to look at it is, 'Wow. Maybe I'll see these guys on ESPN one day,'" said Sayre junior Cabot Haggin the night before playing Scott County. And, as expected, it was a joke of a game. Hicks played his starters for only a half, treating the contest like a late-season scrimmage. There were less than hundred fans in Sayre's gym and there was none of the usual screaming. As the second half ticked away, with Scott County in control, up twenty points, then thirty, Ge'Lawn's father leaned back in the stands, his hands folded on his chest—the very portrait of peace. Even the referees seemed to enjoy a low-stress Saturday night on the hardwood. At one point late in the fourth quarter, one of the refs appeared to be chuckling as he trotted down the court.

"What are you laughing about?" Sayre coach Ted Hall shouted at the be-mused referee. "What's funny?"

"That's enough," the ref replied.

"That *is* enough," Hall answered. "I don't think it's funny."

The ref blew his whistle and hit Hall with a technical foul, giving Scott County two free throws and the ball. Not that it mattered. Scott County won 85–47 and, not surprisingly, the county boys were loose after the game, with a shirtless Dakotah flexing for his teammates inside the visiting locker room.

"That's a ballplayer's body right there," he joked.

"Tell me," Tamron replied, "what ballplayer has that body?"

The boys busted out laughing. And why not? They had won eleven games in a row, not losing since the Lexington Christian debacle over a month earlier. But the laughter was about to end. Hicks was in no mood for it—not now, not two weeks before the postseason was set to begin. To him, the Sayre victory meant nothing. Scott County's jayvee team could probably beat Sayre. And the Henry Clay win meant even less. As Hicks saw it, the Cardinals should have lost that game. And so when the boys showed up for practice the day after the Sayre victory, a Sunday, there was their coach, a whistle around his neck, ready to work.

When the boys failed to rebound a missed shot, Hicks lost it. "Guys," he shouted, "how in the world can you get four people down here and not get a rebound?" When Ge'Lawn failed to defend a lazy pass and let his man get the ball, Hicks stopped practice and lost it again. "That is unbelievable," he hollered. "*Un-be-lieve-able.* How in the world can that happen?" And when Hicks felt Chad wasn't hustling—on the very first play of the intersquad scrimmage that afternoon—he dispatched him to the sideline. "Just get over there, sit down, and be quiet," Hicks told Chad. "Just sit down and watch."

They had a big week ahead of them. On Monday, they were scheduled to play the No. 1 ranked team from West Virginia. On Tuesday, they faced neighboring Bourbon County. And then, in a mere six days, came the game the boys had been waiting for all year: a Saturday night showdown against their most hated rival, Lexington Catholic. There was vengeance in the air—and it felt good.

But soon, the schedule was all fouled up. That night, the West Virginia school called to cancel. Too much snow out east. Couldn't make the drive. Then a storm rolled through Kentucky, dumping a couple inches of snow on Scott County. By midmorning Tuesday, all the main roads were cleared. But Bourbon County, with its 4-18 record, had already called to cancel, and said it was unable to reschedule the game this season. It was the fourth time that winter that an inferior opponent had pulled that trick on Hicks, using weather as an apparent excuse to dodge his team, and he was getting tired of it.

"Isn't that sorry?" he grumbled in his office that night. "It can't just cloud up and rain and you call the game off."

He needed a game. He needed a team willing to play his boys before the county faced Catholic that Saturday and, to make it happen, he was even willing to pay for the other school's transportation and provide postgame pizza—whatever it took. Still, no one jumped on the offer. No team wanted to face Scott County. Not in the middle of February. Not on an eleven-game win streak. And not with the postseason looming. The last thing any coach needed right now was a confidence-shattering defeat. But then, after practice that Tuesday night, the phone rang in Hicks's office. Shane Buttry, Madison Southern's basketball coach, was on the line.

"Hey, Shane," Hicks said. "Shoot, Shane. How y'all doing?"

Madison Southern was up for a game.

THE DIRECTIONS WERE CLEAR: If it was snowing when the bus was set to leave Madison County, one hour south of Georgetown, Shane Buttry was to call Billy Hicks and cancel. And now it was snowing. Again. The flakes that had begun falling on Monday night were still coming down two nights later, melting against the windshield of Madison Southern's bus as it lurched on to the interstate, headed north. But Buttry wasn't calling off anything.

Snow might have canceled school in Scott County for the last two days, but it wasn't going to interfere anymore with basketball. The game, thanks to Buttry, was on—even if some people thought he was crazy.

Madison Southern was no basketball power. The Eagles, starting two guards under five foot ten that season, had never made it to Rupp Arena. Not once. Most years, they weren't even the best basketball team in their own county. That title usually went to Madison Central. And Buttry, in his eighth season at Madison Southern, could sense that some of the boys were afraid of Scott County. He had seen it in their eyes the previous night when he told them who they were playing next. "Some of them," Buttry said, "looked like they'd seen a ghost."

But the upbeat, thirty-eight-year-old coach and Madison Southern graduate—class of '89, the school's inaugural year—believed they could compete. Buttry's Eagles were 18-6. They had almost as many wins so far this season as they had in the previous two seasons combined. "And who knows?" Buttry told his boys in the visiting locker room after their bus had arrived safely in Scott County. Maybe, the less talented, outgunned, too-slow Eagles could catch the Cards looking ahead to Lexington Catholic. Maybe, just maybe, they could pull off a stunner.

"This is a big, big opportunity right here," Buttry told the Madison Southern boys before they took the floor. "This is the best team in the region. If we can play with them, we can play with anybody, okay? This might be the best team in the state. So you can make a name for yourself—more so than what you've already done—*tonight*, playing this game, all right? That's why we're over here. We're not over here to play dead. We're over here to play.

"All right," Buttry added, "let's go."

The gym, at tip-off, couldn't have been much emptier. There were maybe a dozen kids in the student section and another couple hundred fans, at most, scattered like flotsam on an open sea of red bleachers. The snow was killing the gate tonight—and killing the atmosphere, too. It felt a little bit like practice, like it was a chore to be here, and Madison Southern took advantage of the apathy, going on a 10–0 run midway through the first quarter and outplaying the county on both ends of the floor. Even the Eagles' biggest mistakes seemed to break in their favor. When they air-balled a three-pointer with under a minute to play in the period, Ge'Lawn was in position to reel it in. But a Madison Southern player bodied him out of the way, gathered in the errant shot, and then stuck the put-back while Ge'Lawn went for the block and missed.

"Foul him, grab his elbow, grab something!" Hicks shouted in the team huddle at the end of the first quarter with Scott County down five, still stewing over that play. "Don't sit there and let a guy whip you and just take it. I'd rather you foul out. At least that would say you were a competitor. Now *get out there* and *compete!*"

The second period started with yet another gaffe: a terrible pass to Dakotah in the low post, leading to a turnover—Madison Southern's ball. But the Eagles were now as cold as the temperature outside. In eight minutes, an entire quarter, they made just two baskets while the county boys found their footing, scoring at the rim and from the three-point arc. Ge'Lawn scored five in a row. Will added four in a row. At halftime, the Cards were up ten. And a few minutes into the third quarter, the county extended the lead to twenty.

But Buttry's boys weren't giving up. "I feel like we should have the lead," he told them at half. And now they began climbing back into the game. The Eagles got a broken-play layup; Dakotah missed a three. The Eagles dropped a floater in the paint; Ge'Lawn missed a three. The Eagles, running now, scored in transition while the Cards missed again and again. A Madison Southern three-pointer from the left wing—*good!* A Madison Southern three-pointer from the right wing—*yes!* Buttry could barely stay in his seat now, clapping as he bounced up and down the sidelines, while Hicks could barely watch.

It was as if the Scott County boys had two gears: all out and cruise control, playing hard only when they wanted to, only when they decided it mattered. Their 20-point lead shrunk to two points before the county rallied in the fourth quarter and pushed it back to fifteen. But back came Buttry's never-say-die Eagles, nailing back-to-back three-pointers to fuel a 13–4 run that cut the lead to six with a minute to go.

"*Gosh almighty!*" Hicks hollered.

It shouldn't have come to this. Everyone knew that. And afterward, even though the Eagles ultimately lost 79–69, Buttry praised his team for showing something that Scott County seemed to lack: grit.

"Listen," Buttry said in the locker room. "Let me tell you something. I had people today question whether we should come over here. I did. But I told them we've got a team. *We've got a team* . . . Now, we didn't win. Yeah, so what? Billy Hicks just told me we may see them again in the regional finals. And we might."

The regional finals?

Hicks was just being polite. Madison Southern might get there, all right. But the way Scott County had played tonight, Hicks couldn't be sure that his own team would be there come March. And neither could the boys, who seemed to limp toward the locker room after the game, defeated in victory.

But just as they hit the doorway, the public address announcer came over the speakers with an announcement.

"It's official," he declared. "No school in Scott County tomorrow."

Another snow day, the county's third in a row. And upon hearing the news, the boys began cheering and hollering—louder than they had all night, louder than they had in weeks.

"No school, baby!" Ge'Lawn bellowed. *"No school!"*

The celebration didn't last long.

"Daggone, guys. I'm amazed some of you guys can get fired up," Hicks said, stepping into the locker room and managing to derail the fun parade with just a few words. "I wish we had that enthusiasm out on the basketball court. They announce no school. You guys start screaming and hollering. I wish we'd do that out on the basketball court, get fired up like that."

Hicks was pacing now, hands in his pockets, hands on his forehead, back to his pockets, back to his forehead. He wasn't finished.

"I didn't know you guys had emotion," he continued. "They announce no school, and you jump up and down, screaming and hollering. Just think if you were that motivated to play basketball, guys. Just think if you were that moti-vated to play, ready to scream and holler."

He couldn't believe that they had let Madison Southern hang around.

"They went on—what?" he asked. "A 16 to 0, 18 to 0 run?"

"Twenty-four to eight," replied assistant coach Tim Glenn.

"They outscored us twenty-four to eight in the third quarter?"

"I wrote it down," Glenn nodded.

"So they got twenty-four points in—what?—five minutes there?"

"Yep."

"Guys," Hicks said. "*Gawsssh almighty*. Fellas." He was lunging for the words now, searching, reaching for the answers. "You gotta help me on this, guys," he said. "I can't come out, get in your heads, and make you want to play."

Hicks said little else before retreating to his office. But at least one player wasn't celebrating. While his teammates jumped into the air hugging one another over the snow day, Dakotah sat motionless in front of his locker. While his teammates whooped and hollered, Dakotah said nothing. He was hunched over, elbows on his knees, his blue eyes studying the cracks in the concrete floor.

He and Hicks didn't agree on much. But this time, Dakotah thought Hicks was right. How was it possible that his teammates got more excited for a snow day than for a win? How was it possible that his teammates showed more emotion for a day off than they did on the court all night? Sitting in his locker, sweat pooling around his feet, Dakotah began muttering to Ge'Lawn about how they had almost botched it tonight, failing to play defense and, really, failing to match Madison Southern's will to win.

"That white kid—*gawd*," Dakotah moaned. "You're telling me that kid is that friggin' good?"

"He was shooting it from the volleyball line," Ge'Lawn replied.

"What the frig?" Dakotah said. "He didn't take it to the rack one time. All you had to do was get up on him."

"I wasn't guarding him." Ge'Lawn shrugged. "Oh, well. It happens."

"Yeah, it happens," Dakotah snapped. "And that's why we're gonna get beat."

"I agree," Ge'Lawn said.

But Dakotah wasn't finished just yet. A moment later, he turned to Chad, asking him how it was possible that he let his man, a lanky six-foot-five post man bound for a job after high school, not a basketball scholarship, drop twenty-two points on them tonight.

"Before the game," Dakotah said, "that was the one guy that everyone was talking about."

"But was he good?" Chad replied.

"Yeah," Dakotah answered.

"He was good?" Chad said.

"Yeah," Dakotah chirped.

Chad was just looking to get a rise out of his friend now, but Dakotah wasn't speaking anymore—period—not to Chad, Ge'Lawn, or anyone else. He dressed quickly, saying nothing. He pulled the gray hood of his Scott County sweatshirt over his head and barreled out of the locker room. Outside on the gym floor, students were still lingering beneath the lights, and it was common for the players to linger, too, to socialize and flirt with girls, then maybe head over to Applebee's for plates of fried cheese sticks. But tonight, Dakotah had no stomach for the usual postgame rituals, girls or not, and he certainly didn't have an appetite for fried cheese. He hugged his mom without a word to anyone else and then headed home to soothe his aching body in an ice bath.

He would fold his long frame into the bathtub of their home, like a horse trying to squeeze itself into a trough of water. And then he would sit there, relishing the icy cold of the bath until it burned, relishing the pain surging through his bones until it was gone, until he was numb, until there was nothing.

Dakotah could feel it coming. They were going to lose.

12

HOW STUPID DO WE LOOK?

I T WAS THE ONE THING on which everyone could agree. It didn't matter
if you were smart or stupid, a jock or a cheerleader, a hick or a dirt, the lowest of the low in the halls at Scott County High. It didn't matter what your
daddy did, if he farmed tobacco, drew unemployment checks, or worked at
Toyota. And it didn't even matter if you liked the basketball players, if you
thought Dakotah, Chad, and Ge'Lawn were cheaters for having transferred
and, therefore, not deserving of your applause. No matter where you stood,
where you were going in life, or where you laid your head at night—in Georgetown, Stamping Ground, or elsewhere—if you were a county kid, a true Scott
County kid, then you awoke in the morning giving thanks to God, loving your
mother, and hating Lexington Catholic.

There was simply nothing redeeming about Catholic, as far as county kids
were concerned. Catholic students were preppy and snobby, high class in nice
cars. They got what they wanted, when they wanted it, or at least so it seemed
to county kids since their Lexington rivals somehow managed to afford $7,000
a year in high school tuition. None of that would have mattered, of course, if
Catholic was an overrated, underachieving diploma mill. But it wasn't. Catholic kids were good at almost everything. Most seniors—roughly 90 percent—
attended a four-year college, and not just at state schools, but at Duke, Cornell,
and Northwestern, among others. Catholic's average ACT score was 24—about
four points higher than Scott County's. National merit finalists were a regular
occurrence. And perhaps most insulting, the smart kids were good at sports, too,
particularly basketball, beating Billy Hicks in the postseason the previous two
years and denying the county its rightful trip to Rupp Arena.

And so, yes, jealousy was part of the problem. But that alone could not
explain the animosity that county kids at times felt for Catholic. It was, it

seemed, a sort of cultural divide. The two schools might share a county line and
a love for great basketball, but that was about it. Catholic was the big city and
Scott County was the sticks. And although kids at both schools shopped at the
same mall and bought the same clothes, friending each other on Facebook and,
at times, even dating each other's girls, neither seemed to understand the other.

"They think we're a bunch of rednecks who drive our tractors to school,"
said Scott County senior Mallory McGhee, cocaptain of the cheerleading
squad. "We really had someone ask us one time if we drove tractors to school."
But that was a stupid thing to ask. Even Catholic kids should know what their
so-called redneck rivals like to drive most of all. "In our parking lot, we've got
a hundred thousand pickup trucks covered in mud," said Scott County junior
Jay Willmott, the school's off-beat, blond-haired, 220-pound placekicker who
enjoyed hunting deer and kicking footballs. "Theirs?" Willmott added. "Nothing but Mercedes-Benzes."

The annual basketball game between the two schools, played in mid- to
late-February, offered a chance for the kids to settle these differences on the floor.
The winner didn't just get bragging rights, but validation for their way of life—at
least until the two schools met again in the regional tournament in March, which
was inevitable most seasons, given their hardwood dominance. It was Cards
versus Knights, Red versus Blue, and Good versus Evil, with the devil being
determined by your zip code, religion, or the color of the shirt on your back.

Hopefully, the snow would hold off for this one. Hopefully, the game
would go on, Saturday night, in Scott County's gym, as scheduled. The postgame parties were already being planned. And there was even talk of mayhem,
of theft. Willmott, the county's placekicker, wanted to steal the Knight statue
at Catholic. "For years," Willmott said, "we've always talked about doing that."
Of invading Catholic under the cover of darkness, plucking the Knight from its
pedestal, and then ferrying him away in the back of one of those mud-splattered
pickup trucks. That, Willmott said, would show them. "If we could steal that
knight," he explained, "that would probably make the whole year."

It was just big talk, of course, teenaged bluster, the stuff of dreams and
movies. But it was further proof of just how far the little private school from
Lexington had come. Two decades earlier, few students would have bothered

plotting late-night raids on Lexington Catholic. The school was almost irrelevant. Enrollment in the 1980s was in a freefall, down almost 50 percent, and so was school morale and discipline. People in Lexington liked to talk about the priest who had stepped down as principal at Catholic and then married a teacher—juicy gossip. And almost no one talked about Catholic's sports programs. The school didn't even have a football team. But then in walked Robert J. Bueter, a forty-seven-year-old Jesuit priest who wasn't going to let his cleric's collar or his personal vow of poverty stand in the way of Catholic glory.

THE BESPECTACLED PRIEST hadn't wanted this gig. The job that had interested Bueter the most in the spring of 1990 was in Wilmette, Illinois, north of Chicago, running a prep school where he had taught as a young man. But the Wilmette folks hired another man for that job. Bueter, it seemed, had not interviewed well. The head of the search committee seeking to fill the Wilmette post—"a university type," Bueter scoffed, "I forget his name"—informed the priest as much after the fact, telling him in a letter that he would be more than happy to sit down with Bueter and discuss interviewing tips.

Bueter was insulted. If he came off as blunt or bold in interviews, it was only because he *wanted* to be blunt or bold, because he knew what he wanted to do and how he wanted to do it. In the 1970s and '80s, he had served as principal at St. Ignatius College Prep school on Chicago's South Side, before going on to posts in New York and Indianapolis. He wasn't afraid of change. Under his tenure at St. Ignatius, the school had gone coed, growing enrollment. And he wasn't afraid of a little flair, either. Bueter understood that people needed excitement—"The secret in fund-raising," he said once, "is to find an event that excites your people"—and he understood what tended to excite people the most: sports.

Bueter, raised on the Kentucky side of the Ohio River near Cincinnati, wasn't much of an athlete himself. As much as he wished he could've played point guard, quarterback, or shortstop, he was too small and too slow. There would be no spot on the team for him at St. Xavier High School in Cincinnati. The ministry was his calling, serving the Lord, a man for others. That's what he would do, getting ordained in 1973. But Bueter's knowledge of the Bible didn't make him some sort of holy-rolling pushover whispering in the sacristy—anything but. He was partial to martinis—extra dry, dirty and up. He could quote from Karl Marx or Voltaire in conversation, but he was just as comfortable cursing, which he did with regularity. He was a man of the cloth, but also just a man, "a flaming heterosexual," he said, who happened to be committed to God.

The fact that Bueter was a clergyman impressed Sheila Hardy, a mother of five and the chairwoman of the search committee to find a new principal at Lexington Catholic in the spring of 1990. Jesuits, like Bueter, are known for educating. But what impressed Hardy even more was Bueter's vision. He wanted what the parents wanted: better academics, stronger athletics, higher standards, and tougher rules. And he seemed to realize that the job wouldn't just require administrating, but schmoozing for donations. The school offered him the job—Hardy thought the priest interviewed just fine—and Bueter accepted the offer, confident that he could resurrect Catholic. "It's the first job I've ever had that I am actually prepared for," he announced after his hiring.

Changes, swift and sweeping at times, began taking hold before classes even started that fall. Bueter thought the school offered too many remedial courses. So he cut classes and added new ones. He instituted a foreign language requirement and shut down the home economics department entirely. "Do I have a job?" the school's home ec chair, Helen Wheat, wanted to know. She did, but it was worth asking. Bueter bragged that the school board of trustees had given him a gun with instructions to shoot anyone who stood in his way. And he made sure that students got that message loud and clear. The school's dress code—khaki pants with collared shirts—was enforced with new vigor. No long, gaudy earrings for girls. No hooded sweatshirts for boys. No sassing teachers or loitering in the halls. A year earlier, one student admitted, it wasn't uncommon for kids to slip away in the middle of the day and have a few beers at a friend's house before returning to class. But not under Bueter's reign. "He kind of ended that real quick," recalled Alissa Tibe, Catholic's senior class president in 1991. "About a month into senior year that all kind of stopped real quick."

Bueter made it known: He was not to be trifled with. But he also kept it fun, playing basketball with the students, attending practice, and even suiting up for summer leagues with players far more talented than he was. "He'd get in the game with them," said Tommy Huston, a Catholic coach at the time. "And if they weren't passing the ball, he'd be yelling at them, cussing: 'Pass the damn ball!' I thought: This is a different guy."

Bueter wanted to win—that's all. In everything he did, just win. And so, he didn't just raise expectations in the classroom, but on the playing fields as well. When he realized that the school's athletic director and basketball coach Danny Haney was teaching six gym and health classes on top of his other duties, Bueter removed Haney from the classroom. He wanted him to focus on athletics, basketball, hiring the best coaches and fielding the best teams, and he also wanted a football team—as soon as possible.

Bueter asked Haney to raise the $125,000 needed to start the Knights' inaugural football team. Haney did as he was told—raising the sum in short order—and the football team took the field for the first time a year later. With just thirty-five players on the roster, the Knights played a wishbone offense and struggled, going 1-4 in an abbreviated schedule. But the following season, there were more than fifty boys on the varsity roster at Catholic, plus a feeder system in place that allowed younger students at local parochial middle schools to suit up in Knight uniforms. Now there were fans in the seats on Friday nights. Young boys were believing they were Knights before they could even enroll at Catholic. And, just like Bueter had planned it, enrollment was soon rising, up from a low of 332 in late 1990, to 400, then 500, then beyond, improving everything: morale, finances, and, of course, athletic success.

There was the football team going undefeated or the basketball team going to Rupp Arena. Here came the athletes, transferring to Catholic, and the allegations that the school was recruiting them by doling out scholarships. And there was Bueter, flitting about town in a white Mazda Miata convertible with blue pinstripes—the school's colors—and vanity plates that read LXCATH. The priest was working hard, selling the school at small gatherings and big events, coffees and fund-raisers. But what people tended to remember were all those wins and that hot, little sports car that Bueter had wanted to drive for maximum visibility. "That's what he wanted was a Miata," recalled Hardy, who led the search committee that ultimately hired him. "That's all there was to it. It wasn't going to be anything else."

By the end of the decade, enrollment was over eight hundred and Lexington's public high schools would vote to boycott Catholic, refusing to play the Knights due to their belief that they had to be cheating. Bueter responded by portraying his critics as whiners who couldn't compete—the verbal equivalent of pouring gasoline on a brush fire. But Bueter didn't care. The debate, he figured, was like free advertising for the high school. It gave Catholic mystique and forced the basketball team to travel to Alaska or the Bahamas to find games. Facing elite prep schools on a regular basis only made the boys stronger come March, when the local public schools would have to beat Catholic to get to Rupp Arena, rendering the boycott, the hatred, and the allegations of wrongdoing into something of a running joke at Catholic. At Bueter's departure in 1999, faculty members even rewrote the Lord's Prayer in his honor, ending it like this:

Forgive us our enormous success
As we forgive those who hold our success against us.
Lead us not into recruiting
But deliver us from violations.
For thine is the library, the fieldhouse, the second story,
the academics, the fine arts building, and the glory forever.

SUCH THINGS, the cleverness and the arrogance, made it easy for public school kids to hate Lexington Catholic. But Scott County's rivalry with the Knights began over something else, something purer: an actual basketball game, played in March 1998, in the state semifinals at Rupp Arena, at the end of Billy Hicks's fourth season in the county. Catholic, at the time, was 33-2, celebrating its third consecutive thirty-win basketball season, and ranked No. 3 in the nation. Scott County, at the time, was slotted in a different region and faced rural competition to make it to Rupp. The Cardinals, though 32-3 and averaging eighty-six points a game, had little chance of beating Catholic—on this, most people could agree. "It could be a *long* morning for Scott County," the radio play-by-play man warned listeners just before the opening tip. And the game, played before nearly 17,000 screaming fans, mostly followed the agreed-upon script—at least right up until the end.

The county was down by as much as eleven in the first half, unable to stop Catholic's seven-foot-one center or beat the Knights' smothering full-court press. The Cards had committed seventeen turnovers by halftime. And though they clawed back into the game in the second half—managing to take a two-point lead heading into the fourth quarter—Catholic answered, too good to lose. With forty-eight seconds to go, the Knights were up five, 79–74. On the Scott County bench, players sat dejected with towels over their heads while the team manager had already retreated back to the locker room. This one was over.

But Hicks, wearing his signature red sport coat over a crisp, white button-down shirt, red tie, and black pleated slacks, was still coaching—up and down the sideline, a hand in the air, talking to his players, calm. There was still time, Hicks assured them. They could still win this. They just needed to score.

Thirty-five seconds to go.

A stick-legged, backup Scott County guard finds himself alone with the ball behind the three-point arc on the left wing. Casey Alsop has played six minutes in the entire game. But when he fakes a shot and gets a Catholic player in the air, he goes up for the three, gets fouled, nails the basket, and then adds the free throw. A four-point play, a basketball miracle. Scott County down one, 79–78.

Twenty-nine seconds to go.

Catholic brings up the ball and the county isn't fouling—not yet. And here comes the trap—a classic Billy Hicks in-your-face trap—and the Catholic player throws it away. A bad pass. Scott County ball. Running in transition, to the hoop, a county boy takes a one-handed floater that caroms off the glass and then kisses every inch of the rim, rattling around before finally falling in, good. Scott County up one, 80–79.

Fifteen seconds to go.

Get back, Hicks hollers. Back on defense. Catholic is coming. The next shot could win it. But Catholic misses a short jumper on the baseline. A county boy pulls down the rebound, gets fouled, and then drains both of his free throws. Scott County up three, 82–79.

Eight seconds to go.

"The Scott County Cardinals smell an upset," the radio color man crows. But back come the Knights, dribbling up the court and getting the ball to their senior point guard. He swings from the right wing to the top of the arc, then spins back around to his left, with his back to the hoop for a moment and his left foot barely outside the three-point line. Then he throws up a prayer. This shot—off-balance and double-pumped with a county player defending—has no chance of going in. But it does.

Tie game, 82–82.

Six seconds to go.

Hicks could call a time-out, but he doesn't. It's part of his philosophy. Let the players play. Coach them hard, but then trust them. Trust them to know what to do. The ball is in his best player's hands. Rick Jones—that year's Mr. Basketball, the first Mr. Basketball the county could ever claim—rambles up the court, trying to get an open look with two Catholic players closing in around him and the radio broadcasters shrieking over the airwaves.

"It's going to Jones!"

"Rick Jones!"

"He shoots the three . . ."

They say in Scott County that traffic stopped, that cars sat through entire green lights, and that no one laid a hand on their horns. They say that everyone not at the game was listening, leaning into their radios, ears cocked and waiting, pregnant with dreams that the shot might fall, that they might win, and Catholic might lose, while at Rupp Arena the fans stood up on their feet, in silence, in awe.

The shot is a twenty-four-footer, taken while leaping on a dead-sprint run. Jones has a good look at it. But the momentum of the shot alone carries him nearly four feet through the air before his feet touch the court again. It's a 1-in-100 shot, a desperation heave that Jones has practiced before, but has never taken in a game of this magnitude. And as it flies through the air, everyone tracks it, following the arc of the orange ball as it sails, curling toward the orange hoop: Bueter and Hicks, the fans, and, really, an entire state.

It's good. All net. Game over, at the buzzer.

Scott County beats Catholic, 85–82.

· · · ·

THAT NIGHT, the county went on to win the state title, hanging its first boys basketball banner in the rafters of the gym. But what fans tend to remember most is the Catholic game, Rick Jones's improbable shot, and the celebration that followed. As the ball settled into the net—*swish*—Jones took off running for the far basket with his hands reaching for the rafters. His teammates followed like stampeding cattle. And then so did their coach, Billy Hicks, jumping into the air once, twice, five times in all, before breaking into an awkward, high-stepping gallop. The coach, with the tails of his red sport coat flying, just had to be part of the celebratory scrum with his boys, reaching in to rub Jones's head and then picking up his wife, Betsy, on the way to the locker room and carrying her in his arms—the first and only time, Betsy said, that ever happened.

"Ladies and gentlemen," the radio play-by-play man declared, as his voice quivering with excitement, "you have witnessed one of the greatest basketball feats in Kentucky state high school Sweet 16 history."

That was no consolation, however, to Catholic fans. Cheerleaders and players alike were weeping. One player, weak and broken, needed to be helped off the floor as if he had been shot through the chest. And there was nothing that Bob Bueter could do to stop the pain or the photographer who found his way into the Catholic locker room after the game to snap the image that appeared on the front page of the *Lexington Herald-Leader* the next day. There, in the photograph, is Catholic's starting forward, Steve Searcy, crumpled to the floor near the bathroom stalls, shirtless and crying with a hand over his face.

The kid, who played twenty-two minutes and pulled down five rebounds in the game, just wanted to be alone. But Searcy couldn't escape the media's glare that day in the bowels of Rupp. Reporters would be there to chronicle both his life—and his death. Almost exactly two years after Scott County's epic comeback against Catholic, Searcy was found dead at a friend's apartment three miles south of the arena where he had played his final high school basketball game. As with any story of someone dying young, Searcy's tale was complicated, with more questions than answers. He had dropped out of school not long after the painful loss to Scott County and had more recently fathered a child, a daughter, born just a couple weeks before his death. Perhaps, his mother, Jo Ann Muir, suggested years later, her only son couldn't handle the pressure of being a father so young. Perhaps, she said, a mild heart condition helped to hasten his death. Or perhaps there were other factors at play. At the time of his death, the medical examiner noted, Searcy had traces of cocaine, methadone, and diazepam, a generic form of Valium, circulating in his body—a body that had once been described as strong, quick to the boards, and willing to do anything to win.

But the story told in the newspaper that week and in conversations around Lexington in the years ahead was more simplified: Without basketball, it was said, Steve Searcy had lost his way. Without basketball, he was dead, he was gone. It was as if the Scott County game alone had destroyed him.

CATHOLIC WAS THE ONLY THING the county boys were talking about now: how the Knights were coming to town on Saturday, how the Cards needed to avenge last year's one-point loss in the regional finals, and how they needed to win to prove to themselves that it was possible—that, yes, they could beat the private school boys from Lexington.

But two days before the big game, Dakotah wasn't looking ahead; he was still looking back, still stewing over how they had almost lost to Madison Southern the night before. It bothered him so much that he could barely enjoy the snow day that Thursday. Instead, he padded around his house with a pencil in hand, jotting down a list of talking points on a piece of notebook paper.

"Heart," he wrote.

"Sprint back on defense."

"Dive on loose balls."

And then, finally, this one: "Fix it tonight!"

The West Virginia team that had canceled earlier that week due to the snow was coming to Scott County after all, giving the boys one final tune-up before Catholic. And Dakotah, who was determined to use the game to get things right, called a team meeting beforehand to discuss the problems made obvious by the lackluster Madison Southern outing.

"Can we get this over with?" Chad said, joking, before the meeting started.

"It's your fault we're having it," Dakotah replied.

"Yeah," Ge'Lawn agreed.

"I know," Chad said, playing along.

"All right," Dakotah said. "Seriousness."

He felt like his teammates didn't always play hard. "Right now," he told them, "I'm going out there and giving 100 percent every second of the game for thirty-two minutes—and some of us just are not doing that." He felt like he was alone out there at times, fighting for rebounds while his teammates just watched. "I don't want you all to watch me rebound," he said. "Get in there and fight for it with me." And he felt like it was time to throw down a challenge. "I'm just asking y'all to go out there and put it on the line with me for thirty-two minutes," Dakotah said. "And if you can't do that for yourselves, then do it for me, do it for this team, do it for the eight guys sitting right here."

That night, playing hard from the opening tip, the Cards ran out to a 31–6 lead, never looking back and never letting up as they crushed the previously undefeated George Washington Patriots, who were 15-0 coming into the game and ranked No. 1 in West Virginia by a score of 77–58. Dakotah's speech had worked. Something, anyway, had worked. And it was just in time.

"Well, boys," Hicks said after the game. "We got the Knights."

Everyone was gearing up for the game now. The cheerleaders were painting a towering sign through which the basketball players could run as they took the floor against Catholic. CAN'T TOUCH OUR SWAG, the sign said. WISH YOU COULD. One student was trying to acquire a pope costume, which he planned to wear to the game, mocking Catholic. And there was much discussion about how much trouble senior Alan Mastin would get into for the nifty little pope stunt.

"Don't you think they'll kick you out?" Dakotah asked that Friday over a lunch of several bologna, cheese, and salami sandwiches.

"No," Alan replied.

"Isn't that like making fun of their religion?" Dakotah continued. "I'm telling you, they'll probably kick you out."

But Alan was unconcerned.

"Dude," he replied, "I run this school."

"All right," Dakotah shrugged. "We'll see."

Scott County's center had been looking forward to this game for months.

And he wasn't going to be satisfied with just any win. Dakotah wanted to win big, embarrassing the Knights, if possible. He talked about it all the time lately. And he didn't want anyone casting doubts on Scott County's chances, especially total strangers, who, of course, were talking about the game, too, breeding negativity with snarky comments in town. Instead of being pleased with the Cards' nineteen-point victory against George Washington in the lead-up to the Catholic game, some fans were wondering if the boys wasted too many bullets on the West Virginia team. Some fans were saying that the boys should have saved some points for Saturday night—a notion that inevitably made its way to the locker room, where the players greeted it with shaking heads and icy stares.

"Who said that?" demanded Ge'Lawn.

"Tell them," Dakotah added, "to stay home."

But it didn't matter. The boys were ready—and so were the girls. In the hours before the big game that Saturday night, more than a dozen of them gathered inside a house not far from the high school, getting dolled up as Catholic schoolgirls, complete with short, plaid skirts, revealing white button-downs, knee-high socks, and pigtails.

They haggled over bobby pins. "Who has a bobby pin?" They wailed with excitement and then hushed one another. *Stop yelling!!!* They worried about being late. "Are we leaving? Are we ready?" And they kept jostling for space in the bathroom, passing around the hair spray, applying lipstick, and examining their faces in the mirror.

"Does my hair look okay?"

"Yes."

"Are you wearing it on the side like me?"

"Yes."

"Omigod," said senior Shelby Bennett. "I'm so excited."

And on it went, an all-out verbal assault on the brain that grew louder with each passing minute until finally, yes, yes, indeed, the girls were ready for Catholic, ready for anything—ready, they said, to raise.

"And what does raise mean?" shouted senior Bree Saunders, standing amid the throng of county girls dressed as trashy Catholics.

"Raise hell!" they replied.

• • •

REPORTERS HAD BEEN CALLING all week. Brandon Salsman, Catholic's head coach, told his boys that he must have received more media requests for tonight's game than any regular season basketball game he had ever coached, or seen coached, at Catholic. And that was saying something. Salsman, though just thirty-five, had been around. He was a 1992 graduate under Bob Bueter's tutelage, a six-foot-four, 225-pound senior leader on the first Catholic team to make it to the state finals, and then an assistant, before being hired as the head coach in 2005. Salsman was heavier now than he was during his playing days and starting to lose his sandy brown hair. But he was still a winner, cut from the Catholic cloth. He had led the Knights to back-to-back regional championships, back-to-back trips to Rupp Arena, and he seemed to excel in particular at beating one man.

"What's up, Billy?" Salsman said, greeting Hicks during warm-ups.

"Hey, Brandon," Hicks replied.

The two coaches quickly downshifted into small talk: about their families and their health, the sports coverage that season and the general lack of crowds at basketball games. "I guess it's a sign of the times," Hicks said, "that this place ain't packed tonight." Then Hicks turned to the topic of the game itself and the coaching job that Salsman had done that season, guiding a young team to the No. 5 ranking in the state.

"Brandon," he said, "you've done a heckuva job this year."

"I appreciate that."

"Nobody in the state," Hicks added, "has overachieved like you all have. I never dreamed that you all would be five in the state right now."

Hicks meant it as a compliment, but the word choice could have been better. *Overachieved*—it sounded as if Catholic was in over its head. And returning to the locker room moments later, Salsman didn't miss the opportunity to use the comment as motivation for his team in his final pregame speech.

"This is what Coach Hicks told me in the twenty-minute conversation I just had with him," Salsman told his boys. "He said, 'Coach, you're the coach of the year.' And I was like, 'Wow, thanks. I appreciate that.' He's like, 'You really are.' He goes, 'There's no way in hell your team should be ranked number five in the state.'"

Salsman stopped talking for a moment and let that idea sink in: that Billy Hicks thought the Catholic boys weren't that good, that Billy Hicks thought they were overrated.

Finally, he spoke up again.

"Boys," Salsman said, "it's ass-kicking time. It is *ASS . . . KICKING . . . TIME*. Right here. You hear what I'm saying? He wants to throw crap out like that? Let's put it on 'em, boys."

Then, together, the Catholic kids began to pray.

"Our father, who art in Heaven, hallowed be thy name . . ."

"God," Salsman added at the end, "give us the strength to handle whatever happens today: good, bad, or indifferent."

"Team on three."

"One, two, three . . . TEAM!"

G E'LAWN SCORED off the opening tip. Chad added a layup. Ge'Lawn drained a jumper. Dakotah followed suit. And then, here came Ge'Lawn again, darting down the left baseline, past two Catholic defenders and over a third to lay the ball into the hoop, soft and easy, like an egg into a basket. The Cards had bolted out to an early lead and the Catholic students, getting frustrated, took this opportunity to mock the county girls in their plaid skirts and fake tans.

"Sun Tan City!"

Clap, clap, clap-clap-clap!

"Sun Tan City!"

Clap, clap, clap-clap-clap!

But Dakotah quieted the Catholic fans a moment later by scoring yet again, backing it right into the hoop for another easy two and giving the county kids their reply, which they began chanting now toward the upper deck.

"We can't hear you!"

Clap, clap, clap-clap-clap!

"We can't hear you!"

Clap, clap, clap-clap-clap!

Scott County's pep band wasn't there. There wasn't a single sousaphone in the house, which, to Hicks, was inexplicable. But the student section was representing tonight with the girls all done up in their outfits. Alan Mastin was standing amid them in his pope costume, complete with a white, gold-trimmed papal mitre perched on his head. Just as Mastin had suspected, no one was throwing him out of the gym tonight. He was free to shout and hold up his sign that said, GIVE UP BASKETBALL FOR LENT. And for most of the first half, it appeared that Catholic had done just that.

The Cards opened up a ten-point lead in the second quarter and then fought off a Knights rally, punching back every time they got hit and throwing a haymaker just before the intermission. With less than twenty seconds to go in the half, Catholic's star guard, Jaylen Beckham, gathered in a long rebound, ran the length of the floor, and threw down a dunk, cutting the Cards' lead to seven and saluting the Scott County student section for good measure as he bounded back down the court. But the county answered, swinging the ball from Tanner to Tamron to Chad and then Dakotah, who was all alone behind the three-point line, deep in the right corner. Dakotah lined up the shot just before the halftime buzzer and sank it. The county boys had the lead, 36–26, and they were fired up about it. As the half ended, Dakotah yanked his white, double-XL jersey from the waistband of his shorts and screamed.

With just sixteen minutes left to play, everyone was confident—even Hicks. "You know and I know, *shoot*," he told the boys at halftime, "we're better than ten points better than this team." And briefly, Hicks was right about that. Less than a minute into the third quarter, after baskets from Ge'Lawn and Chad, the county had stretched its lead to fourteen points, going on top, 40–26.

Catholic couldn't hit anything. The Knights, for the game, were shooting a dismal 28 percent from the floor. And somewhere on the Catholic bench, there was talk of moral victories, of using tonight's game as a learning experience, something for the young team to build on for the postseason. But Salsman didn't want to hear it. He wasn't conceding anything.

"Let's go!" Salsman told his team. "C'mon! Get us in this thing!"

And now, about halfway through the third quarter, his team responded, driving to the basket and getting fouled, knocking down free throws and three-pointers. While Chad and Ge'Lawn picked up their third fouls, and Austin picked up his fourth, Catholic started to roll and its shots began to fall.

Within four minutes, Catholic cut the county's fourteen-point lead in half. By the start of the fourth quarter, the Knights were only down six. Then, on the very first possession of the last period, they dropped a three from the left corner. Chad promptly traveled, turning the ball back over to the Knights, who would soon score, of course, cutting the county's lead to just one, 51–50. With six and a half minutes to go now, the cushion was gone. And so was the confidence. Just as they had allowed Henry Clay and Madison Southern to hang around and sneak back into recent games, the county boys had left the door open for Lexington Catholic—and the Knights, being Knights, had kicked it in, ripping the door off its hinges and starting to ransack the kitchen while the women and children screamed.

"We can't do nothing about what we've done so far," Hicks told his boys during the time-out that followed. "But daggone it, guys—Chad, Ge'Lawn, all you guys—we got six minutes right here on our home floor against Lexington Catholic. And some of you guys are already starting to stand around out there."

The boys were tired. Catholic's full-court and three-quarter press was killing them. But it was time to play. This was it.

"Let's go, man," Ge'Lawn said. "Let's get this."

The county went up three, then Catholic tied it. The county went up two, then Catholic tied it again. Any question the Cards seemed to raise, the Knights seemed to answer. When Dakotah hammered home a three-pointer with 3:45 to go, giving Scott County yet another lead, Catholic came right down and dropped a three of its own. Tie game. Back and fourth, right up until the end.

It was 71–71, with thirty seconds to play. Catholic's ball, with a simple plan: look for an open layup or open three for the team's best outside shooter. "We're playing defense right here," Hicks told his boys. But the Knights got that open layup, just as Salsman had scripted it, got fouled, and then nailed both free throws to take a two-point lead with 14.7 seconds to go.

The Cardinals were on the run now, looking for their last chance with the fans on their feet. But it wasn't pretty. They nearly threw the ball away—

twice—then finally got it to Chad at the top of the three-point arc. This wasn't his shot. Chad Jackson had made a grand total of six three-pointers all season—and none of them had come tonight. His best move was to drive or to pass it. There were still a few seconds left on the clock, with Ge'Lawn wide open to his left and Dakotah standing to his right, shooting a gaudy 41 percent from downtown.

But Chad fired up the shot, anyway. It clanged off the rim, wide left and long. A Catholic player got the rebound, got fouled with a second left, made one free throw and missed his second on purpose. And that was it. There would be no Rick Jones miracle tonight, just more of the same agony that the boys had felt the year before.

Catholic had beaten Scott County—again: 74–71.

"Great game, Billy," Salsman told Hicks afterward on the floor. But as he reached the locker room, the Catholic coach was decidedly less gracious, opening with a simple question. "Who the hell said we weren't five in the state?" he asked his team, his voice cracking with emotion. "We ain't five in the state," he added. "We're number one. That's what we are."

THE COUNTY BOYS had been talking about Rupp Arena for an entire year. They had been thinking about what it would be like to step on that floor, to play under those lights, and bring a state title home to Scott County, just like the basketball heroes who had come before them. Many of the boys had been dreaming about it since they were old enough to dribble a basketball. But after losing to Catholic—a team they most likely would have to beat to make it to Rupp—it felt like that dream was dead. Salsman himself said it best, giving a postgame interview that night. "I think we've served notice," he said. "We're going to be a tough out."

In the Scott County locker room, Hicks tried at first to be upbeat. "The season's not over, guys," he told his team. "The tournament's getting ready to start." But then, thinking about the tournament, he started harping on their failure to play defense in the second half against Catholic and how, if they played the same way in the postseason, they weren't going to be playing for very long. Hopefully, he said, they had learned something tonight. "If we don't learn from this, if we don't learn from this right here, guys," Hicks said, "then dag-gone it, we won't learn from anything."

There wasn't much else to say. But the boys didn't leave, scattering into the night like usual. They lingered over this loss, sitting in the locker room and then outside in the empty gym, like mourners who couldn't bear to leave the funeral.

"Boys," Hicks prodded them, "let's go home."

But Chad and Dakotah didn't listen. For over an hour, the two friends sat in the empty gym amid discarded popcorn buckets and candy wrappers, talk-ing about everything that had gone wrong. Chad was miffed that Hicks had called him out after the game for letting a Catholic player clap in his face. "What was I supposed to do?" Chad said. "Get on the court and beat him up or something?" And Dakotah, only half-jokingly, said he was ready to start pray-ing: praying that some other team would knock off Catholic in the regional tournament because, Lord knows, Scott County wasn't going to do it. "Some-thing about *that team*," Dakotah said. "They freakin' beat us every time."

Chad didn't reply. They couldn't beat Catholic—it was true. They would probably never beat Catholic, which meant they weren't going to make it to Rupp, which meant they weren't going to play for a state title, much less win one, which meant they were going to go down in the record books not just as trans-fers and not just as cheaters, but as losers. Completely and totally forgettable.

Not far away, in the subdivision behind the school, a few dozen students were hanging out at a girl's house, drinking beer and listening to music in the basement. The basketball players were supposed to be there for the party. But now that they had lost, they didn't want to go, least of all Chad and Dakotah, who still hadn't left the gym. For a long time, they just sat there, saying noth-ing at all.

"How stupid do we look?" Chad said finally.

Dakotah just shrugged. "I'm getting used to it," he replied.

Part III

THEY SAID WE WERE SOFT

AT THE TEAM'S FIRST OFFICIAL practice, four months earlier, Hicks had forced the boys to watch the game tape of the previous year's season-ending loss to Lexington Catholic in the postseason—a terrible thing to see, but Hicks figured it was good motivation. Now, with a new postseason about to begin, the boys were back in his office, watching another loss to Catholic—only it was the previous night's game. And this time it wasn't motivating. It just hurt. "I'd rather take two shots to the balls," Austin said as he walked into Hicks's office, "than watch this film."

Hicks, initially, felt about the same. As he came into his office that Sunday morning to watch the tape, he had no intention of showing it to the boys. But the more he watched, the better he felt. No one had quit out there. They were all playing hard, right down to the end. The problem was defensive breakdowns in the second half. Everyone was guarding their man, not moving to the ball. And there was time to change that, Hicks believed, time to still coach that. He wasn't panicking at all; he was almost at peace. Maybe, he decided, losing was the best thing that could have happened. Now Catholic would be the favorite to win the region and go to Rupp. The pressure would be on the Knights. And now, perhaps, his boys would listen. Perhaps, with the loss, he'd have their attention when it mattered most.

"Let's start watching that tape," Hicks said, cuing up the video with the boys in his office. As the game began playing in the dark, Hicks opened with an apology. He admitted that he'd made at least one mistake. "I probably underestimated this team," Hicks said. "To be honest with you, I probably underestimated them." And, he conceded a little while later, he also probably spent too much time yelling at the referees during the Catholic game. "I let the referees get to me," Hicks said. "I got mad."

But the boys had made mistakes as well—simple, correctible mistakes. They could all see that now. They had failed to make the extra pass. At one point, late in the fourth quarter, Dakotah was wide open in the corner. "He could have eaten a bologna sandwich hitting that shot," Hicks said. But no one passed Dakotah the ball. At another point, late in the game, they were just standing around on defense. "That's just bad team defense, guys," Hicks said. And, at times, the boys seemed almost too amped up for the game, missing easy baskets. As Chad sat before the television watching himself miss a layup, he just shook his head.

"Gotta take those layups seriously," Hicks said, "don't you?"

"Yeah," Chad whispered in the dark.

For more than an hour, they watched the tape, reliving every second of the game. Then Hicks stood up, turned off the television, and flicked on the lights. He knew that everyone was talking about why Scott County had lost. "How many opinions have you all heard?" Hicks asked them. "Even my mother—ninety years old next month—she watched the game last night. She has an opinion on it." But he wasn't worried about the critics. "Let's let everybody have their say so," Hicks said. There was still a lot of basketball left to be played—and he, for one, was ready to play it. They might face the Knights again in the postseason, he told the boys now, or they might not. Catholic could reach the regional finals, he said now, or maybe not. There was no guarantee that Catholic would make it that far. Hicks was only sure of one thing.

"We're gonna get there," he said. "We're gonna get there."

The push was on now. With only a few days left to work before the postseason began, Hicks threw himself into practices, bounding up and down the court in a long-sleeve, burnt-orange thermal shirt and black sweatpants—a wardrobe combination that seemed pulled off his closet floor. But it hardly seemed to matter at the moment if his socks matched. Hicks was focused solely on the boys, specifically their defense. "Everybody," he said, "is going to play team defense." At times, he even broke things down like a third-grade teacher, asking the boys to repeat after him: Move toward the ball. "Say it with me," he said. "Say it so we can *hear you*." Other times, he was calmer, just coaching.

"You can't forget your man. But play the ball," Hicks said at one practice that week. "*Play . . . the . . . ball*. Because you know what they score with?" he said, turning now to Josh Harris, a sophomore with dreams of one day starting for the county. "What do they score with, Josh?"

Josh froze.

"Layups?" the boy guessed.

His teammates burst out laughing. Hicks just shook his head.

"The *ball*," he replied, correcting poor Josh. "They score with *the ball*."

The exchange seemed typical of this team—and this season. They were dialed in one minute, but not the next. They played well one night, but not the next. They looked like they might blow out Lexington Catholic, then they lost. Up and down, all year long, the team had left Hicks searching for answers. Even the boys seemed to know that something was wrong with them—especially Ge'Lawn, who was scoring fewer points a game as a senior than he had as a junior.

"Dakotah," Ge'Lawn said at one point, "what's up with our stroke this year?"

"I don't know," Dakotah replied. "But we're going to get hot at the right time."

"I hope we do."

"At tournament time," Dakotah nodded, "we're going to get hot."

Now, that time was here. Soon, entire towns—sixteen to be exact—would be emptying out to make the trip to Rupp, an occasion so grand that schools are known to cancel classes and city governments all but shut down. Mayors and judges often don't have the time, nor the interest, in running the government when the local boys are playing at Rupp. And even if they did, their secretaries, clerks, and bailiffs wouldn't be there. The week of the tournament, headaches and mysterious viruses run rampant across the state as adults call in sick to work and then go to Rupp.

High school administrators have called it the best time to be in the education business. Students are happy and spirits high. But it's not a great time for local sheriffs who must arrange motorcades for the winning teams or patrol communities reduced to ghost towns overnight. With so many people gone to Rupp, extra deputies are sometimes forced to work on game days in March, guarding against opportunistic burglars or chicken thieves. It's all about the boys, and the score, sometimes to the extreme. In one remote, eastern Kentucky community, Clay County, where the high school won the state title in 1987, officials named a street for the team's star player, future University of Kentucky standout Richie Farmer—shortly after Farmer's high school graducation. If you wanted to mail a letter to Farmer, you could address it to him at Richie Boulevard.

It's the sort of honor typically bestowed upon a professional athlete. Larry Bird, Jackie Robinson, and John Elway, for instance, all have streets named after them. But in Kentucky, there are no professional franchises to overshadow the high school teams en route to Rupp. No LeBron James to soak up the spotlight or NBA team to dwarf the moment.

The folk heroes here have to be boys.

THE SCOTT COUNTY HIGH SCHOOL DANCE was scheduled for the Friday night before the postseason started. Posters advertising the event—THE BLACK TIE AFFAIR, it was called—had adorned the walls at Scott County High for weeks, and many basketball players planned to go. But not Ge'Lawn.

The problem wasn't finding a date. There were plenty of girls who might have gone with him, including, but not limited to, the girl who kept flirting with Ge'Lawn in English class, passing him notes in recent days.

> The girl: "Sooo what about me & you, Ge? Or do you got too many girls on
> you?"
> Ge'Lawn: "You not being real rite now are you?"
> The girl: "YES I AM!"
> Ge'Lawn: "I don't think so. But hmmmmm. You kool and everything.
> Ummmm look it's to hard to decide."
> The girl: "Well it shouldn't be! Make the decision."
> Ge'Lawn: "I CAN'T RITE NOW!!!!!!!"

Ge'Lawn kept the note, stashing it in his locker along with the mail still pouring in from college coaches. But he had no intention of getting involved with the girl at this point. "I got out of it," he explained. Like it was a relief.

Like a burden had been lifted. With the postseason upon him, Ge'Lawn was going underground now, deeper than usual. He didn't want any distractions. So, no, absolutely not—there was no way he was going to the dance that Friday night.

"You got anything to do now?" Hicks asked Ge'Lawn as practice ended that evening.

"No," he replied.

"Come on back to the office, then."

Ge'Lawn, wearing a gray hoodie and jeans, followed his coach into the small cinder-block office, taking a seat on the couch against the wall. Dinner was procured from the concession stand, which was open that night for another team's game. And soon Ge'Lawn was eating a barbecue sandwich while Hicks played some recent game tape, hoping to show Ge'Lawn how he could improve his game. Mostly, it seemed, Hicks just wanted to remind Ge'Lawn of who he was, or who he used to be, or what he could still do with the time they had left.

"I'm not picking on you," Hicks assured Ge'Lawn as game tape flickered on the screen. "I want you to be Ge'Lawn Guyn. I want you to be Ge'Lawn Guyn, the stud-hoss. Not a little role player out there. How many points did you get in the regional championship last year?"

"Thirty-one," Ge'Lawn replied.

"Thirty-one in the regional championship," Hicks answered, nodding. "You ain't took enough shots this year to get thirty-one points in one game."

Part of the solution, Hicks said, was working harder. But the other part of it, Hicks seemed to suggest, was confidence. It was mental. It was almost like Ge'Lawn needed to remember that he was fast enough to pick off passes on defense or take his man one on one on offense. "You gotta look to drive," Hicks told him, "and take advantage of your talent, son." Because he still had it, Hicks told him. It was still there. As difficult as the season had been for Ge'Lawn, he still had a chance to redeem himself. "It ain't like the season's over," Hicks told Ge'Lawn. "Really, it's just starting." And if Scott County was going to win, it was going to need Ge'Lawn—the *old* Ge'Lawn—to resurface.

"You know what I'm saying?" Hicks told him. "You're the best athlete on the floor. You could be the best player in the state of Kentucky. And I expect that out of you. I expect you to go out there and just dominate a game. We're gonna put that ball in your hand down at tournament time here. You want it, don't you?"

"Of course," Ge'Lawn replied.

As they spoke, Ge'Lawn was icing his knees. *"Man,"* he'd exclaimed at practice that night, "my knees are killing me." The pain—and the discussion of it—simply would not go away. But finally, recently, George Guyn had made a breakthrough, convincing a new doctor to order an MRI. He hoped that it would settle the matter once and for all and, one afternoon after school, he met his son at a medical park in Lexington to get the results from the doctor. For over an hour, the Guyns sat in the waiting room and then inside an examining room with teal walls and white floors, until finally Dr. John Balthrop appeared in his white coat.

"Sore right here?" he asked, examining Ge'Lawn's knees.

"Uh-huh."

"Here?"

"Uh-huh."

"Which one's worse?" Balthrop inquired.

"This one," Ge'Lawn said. "My right one."

The MRI confirmed the previous diagnosis: Ge'Lawn was suffering from tendinitis. There was no other structural damage, which was good news. But there was no way to cure the tendinitis, either, which was bad news. The only thing Ge'Lawn could do, Balthrop said, was to treat it: heat his knees before playing, ice them afterward, get electro-stimulation therapy, and stretch with exercises—things Ge'Lawn had already tried or been told to try.

"Would rest—?" George Guyn started to ask.

"Oh, rest would help it a lot," Balthrop replied, interrupting him. "But you can't rest and play basketball at the same time."

Ge'Lawn sighed—a long, deep sigh that seemed to fill the small teal room. Hicks and the coaching staff had been right: Ge'Lawn was going to have to play through the pain. But at the same time, the Guyns were vindicated as well. According to the MRI, the inflammation of the patellar tendons in Ge'Lawn's knees was significant.

"Yours is, like, that big," Balthrop said, drawing a thumbnail-sized circle on a piece of paper for Ge'Lawn to see. "Too big to take out," the doctor added. "Plus, if you cut it out now, your season would be over."

That simply wasn't an option, not with the postseason set to begin and the pressure building to make it to Rupp Arena—to win, for once, when it really mattered. It was everywhere now—talk of Rupp, getting to Rupp. The pressure was even coming from people inside the locker room.

"How many big games y'all won?" equipment manager Charles Eddie Doan asked, needling Ge'Lawn a few days before the play-offs began.

"A couple," Ge'Lawn replied.

"When?"

Ge'Lawn couldn't come up with an answer.

"You won any state championships?" Charles Eddie asked. "A regional?"

Ge'Lawn had not. This Scott County team had not. But the boys were trying not to think about that now. It was better to dwell on other thoughts, such as the advice that Dr. Balthrop had given Ge'Lawn before he had left the doctor's office that day. "A little bit of advice," Balthrop said, "that you're not asking for."

"Use basketball," he told Ge'Lawn. "Don't let it use you."

"Yes, sir," Ge'Lawn replied.

SCOTT COUNTY STOMPED ON little Sayre to open the district tournament, crushing the private school 77–40. Then, three nights later, the county boys beat Henry Clay for the third time that season, winning 66–49 after holding the Blue Devils to just twenty points in the first half. In doing so, the boys clinched the district title and earned a top seed in the eight-team regional tournament set to begin five days later at a college arena in Richmond, about forty miles south of Georgetown. "Our business," Hicks told the boys, "is in Richmond."

He was impressed by their performance in districts, but not shocked. Scott County was supposed to win the district. The surprise, in this round, came in Lexington, where Catholic was facing Lafayette High, a city school that hadn't made it to Rupp in nine years. The Knights were on an eleven-game winning streak headed into the contest, and the streak wasn't likely to end against the Generals. Catholic owned Lafayette, winning the last five matchups. And anyway, Catholic always made it out of districts—at least it had since 1986.

"I say Lafayette by six," Chad predicted the day of the game.

"I got Lafayette by ten," Ge'Lawn added, making a prediction of his own.

Dakotah, however, just shook his head. "No," he said, waving off his teammates' wishful thinking. "They're not going to lose. That coach is too good."

But that night in Lexington, it was Catholic's turn to blow a second-half lead. It was Catholic committing the stupid turnovers—twenty-six in all—under pressure from Lafayette's guards. And it was Catholic missing the three-point shots at the end. With thirty seconds to go and Catholic down by six, radio play-by-play man Gary Ball was still calling the action, speaking in rapid-fire from his courtside seat. But his broadcast partner, retired coach Kirk Chiles, who had 603 career wins in Kentucky, interrupted Ball's dramatic account with a flat assessment.

"It's over, Gary," Chiles said. "The Catholic kids have quit."

Hicks, who was listening to the broadcast in his office, was almost a little disappointed by Catholic's 62–56 loss.

"I was hoping we could play Catholic again," he told local preacher Gary Brown the next day.

"You know what?" Brown replied. "I'd take that break."

Hicks was at Brown's church, Grace Christian, so that the congregation could pray over the boys before the regional tournament. "Father," Brown began, "I just ask that you be with this team." But clearly, he already was. Catholic was out. The regional tournament was here. And the boys felt good. Still, there were doubts. To win the region, Scott County, with its 24-6 record, was going to have to beat three 20-win teams—a difficult task, made plain by a headline in the *Lexington Herald-Leader* that week. SCOTT CO., said the headline, HAS A TOUGH ROAD TO RUPP.

Hicks seized on the idea, scrawling the headline on the whiteboard in the locker room. "These birds down in Lexington," he groused, "they think we ain't tough enough. They think we ain't tough enough to do the job to get to Rupp Arena."

He was getting more ornery by the day—so focused on basketball that the sound of his own cell phone ringing would have him muttering. But he was up for a little company at dinner the night before the team's trip to Richmond. When Ge'Lawn had nowhere to eat, with his parents off watching his sister play basketball, Hicks invited him over to his house for heaping plates of spaghetti and towering bowls of spinach salad.

"What kind of salad dressing do you like, Ge'Lawn?"

"You got ranch?" the boy asked.

"We've got everything you want," Hicks replied.

In the dining room, Ge'Lawn began eating, and then began texting. But Hicks urged him to put his cell phone away. "Tell them girls you're busy," he said. "Tell them they can't bother you tonight. You've got the whole rest of your life to fool with them girls now."

Ge'Lawn put down his phone. And for a while, the pair ate in silence, the player sitting across from the coach on the eve of the tournament that would decide everything. Finally, Hicks spoke up.

"Guess what kind of ice cream we got," he said.

"What's that?" Ge'Lawn replied.

"Guess," Hicks said. "I'll give you three guesses."

Ge'Lawn smiled. He knew the answer.

"Black walnut," he said.

It was Ge'Lawn's favorite.

SCOTT COUNTY'S FIRST-ROUND FOES in the regional tournament were familiar: Shane Buttry's scrappy Madison Southern boys, who had nearly beaten Scott County, in Georgetown, three weeks earlier and finished the year with a 21-9 record. And this time, Buttry was thinking upset.

"We can beat them," he told his team. "We really can."

The crowd at the arena in Richmond was on their side. "Everybody in the world is pulling for you," Buttry told his team, "except their own fan section right over there." And if the Eagles could beat the Cards, if they could win tonight, Buttry was convinced that they would win the next two games and go to the state tournament. "If you've ever dreamed of playing at Rupp Arena," Buttry said, "daggone it, here's your shot."

Hicks, pacing in the other locker room, told his team that the key to winning was defense. And the boys seemed to be buying into it now. Dakotah was convinced they would win if they played tough on defense—and if Chad didn't let the Eagles' big man, Joey Wallace, go off for twenty-two points again.

"He gave you buckets," Dakotah told his friend before the game.

"Yeah?" Chad replied.

"And he already said in the paper that he's coming for you again."

"Right."

"I'm just saying it makes you look bad."

"Right," Chad said again.

In the early goings that night, Wallace had six points—a bad omen for the county. But for the rest of the game, Wallace scored only one more basket. No one was giving Chad buckets tonight and no one was stopping Ge'Lawn on offense. While Dakotah was off target from the tip, Ge'Lawn was on, making steals that led to layups and draining threes from outside the arc. Austin chipped in and Will did, too, scoring eight a piece. And the game soon got out of hand.

Buttry, it turned out, was wrong. Madison Southern couldn't beat Scott County. "It's a college team," he marveled to reporters after the game. "Better than a college team. They'd beat Berea College." But standing before his players in the losing locker room, Madison Southern's coach simply wept. "My kids look up to you seniors," he told his boys, choking back tears. "It's unbelievable. Today, I'm getting ready to leave and my two sons are playing ball in their room and one's Trent, one's Rico, one's Joey—they keep naming the names. Hell, they love you guys." The Cards, though, were the victors, winning in a rout, 72–38.

Two more wins to Rupp. *Two more!* Dakotah hollered in the locker room. And now, it was about to get personal. The semifinal matchup pitted Scott County against Tates Creek, a rivalry that had spawned last year's fight between the Lexington cheerleader and the Scott County beauty queen. And predictably, the Creek students were fired up for the game, spewing invective from the stands in Richmond three days later as Scott County took the floor.

"Shave your mustache, Coach!"

"Dakotah, you suck!"

"Ge'Lawn, you suck!"

"Hey, Ge'Lawn—what kind of name is Ge'Lawn?"

But the boys paid the fans no mind. If anything, the insults hurled at Ge'Lawn only motivated him more. As Hicks called the team together in the locker room for the pregame prayer and everyone circled up, placing hands in the middle, one hand on top of the other, Ge'Lawn closed his eyes and gently buried his forehead into Hicks's back.

"Let's get this," Ge'Lawn declared.

The game couldn't have started much worse for Scott County. There was a turnover, then another turnover. Dakotah missed a three, way short. Then he coughed up the ball on the next two possessions. Ge'Lawn got whistled for a dumb foul. Dakotah missed another shot. Ge'Lawn chucked a three on the very next possession and missed, too. And there were the Cardinals, nearly four minutes into the game, without a single point on the scoreboard. Zero points.

But Austin, hustling, collected Ge'Lawn's errant three-pointer and laid it in. Ge'Lawn, not afraid, heaved up a three on the very next trip down the floor. And, this time, he nailed it. Dakotah missed the next shot—Scott County's leader was ice cold, yet again—but Austin pulled in the rebound, another board for him, and scored again to give Scott County its first lead of the game, 7–5.

It was tied at the end of the first quarter. "We're okay," Hicks assured the boys. And Scott County soon began to pull away, mounting a twelve-point lead midway through the second. But Tates Creek answered with a 7–0 run and Scott County was only up five at the half, 34–29. Nothing seemed to be going right. At one point in the first half, the student managers couldn't even find Gatorade for the boys to drink during a time-out.

"Where's the Gatorade?" Hicks pleaded. *"Hurry!"*

The second half started off just as poorly. Both Ge'Lawn and Dakotah lost their men on Tates Creek's first possession, allowing the Commodores to get an easy basket, which cut the lead to three and prompted Hicks to call an immediate time-out, a mere twenty-six seconds into the half. "Stunt and recover," he begged the boys, preaching defense. "We can't win this ball game if we can't guard."

Scott County proceeded to miss its next three shots. But Tates Creek couldn't capitalize, missing layups and failing to rebound. And the Cards jumped out to a nine-point lead, thanks to baskets by Chad and Ge'Lawn and stifling defense that forced the Commodores' sure-handed point guard into seven turnovers. In all, the Commodores committed twenty—the sixth consecutive game the Cards had forced their opponent into twenty or more ball-handling mistakes. And down the stretch, Tates Creek threatened only once. With a turnover and a fast-break bucket, the Commodores cut the Cardinals' lead to five with exactly four minutes to play. Tanner then responded by firing up an ill-advised three at the other end, which missed long, caroming hard off the rim and giving Commodores fans still more reason to roar.

They were on their feet in the arena now. With the rebound and a basket, they could cut the Cards' lead to three or even two. They could win this thing. But Ge'Lawn hustled after Tanner's off-target shot, grabbing it in the paint amid three Commodore players and flicking it into the hoop with one hand as he backpedaled down the floor.

Swish.

"This game ain't over," Hicks hollered in the ensuing time-out.

But it was. Scott County rolled, 69–58.

"One more, baby!" Dakotah yelped after the game. "One more!"

This one, though, was going to be Scott County's toughest test yet. The Lafayette Generals—the team that throttled Lexington Catholic in the district round—awaited the Cards in the regional finals: long, athletic, and hungry, a scary team with nothing to lose. And there were plenty of other reasons for concern. Dakotah's shots weren't falling. He was barely shooting 30 percent in the postseason—well below his season average. And Austin had injured his back in the meaningless final minutes of the Madison Southern game, making it hard to walk, much less run. On a scale of 1 to 10, with 10 being the worst, he told the coaches that the pain felt like a four, maybe a five, sometimes a six, raising questions about whether he would even be able to play against Lafayette in the regional finals on Tuesday night.

"Does it hurt when you shoot?" Dakotah asked him.

Austin, making 50 percent of his shots on the year, shook his head no.

"That's good," Ge'Lawn said, hopefully.

"I am running funny, though," Austin replied. "With every bounce, it hurts." And when Ge'Lawn pressed him, when Ge'Lawn asked Austin if he thought he'd play in the game, Austin sat there for a long quiet moment, until finally nodding his head yes. Yes, he thought he would play. Maybe, he hoped.

Meantime, Hicks, bleary-eyed from watching too much Lafayette game tape—he estimated he'd viewed ten hours in all—was getting a little jumpy. He was worried about spies in the gym who might ferry information back to Lafayette and he wasn't opposed to questioning strangers passing through the building. "Who's up there watching practice?" he said from the floor on the eve of the finals, eyeing an unfamiliar man in the upper deck. "Who's that?"

It was just a repairman. No need for alarm.

Still, it was worth asking. The next game was for everything: a title, a trip to Rupp, a shot at redemption for Hicks, and, for the boys, a chance of glimpsing greatness at least for a moment. "Thank God for the opportunity," Hicks told the boys. It had not been promised to them, and it would not be given to them. They were going to have to earn it, wrestling it away from Lafayette, Hicks said, by keeping the Generals away from the rim, denying them second-chance points, and putting pressure on them by jumping out to an early lead. The Generals, Hicks said, would fold under pressure. But the boys weren't so sure.

"What if it comes down to the last second tonight?" Chad asked on the day of the game while the boys were eating lunch at school.

"Coach Hicks would done have a heart attack," Dakotah answered, not missing a beat. "He'd be on the ground. We'd be reviving him. Coach Willhite would call a play, and we wouldn't run it right, and we would lose."

The boys all had a good laugh over that one. But Chad wasn't finished.

"No, seriously," he said. "What if we lose the same way we did last year?"

Dakotah stopped laughing now, put down his sandwich, and just looked at his friend. "Don't even joke about that," he replied.

The boys picked at their food for a while and then headed back to class, but not for long. The bus bound for Richmond was idling outside soon after the last bell rang. It was time to go, time to play.

"Ready to win?" the bus driver asked Hicks as the coach stepped on board.

"Ready to try," Hicks answered.

·   ·   ·   ·

THERE WAS CHEST-BUMPING, high-fiving, and low-fiving. During player introductions in Richmond that night, the Lafayette players even bowed down to one another, as if worshipping their very existence—all of which perturbed Hicks to no end. "This," he said, turning to his boys on the bench, "is the cockiest team we've faced all year. Let's shut 'em down right here."

The Generals won the tip and launched a three-pointer to open the game. The shot missed. But Lafayette scooped up the long rebound and then scored, driving right around the defense and laying it in over Dakotah. Scott County fumbled the ball on the other end of the floor. And now the Generals were running. Here came the fast break and another easy two when Dakotah couldn't catch up to his man: a six-foot-seven eighth grader who flexed his arms as he bounded back down the court.

In the span of fifty-one seconds, the Scott County boys had managed to do the exact opposite of what Hicks had asked of them. They had given the Generals second-chance points. They hadn't pressured anyone. The layups had been free and easy, there for the taking. And now, worst of all, the Generals had the early lead and the momentum that Hicks didn't want them to have. He had no choice. He had to call a time-out, signaling for time before Lafayette's second basket had barely settled into the net, stomping his foot, and scowling, red-faced, at his boys.

In the locker room, just a few minutes earlier, Hicks had seen no reason to raise his voice, speaking at times in a low, raspy whisper. He had laid out the game plan for the boys. He had slipped on his famous red sport coat, size 46 long. And he had granted radio interviews without a single complaint, quietly giving the reporters what they needed, even though he was itching to be on the floor.

"One last question," said the second of the two radio reporters, detaining Hicks in the tunnel of the arena for a bit longer. "If you were coaching against your team, how would you stop your guys?"

"Shoot," Hicks replied, quiet and reflective. "I'd outscore them."

But now he was yelling, wondering if the boys had listened to anything he had said. "We gave them two layups two times down the court," he hollered. "*C'mon now!* Defense the heck out of them."

Ge'Lawn nodded, then answered. Out of the time-out, he dribbled up the court and drained a three to put Scott County on the board. Lafayette failed to score on its next trip, missing a gimme at the other end. But Austin wouldn't miss his. Hobbled by back pain yet playing—he absolutely had to play—the county's sharpshooter matched Ge'Lawn's three with a three of his own. Lafayette then proceeded to turn the ball over on the next two possessions, leading to a bucket from Ge'Lawn and a three from Dakotah. And then Ge'Lawn stole the ball, lobbing it in transition to Chad, who scored.

The Generals, scoreless for three long minutes, finally hit another layup. But Ge'Lawn responded by scoring again, getting fouled in the process, preening for the crowd, and then making his foul shot to complete a three-point play. Lafayette answered with more turnovers—an errant pass, two more traveling violations, an offensive foul, and bad decisions—while Scott County kept scoring and hustling. At one point, during a fast break, Lafayette had the county outnumbered, four to one, attacking the basket. But Chad, running the length of the floor, raced back, hustling past everyone, and reached the rim just in time to block Lafayette's easy layup off the backboard. At another point, Ge'Lawn, who was right-handed, blocked a Lafayette shot with his *left* hand, swatting it out of bounds and then standing before the Lafayette kid as if to remind him who had done the swatting.

"Let's go," Ge'Lawn bellowed. "Let's finish this."

It was a stunning seven minutes of basketball that produced one very unlikely result. By the end of the first quarter, Scott County, down by four points to start the game, was crushing Lafayette, embarrassing the last Lexington high school still playing basketball in the state of Kentucky. The tally was right up there on the scoreboard for everyone to see.

Scott County 21, Lafayette 6.

The Generals tried to make up ground by dogging the Cards with a full-court press in the second quarter, and the tactic forced a few mistakes. But Lafayette trailed by double digits the rest of the way, never in contention and never a threat. The county was up eighteen at half and up twenty-five when

Hicks finally pulled his starters with about two minutes to go, meaning Chad, Dakotah, and Ge'Lawn were on the bench when Will Schu got the ball, just outside the paint, with fourteen seconds left in the game. Will said later that he knew what he was going to do. He knew how he wanted to end it. Without dribbling the ball even once, the county native took two steps, jumped, and then threw down a two-handed dunk, hanging on the rim for just a moment before dropping back to the court with his arms over his head and the palms of his hands turned up toward the rafters.

Ge'Lawn couldn't stop jumping. Dakotah couldn't stop running. Both boys scampered around the floor in victory, hugging each other, their teammates, and then their fathers.

"Pop!" Ge'Lawn said.

"I love you," George replied.

Scott County had won 76–50. Ge'Lawn had led all scorers with eighteen points. He was named MVP. And as he accepted the award on the court after the game, the television cameras closed in around him with their white lights blazing, angling to get closer and hear what the boy had to say. "They said we were soft," Ge'Lawn announced, bathed in the white lights. "But we showed them." For the first time all season, it seemed, he was exactly where he was supposed to be. Ge'Lawn was the star.

THE SHERIFF HIMSELF escorted the team bus back to Scott County, with the blue and red lights of his squad car flashing in the night. At Iron Works Pike, close to home, more squad cars were waiting to greet the team. And once the bus eased off the interstate, turning onto Route 25 and rolling past the trailer park at the county line, the boys were allowed to stick their heads out the windows and scream into the darkness.

Motorists honked their horns. People at the gas station on South Broadway turned and waved. A little girl standing outside the courthouse downtown held up a sign for the boys to see. NEXT STOP RUPP, it said. And when the bus arrived at the high school, a horde of fans, including school superintendent Patricia Putty, was there to welcome the boys home.

In the postgame celebration back in Richmond, Hicks had reminded his boys not to become boastful in victory. With heads bowed and eyes closed, they shared a long, weighty moment of silence, giving thanks for how far they had come. But now, back in Scott County on their home floor, people couldn't help but brag—at least a little—about where they were headed next.

"Last one out," Putty told the crowd, "turn off the lights."

The county was bound, once again, for the state tournament to play before screaming crowds of twenty thousand fans or more, with reporters live-blogging the action from courtside seats and college coaches watching from the stands. Most of the boys—even those lucky enough to play college ball—would never suit up before such crowds ever again. They were going to Rupp Arena, *their house*.

"Whose house?" the students chanted now.

"OUR HOUSE!"

"Whose house?"

"OUR HOUSE!"

"Whose house?"

"OUR HOUSE!"

"Cards on three!"

"One, two, three . . . CARDS!"

HOPE YOUR HOPE AND PRAY YOUR PRAYER

THERE IS NOTHING ESPECIALLY REMARKABLE about the arena itself. It's beige and boxy, slab-sided and cavernous, rising like a warehouse in downtown Lexington. It's attached to a mall, which is connected to a hotel. And at the groundbreaking in 1974, some people hated it. Locals referred to the still unnamed civic center as the Big Box or the white elephant, confident that the $46-million project was going to ruin everything.

Basketball fans believed the mammoth, ten-story structure was going to destroy the collegiate atmosphere at University of Kentucky basketball games. With a capacity of 22,934, the arena, once finished, was going to be the largest basketball center ever constructed—twice the size of Memorial Coliseum, where the Wildcats had lost only thirty-eight times since 1950. In Lexington, it was said that General George Custer would sooner fight at Little Bighorn again than coach a visiting team in the Coliseum. And it was questionable, at best, whether such success could be recreated inside the new arena. "If anything," conceded then Kentucky coach Joe B. Hall before his first game there, "I'm a little apprehensive about what the atmosphere will be like."

For one thing, the color scheme was all wrong. In the months before UK moved into the new building in late 1976, fans driving downtown nearly wrecked their Buicks upon seeing large reddish-orange triangles adorning the arena's exterior walls. It was the civic center's new logo, patterned after the triangular steel beam towers, which held the arena's 3.5-acre roof in place. "We're working in earth-tone colors," explained Tom Minter, the center's executive director at the time, "and the only colors that will harmonize are red and yellow and those in between."

The logo, technically, was amethyst red. But to UK fans, it looked suspiciously like University of Tennessee orange, leading Tennessee officials to crow.

"I appreciate the show of friendship," Volunteers basketball coach Ray Mears chuckled that summer. "It is a most unusual thing and I appreciate it."

Kentucky fans, unwilling to tolerate such chiding from their neighbors with their subpar basketball, soon began circulating a petition to have the logo repainted with a more appropriate color—namely, blue. But Minter, a self-described nuts-and-bolts man, was forced to explain that blue simply didn't complement beige. And anyway, even if it did, it was too late to change the logo now. "We couldn't change it," Minter said, "for less than $100,000."

Some doubted whether fans would fill the arena. Others wondered if the center would attract other events, such as rock concerts and ice shows—clients deemed critical to the project's success. And then there was the controversial matter of parking. Homes were going to have to be demolished to make way for wide swaths of asphalt parking lots.

Lexington residents—black and white, but almost uniformly poor—were especially angry about the parking lot issue, refusing to leave their homes and turning the new project into a symbol of class warfare. One man, David Taylor, said the city was trying to eliminate the rabble downtown. "So the rich people can come down," he complained, "and have their parties." And the city's efforts to dissuade the soon-to-be displaced residents of this notion often fell flat. In a public meeting in the months before the arena opened, officials assured people that there was money set aside to help them relocate and declared that they were not in the business of putting people out on the street.

But folks weren't convinced. Residents claimed there was nowhere for them to go—at least nowhere suitable or equally affordable as the homes where they already lived. Even with large housing projects like Charlotte Court, Lexington was suffering from a lack of decent low-income housing. By one count, 12,000 families were already in line, leaving arena neighbors like Gene and Mary Lester with few options. "They told us they'd move us cost-free in a trash truck," said Mary Lester, bemoaning the government's offer at the time. "Can you just imagine arriving in a new neighborhood in a trash truck?"

Everything about the project, it seemed, incited arguments, creating stress both inside and outside the building, which was rising now like a cardboard box against the squat city skyline. "If this thing lays a big, fat elephant egg," conceded center president Jake Graves, three months before the opening, "we, the taxpayers, will have to pay for it."

But on one issue there was no debate. The project would be dubbed the Lexington Center and the arena itself would be named for one man, a Kentuckian, by way of Kansas, who was the most successful college basketball coach to ever step on a floor: Adolph Rupp. The man with his passion for discipline was not easy to please and not one for handing out empty compliments. He was bulky and jowly, cantankerous at times and often dictatorial, presiding over basketball practice at the University of Kentucky in starched khaki and making an art out of biting sarcasm. "Someday I'm going to write a book on how not to play basketball," Rupp once told UK guard Tommy Kron, "and I'm going to devote the first two hundred pages to you."

He expected his players to go about their business in silence, much like a student would approach the study of economics or chemistry. "No nonsense," he said once. And he was also down on horseplay, chatter, whistling, and singing. But the man who expected silence from his team rarely kept it himself. When a quirk in the 1954 schedule forced Kentucky to play Georgia a second time, just two nights after thrashing the Bulldogs 106–55, Rupp declared that it was "more ridiculous than kissing your sister." His team had better things to do than play Georgia again. But the Wildcats, adhering to the schedule, did so, anyway, crushing the Bulldogs once more, 100–68, which was, for Rupp anyway, no surprise. His Wildcats that year, he boasted, weren't just undefeated; they were the "finest team ever assembled in the United States."

In death, he would be labeled a racist opposed to recruiting black players, not just mean, but mean-spirited—portrayals that would not play well in Lexington where Rupp's descendants would rush to his defense. In life, however, Rupp himself paid such criticism no mind. He knew people thought he was mean. "But it's not true," he said. "The fact is, I've got an invitation to coach *both* basketball teams when I go through the pearly gates."

Winning was all that mattered. He didn't care if people hated him. The key to success, he believed, was not listening to the critics at all, but rather heeding the voice that raged within one's own soul. "Sing your song," Rupp wrote once, quoting verse by an English poet. "Dream your dream, hope your hope, and pray your prayer."

Kentuckians liked that. They liked the idea that their coach found poetry in the game. They enjoyed the fact that Rupp could be both intellectual and in your face at the same time, that he could recite from the works of Rudyard Kipling in public speeches only to turn around a moment later and call his critics "a bunch of nincompoops." "Just pay attention," he said, "to the next game."

And so, for Kentuckians, there was no doubt about the name of this new arena opening in Lexington in the fall of 1976. It was Rupp's, all his, a tribute to the recently retired coach's 876 wins and four NCAA titles. And the man, though aging and ailing from diabetes, would live just long enough to mark the moment. He'd be there for the grand opening, attending the arena's first event, a Lawrence Welk concert, in October 1976 and the inaugural Kentucky basketball game a month later.

Not unexpectedly, there were problems. Parking downtown was scarce. Thieves targeted cars parked on side streets. There were concerns about the safety of those sitting in the upper deck. It was just so high. "You feel like you need seatbelts," complained one spectator, Vic Ward, at the Lawrence Welk concert. "If somebody should start falling, they're liable to take fifty bodies with them." And at the first basketball game, there were glitches as well. Arena officials had ordered about eight thousand hot dogs—plenty, they figured. But by halftime, most concession stands had sold out of the processed meat product. "How many hot dogs do you order for 23,000 people?" Minter asked. "We've never had to do it before."

But Kentucky won the game, outlasting Wisconsin, 72–64, before a record 23,266 fans. There was no need to worry about attendance, as it turned out. The problem now was *finding* a ticket to games. And Rupp himself loved it. He didn't care about the orange logo outside. "It doesn't look anything like Tennessee orange to me," he said. And he didn't mind signing autographs for fans who gave him a two-minute standing ovation the night the arena opened. The seventy-five-year-old icon had only one request: that people stop calling him for tickets. "Please, do me a favor," he said. "No more calls."

The arena was every bit the success that city planners could have hoped.

The mall outside was bustling. And the attached hotel, a Hyatt Regency, would open the following spring with a soaring atrium and $69,000 worth of planted Ficus trees. The hotel rooms, of course, were sold out that night. Ice shows, rock stars, and conventions were indeed coming, and so, too, was the state high school basketball tournament, the Sweet 16. After years of moving it back and forth between Freedom Hall in Louisville and Rupp Arena in Lexington, officials in 1995 finally settled on Rupp, where ultimately even those orange triangles disappeared, painted over in 2004 with a more palatable beige.

The tournament's move to Rupp was a boon to Lexington. The four-day event generates an estimated $5.3 million in local business. Fans routinely spend an additional $1.2 million on tickets to get inside, where they proceed to spend even more on concessions, consuming 1,600 pounds of hot dogs, 6,700 gallons of soft drinks, 8,200 boxes of popcorn, and nearly 21,000 servings of ice cream. It is not surprising then that some boys, upon taking the floor for the first time, are overwhelmed by the gravity of the moment. Some bow down and kiss the floor. Others tremble with fear. And almost all of them notice the lights, hot and pulsing and burning inside large banks of 1,000-watt metal halide lamps. Going up for layups for the first time in the arena, some boys say the lights are so bright that for a moment they cannot see at all.

"Hopefully, we won't have a urinal knocked off the wall this year," said Cathy Derr, an employee giving tournament officials a tour of the facility the day before Scott County and the other teams arrived that March.

"Or a drinking fountain," replied Julian Tackett, assistant commissioner of the Kentucky High School Athletic Association, walking along beside her. "Adrenaline," Tackett added by way of explanation. "Sometimes," he said, "the adrenaline gets to them."

JUST PLAY BASKETBALL," Hicks told his boys in the locker room before they took the floor against the Corbin Redhounds in their first game in the hallowed building. "You've been playing basketball all your lives. Just go out and play."

Hicks, for once, wasn't trying to get the team pumped up. He knew the boys were excited, probably too excited. So he spent the team's final minutes in the locker room trying to calm everyone down. There were no big speeches. And none of his usual pacing, either. In fact, Hicks pulled up a chair, sat down, crossed his long legs one over the other, and began to sip from a can of Diet Pepsi, chatting with the boys as if they were attending a church picnic. Even a near catastrophe—Tanner had forgotten his uniform back at the hotel—didn't rattle him. Hicks simply dispatched an assistant coach to go get it. No big deal.

"Tanner," Hicks said, smiling, "it's your first rodeo, isn't it?"

"Guess so," Tanner smiled back.

Still, it was impossible not to feel nervous. Tanner was sweating even before the team left the locker room. Austin buried his head in his hands, trying to compose himself. And Dakotah was the one doing the pacing now, plodding around the room and practicing an imaginary jump shot.

Rupp Arena held no particular grandeur for him. He'd been here before as an invited guest of then Kentucky head coach Billy Gillispie. But that was when Dakotah was still considered a prized Kentucky recruit, when Gillispie still had a job coaching at Rupp, and Dakotah still had that scholarship offer to play basketball in Wildcat blue. All of that, of course, had changed months ago. Dakotah was going to be an Akron Zip in the fall now; not a Kentucky Wildcat. And yet some people still refused to leave him be.

With Scott County surging toward Rupp Arena that year, some of Dakotah's own classmates at the high school were attacking him, dredging up the transfer arguments all over again. "I could go out here and beat Dakotah in basketball any day," said Dustin Rodgers, a Scott County senior who had quit the team after the wave of transfers moved in. "He can shoot the threes. But if you guard him, he ain't gonna score." In fact, Rodgers said, he was pretty sure that he and the other players who had quit could beat the current squad. "I guarantee you, I swear, if you took five of us and gave us a good month to two months to play with each other and get back in the groove, we'd beat them," Rodgers said. "I've always thought that in my mind. I don't care what anybody says."

Dakotah didn't really care, either. He had tuned out the critics long ago. What worried him now was his sudden inability to shoot the ball—he'd been off target for days—possibly due to a tweaked back, which left him groaning at times on the basketball court. Yet still, there he was, working in the Scott

County gym with his father, two nights before the state tournament began. The official team practice, on this day, was not going to be enough for Dakotah. He needed a second one.

"There you go, there you go," Clay Euton said, urging his son along. "That's it. Little touch, little glass. Atta boy."

They started with a simple put-back drill: Clay would intentionally miss a shot in the low post. Then Dakotah had to get the rebound and go right back up and score—a routine shot for a big man. But the shots weren't falling tonight.

"Oh, my God," Dakotah muttered after one miss. "I hate this frickin' shot."

The Eutons moved on to free throws, which went better. "Fingertips. Toes. Back of the rim," the father told the son, coaching him now. "You cannot leave it short." Then they turned their attention, finally, to Dakotah's outside shot, his three-point game. And there is where it fell apart. Dakotah's threes just weren't falling.

Perhaps the problem was his form. "Keep your hands up above your head," Clay instructed him, "instead of in front of your face."

But that didn't help much.

Perhaps the problem was his follow-through. "You're shooting the shot and you're moving," his father told him. "Shoot the shot and stay right there."

But that didn't help much, either. The shots continued to miss.

"It's all right," Clay Euton said. "Those will fall."

But it was far from all right. On the brink of the biggest basketball games of his life, Dakotah Euton couldn't hit anything.

Brick.

Clang.

Swish.

Brick.

"Jeez," Dakotah said finally.

"Shoot some free throws," his father suggested.

But Dakotah didn't feel up to it. Suddenly, he said, he felt ill. And without another word to his father or the others in the gym that night, Dakotah walked into the locker room and headed outside to his truck sitting in the lights of the empty parking lot. It would be several minutes before Clay Euton realized that

Dakotah was gone, that his son had just left and driven home. The shoot-around was over. There would be no more basketball tonight.

"He'll be all right," Clay said. "He'll be fine."

But no one knew for sure.

THE CORBIN REDHOUNDS—white mountain boys, mostly—jumped out to an early lead against Scott County. They hit their first jumper, nailed a three, broke down the Cards' defense for a layup, and then drained another jumper. Scott County, meantime, came out cold. Dakotah missed his first shot—of course. Then he missed his second. Chad missed three foul shots in the span of twenty seconds, plus a jumper. And there were the Scott County boys, more than four minutes into their first game at Rupp, without a single field goal. Not one basket.

"Guys, you got your tails between your legs like you're scared to death," Hicks shouted over the crowd—14,000 strong and, for the most part, rooting against Scott County. "Will you get out there and play basketball?"

The Cards had drawn the Redhounds in the first round by pure luck. There were no seedings at state; just a blind draw to determine the sixteen-team bracket. The eleventh region champs, Scott County, had drawn the thirteenth region champs, Corbin, and the Redhounds, though favored to lose, were not afraid.

They had played in Rupp the year before. They had senior leaders, who had won 105 games in four years, and a coach who knew exactly what Billy Hicks was going to do. Tony Pietrowski not only knew Hicks's system; he had *played* in the system, starring for Hicks at Corbin twenty years earlier. And the Corbin boys knew first hand that they could hang with Scott County. Back in December, the two teams had met at a showcase in the mountains. And though Corbin ultimately lost by eleven, the score at the end of three quarters was tied: 46–46.

Now, at Rupp, Corbin was winning: up the entire first quarter, until the waning moments of the period when Dakotah Euton finally found what he had lost. It started with a rebound. Dakotah pulled in a shot that Ge'Lawn had missed, went right back up with the ball, and scored to cut Corbin's lead to three. On the next possession, he got open and drained a three-pointer from the right wing. And then, with just seven seconds to go in the quarter, Tanner set a screen for Dakotah, who ran straight to the same spot again. Austin saw that his friend was open, passed him the ball, and Dakotah fired up another three—all net, again. In less than two minutes, the county's big man had scored eight points. The ice had thawed and the Cards had taken their first lead of the night, 16–13.

The Redhounds, however, refused to quit. They held the Cards to just ten points in the second quarter. Dakotah was courting foul trouble; he had two personals by halftime. And Chad was courting disaster; he had just one point in sixteen minutes—all of which had the Redhounds feeling good in the locker room at half, down by four. Pietrowski was convinced that Corbin could win now. "We can beat them," he told his boys. And he was convinced that Scott County's players—frustrated by not scoring—would soon start turning on each other.

"They're pissed because they only got twenty-six points," Pietrowski told his team. "Euton ain't gonna get his seventeen. Chad ain't scoring. He's not gonna get his fifteen or twenty. So they're mad about that. If you get down and guard them, they will force up shots. They are impatient. *They are impatient.*"

Corbin responded by taking a two-point lead early in the second half. But in the Scott County huddle, there was no bickering and no shouting. Frustration, maybe. But impatience, no. Dakotah just clapped his hands and looked his teammates in the eyes.

"Let's go, y'all," he said.

Will Schu started the run by nailing two free throws. A sophomore off the bench, Isaiah Ivey, added a jumper. Then it was all Dakotah and Ge'Lawn, Tanner and Chad.

"Be Chad Jackson," Hicks implored his quiet star.

"Yes, sir."

"Play like Chad Jackson," he said again.

"I will," Chad replied.

And finally, with thirty-seven seconds to go in the third quarter, Chad showed up, scoring four points in a row to cap off a 15–2 Scott County run. There was still an entire quarter left to play. But this game was over. With the fans booing him from the stands, Dakotah had played at Rupp Arena—and won. Scott County had rolled, 68–49.

"It was," Dakotah told reporters afterward, "a dream come true."

HICKS WAS RESTLESS the night before the next game, the quarterfinals. At the team hotel in Lexington, he couldn't sleep. Hours ticked away while he thrashed around in bed, thinking about basketball. Everyone, it seemed, wanted a minute of his time now: radio show hosts and newspaper reporters, total strangers and old friends. He just wanted to get back on the court. But even there, he couldn't escape. Taking the floor for the quarterfinal game against Christian County that Friday afternoon—thirty-six hours after the Corbin victory—Billy Hicks turned around and ran into a Kentucky legend, former UK basketball star and current state agriculture commissioner Richie Farmer, who, of course, had something to say. "Hey, Coach," Farmer said, greeting Hicks from his seat just behind Scott County's bench. "You ought to take a look at my son. He's six-one and he's growing."

Hicks managed to smile at Farmer, but barely mustered a reply. It was game time now and he was thinking solely about Christian County. The Colonels, from Hopkinsville in far western Kentucky, had made it to Rupp in four out of the last five seasons. They had thirty wins this year—two more than Scott County—and one unstoppable point guard: Anthony Hickey, a shade under six feet tall with the speed of a jackrabbit and long hair pulled back in a bun. The Colonels would go only as far as Hickey could carry them. Everyone knew that, especially Kerry Stovall, their forty-seven-year-old coach with a buzz cut going gray, a neatly trimmed goatee on his chin, and a taste for Skoal chewing tobacco.

"You gotta be grown, son. You gotta be a man," Stovall said, singling out Hickey and pointing in the boy's face at Christian County's final practice the day before the quarterfinal game. "Because they're coming at your butt. They're coming your way. And we're going to come at them. The first person that flinches—that's what I want to see," Stovall continued. "Because I don't think they can handle what we bring."

Early in the game, it looked like Stovall was right. Christian County was

as speedy as advertised, scoring six points off early turnovers while Scott
County struggled to score at all. The Cardinals missed their first five shots. But
Dakotah stepped up yet again, scoring six of the county's first ten points, and
the Cards kept pace with the Colonels. They trailed by one after the first quar-
ter and then mounted a seven-point lead going into the half, outrebounding
Christian County and shutting down its celebrated star. The great Anthony
Hickey had just three points.

"I'll give them credit," Stovall told his boys in the locker room at half.
"They're a pretty good defensive team."

But they weren't *that* good, Stovall added. In fact, the more he talked
about it, the more he seemed to convince himself that the Colonels could
come back. They were going to push the ball more, Stovall said, and penetrate
to the basket better in the second half. They were going to be just fine. His
boys sat before him, silent and seemingly defeated. But Stovall wasn't ready to
quit.

"Have we played as well as we can play yet?" he asked his team.

"No, sir," they replied, weakly.

"Then let's go out and do it in the second half."

It was Scott County's ball to start the third quarter. And the county boys
were ready to bury the Colonels. "Right here at the beginning, we gotta bust
'em," Dakotah told him teammates. *"Bust 'em right here."* But when Ge'Lawn
got the ball on the first possession and Christian County double-teamed him
in the backcourt, Ge'Lawn immediately threw it into the hands of Anthony
Hickey. Hickey dished to a teammate, who scored as Ge'Lawn fouled him—
his second personal. And the foul trouble for Scott County was just beginning.
In one thirty-second stretch early in the third quarter, Dakotah picked up his
third and then his fourth foul of the game. On the brink of fouling out, he had
to go to the bench while Hickey kept scoring—accounting for fourteen of
Christian County's twenty-three points in the third quarter alone.

"We'll get a stop right here," Hicks told his boys during one third-quarter
time-out. "We *will* get a stop right here."

But once again, they didn't. Hickey zipped right around the defense, scoring with ease. In seven minutes, Christian County had come all the way back

to tie the game, and then briefly took the lead, before Chad ended the period with a three-point play to put the Cards up by two.

Eight minutes to go. One man to stop.

But they couldn't stop him.

Hickey scored again to start the fourth quarter, running past Ge'Lawn for a back-door pass and bucket. Chad answered with yet another drive, basket, foul, and three-point play. Dakotah reentered the game for the first time in six minutes. But Christian County's lead swelled to five. It was starting to slip away now. The county boys could feel it. But here came Chad yet again, running the length of the court for one more drive, basket, foul and three-point play. And so it went. Hickey, then Chad. Chad, then Hickey—then disaster.

Dakotah fouled out with 3:09 to go and Ge'Lawn fouled out seventeen seconds later, grabbing his head in disbelief before walking to the bench.

"That's five," a referee informed Hicks.

"That's unbelievable," Hicks replied.

But it was just the beginning. Tanner fouled out on the very next play, picking up his fifth foul as he tried to stop Hickey from scoring. And then, shortly after that, Tamron joined him on the bench, fouling out as well. In less than ninety seconds, four of Scott County's top six players had been disqualified. Only two regulars were left: Chad and Austin. And only one boy could fill the void now.

"Get Will," Hicks told his assistants.

Will Schu had dreamed of this moment all his life: a tie game, at Rupp Arena, the coach calls his name, the county needs him. But as Hicks waved Will into the game, pausing to put a hand on the boy's shoulder, Will froze. *Don't screw it up*, he thought. *Whatever you do, don't screw it up.*

Everyone seemed to be talking about Will now. The cheerleaders were chanting his name—"*We want Will! . . . We want Will!*"—and the radio broadcasters were mocking him. Good thing, they said, his parents hadn't named him *Jim Schu* or *Tap Schu*. There was laughter all around. And then it happened. As Scott County inbounded the ball to Chad, Christian County double-teamed him. Chad, worried about getting trapped in the backcourt, flung a high, twenty-foot pass to Will, who lost it off his fingertips. Christian County could take the lead now. Here came Hickey, driving. But Austin, all six feet two inches of him, blocked Hickey's shot and then somehow ended up with the ball in his arms.

Time-out, Scott County; 1:17 to play.

Will was off the hook. The game was still tied.

"Don't worry about that, Will," Dakotah assured him.

"It's all right, Will," Ge'Lawn agreed. "C'mon."

Ge'Lawn rubbed Will's head. Will clasped his hands together, as if in prayer. And Hicks turned to the team, scripting the next play. Austin was going to inbound the ball to Chad, he said. And Chad was going to run.

Just get it and go.

"Get a good layup," Hicks told him. "Get a good shot."

Two Colonels players flanked Chad from the moment he stepped on the floor after the time-out. But Austin still managed to get Chad the ball. And once he had it, no one could catch him. Chad ran ninety-four feet, the length of the court. Past both defenders on his back. And right through the other three Colonels players waiting for him in the paint. Everyone in the building—all 14,340 fans—knew what Scott County was going to do and still Christian County could not stop it.

Chad scored, kissing the ball off the glass, and then he planted himself in the lane at the other end. He knew Hickey was coming and this time he was ready for him, picking up a charge and knocking down two foul shots, a moment later, to put Scott County up by four.

Christian County would have its chances in the waning moments: five more shots at the basket, to be exact. But not a single one of them found the net. Even Anthony Hickey was off target now, missing a critical layup with thirty-two seconds to go and a meaningless three-pointer at the buzzer, which rattled off the rim and into the hands of Will Schu.

Game over.

Scott County had survived, 69–64, thanks in large part to Chad's twenty-six points, eleven rebounds, and his refusal to lose with his teammates reduced to spectators. The Cardinal mascot was hugging the players and the players were hugging each other. The Cards were back—back in the state semifinals for the first time in three years. Out of 269 boys high school basketball teams in the state, they were among the last four still playing. And the next game was just seventeen hours away. The celebration would have to be brief. The boys needed to get back to the hotel to rest and watch game tape of their next foe: Ballard, one of just six teams that had beaten the Cards all year.

"Remember that?" Hicks asked the boys as they all crammed into a single hotel room to watch tape of the Bruins. "They just killed us on the boards."

The boys nodded. They were sore and exhausted. Ge'Lawn's knees were aching and Dakotah's eyes were half open. But they needed to see this.

"Look at this," Hicks said. "My goodness."

Ballard looked good. Really good.

GE'LAWN COULDN'T FIND his knee medication in the morning. It was dark in his hotel room. Too early for basketball. But with the game scheduled for 10 A.M., the boys had to be up by eight, so they could get to Rupp by nine. But now Ge'Lawn's pills were missing and Chad was running late. As the team bus idled outside, Chad was still walking the halls of the hotel, shirtless in his sock feet. One player boarded the bus only to realize he'd forgotten his shoes, leading to still more delays. There was no time for a real breakfast. They'd take the floor at Rupp Arena this morning fortified by bananas and Krispy Kreme doughnuts.

The building, at first, was slow to fill. Basketball fans were just as weary as the players themselves. But soon they began streaming to their seats with trumpets playing, drums thrumming, and the brass of the high school pep bands picking up the lights of the arena. Some fans had painted their faces and dyed their hair to match. Others wore glitter or eye black. And some, already, were praying. Scott County band member Brittany Carr had even painted a cross on her cheek. "She loves Jesus," shrugged Carr's friend Grayce Courtney, sitting beside her. "Jesus will help us win."

It was at least worth asking for help from above; others were, too. Down in Ballard's locker room, head coach Chris Renner began his pregame comments by quoting from Psalm 121—"I raise my eyes toward the mountains," he said. "Where will my help come from?"—and then he downshifted into strategy, sounding almost Hicksian at times. The game, Renner said, was about re-bounding and hustling. The game, Renner said, was about defense and toughness. They weren't going to play like punks, he explained. They were going to play like *predators.*

"That's what we are," said Renner, shaved bald and wearing a black Ballard vest over a long-sleeved maroon shirt. "We're not gonna sit back. We're gonna freakin' punch them in the mouth first, okay? That's what we're gonna do. And then they've gotta respond to that. This is our game, fellas—I'm tellin' you," he added. "This is our basketball game."

Out on the court, Renner greeted Hicks with a smile and a handshake. "If we're going to lose," he told Hicks, "I'd rather lose to you." And Hicks, smiling, returned the compliment. But for him, there was more on the line than just a spot in the state finals that night. A win this morning would give Hicks more career wins in the state tournament than any other coach in Kentucky history: twenty-one. It would be a momentous achievement for anyone, but especially for a man who'd begun his career in Harlan County, shoveling coal into a furnace to heat the gymnasium before basketball practices on cold winter nights. The old gym in tiny Evarts was now vacant, a target for vandals and copper thieves, too dangerous to enter, some believed. But Hicks was still coaching, still here, on the cusp of a record that most thought he'd never have. And yet he didn't mention it. Not a word about the record. It wouldn't mean anything if Scott County won this morning only to lose tonight in the state finals. And it certainly wouldn't mean anything if the Cards lost to Ballard.

In the locker room now, he held out his left hand and asked the boys to take it. They all piled in, one hand on top of the other, Austin and then Chad, Ge'Lawn and then Dakotah, Will and then Tanner—everyone. And then Hicks took his right hand and placed it on top as together they began to pray.

"Hey, guys," Hicks said in a whisper. "Let's go now."

SCOTT COUNTY SCORED first, but Ballard answered. The Bruins pushed ahead and then the Cards pushed back to reclaim the lead. In the first half alone, there were seven lead changes, six ties, and still more foul trouble for the county. Tanner quickly picked up three fouls while Ge'Lawn and Chad each had two. "You gotta be careful," Hicks pleaded. "You gotta be set with roots in your shoes."

He was worried about living through a repeat of the Christian County nightmare when so many players had fouled out. But there were other concerns as well. Chad scored eight points in his first thirteen minutes on the floor, picking up right where he'd left off the day before. At times, though, it seemed like the boys weren't getting him the ball enough. "Look for Chad inside," Hicks told them. "He's wide open in there." And he was concerned, too, about his star with the tender knees. "Ge'Lawn," Hicks said late in the first quarter, "be aggressive. Don't be afraid to drive on these guys." Then, placing an arm around the boy, he asked him a simple question.

"You all right?"

Ge'Lawn nodded—yes, he was fine. As if to prove it, he went out and scored five points in a row. But it was Dakotah and Chad who carried the Cards in a bruising first half, combining to score twenty of the county's thirty-two points despite the Bruins' best efforts to stop them.

The first time Chad got the ball in the post, a Bruins player hammered him, sending Chad to the floor, where he lingered, wincing in pain. And anytime Dakotah touched the ball, the Ballard students took great joy in taunting him with boos and insults, chanting the name of the Kentucky basketball coach for whom he would not be playing next year: John Calipari.

"*UK reject!*"

Clap, clap, clap-clap-clap!

"*Calipari!*"

Clap, clap, clap-clap-clap!

Ballard was leading by a basket at the half, 34–32. But Hicks was OK with that. "Ballard," he said, "always gives you their best lick in the first half." The Cards just needed to avoid foul trouble, he said, and avoid mental mistakes. He begged his boys to set up and take a charge. He pleaded with them to finish their layups—"And we will," Hicks assured them—and he asked for more from Ge'Lawn. "We've worked all our lives for this," Hicks told him as they headed out for the second half. "Sixteen minutes, Ge'Lawn. Sixteen minutes right here."

"Yes, sir," Ge'Lawn answered.

"Let's go y'all," Dakotah hollered.

"We got this," Austin added.

"Let's go right here," Dakotah said again. "Defense on three."

"One, two, three . . . *DEFENSE!*"

Austin started the half with a three-pointer from the left corner—*swish*—and then another three-pointer from the right wing—*money*. Dakotah scored, knocking down a turnaround jumper, and then, two possessions later, Austin wanted the ball again. This time, he was in the right corner. And this time, he was covered. But as Ge'Lawn drove with the ball into the lane and the defense collapsed upon him, Ge'Lawn flicked the ball to Austin, who eyed the hoop, pulled up once again, and drained another three.

The county led by as many as five. But Ballard wasn't quitting. The Bruins stormed back with three-pointers of their own, steals that led to layups, and points from the free throw line. The foul trouble that Hicks had hoped to avoid was now a reality. Austin picked up his third foul while trying to draw a charge and Chad picked up his fourth while trying to do the same.

"What?" Chad said, pleading with the refs.

But it was no use. Hicks had to rest him. Chad was headed to the bench. And with him watching, Ballard tied the game, stealing the ball after Ge'Lawn made a long, ill-advised pass in the final seconds of the third quarter and laying it into the hoop just before the buzzer. It was 51–51 headed into the final frame.

"We're fine," Hicks assured his boys. "Daggone it, the score's tied."

There was no reason to panic. Chad was heading back into the game, checking in with 6:59 to go. The county's starting five were once again together on the floor. And reunited, they scored quickly, as Ge'Lawn knocked down a seventeen-footer from the right corner. *All net.* Scott County up two.

But back came Ballard, on the run, slicing into the lane at the other end. Chad, playing with four fouls, needed to be careful here. He couldn't be too aggressive on offense—or defense. But as the Ballard player cut to the rim, Chad found himself in the paint, with nowhere to go. The two boys collided. Chad crashed to the floor. And a referee's whistle sounded. Chad was guilty of yet another foul: his fifth—and his last—a mere twenty seconds after checking back into the game.

"He's out of there!" screamed radio broadcaster Stan Hardin over the airwaves.

"Chad Jackson just fouled out," replied Hardin's broadcast partner, Gary Ball, mystified by what he had just seen. "Chad Jackson has fouled out," Ball said again a moment later, still not believing it. "The superstar for Scott County."

Gone.

"Go figure," Ball added.

On the floor, Chad grabbed his head with both hands and for a long spell just sat where he had landed beneath the hoop. The game, for Chad, was over. Dakotah had to help him up and Ge'Lawn almost needed to carry him to the bench, wrapping both arms around his teammate and telling him it would be OK. It would be all right.

Ge'Lawn was going to finish this.

Dakotah missed a jumper. But Ge'Lawn drove, got fouled, and nailed both free throws. Dakotah missed again and then a third time. But Ge'Lawn bailed him out, draining foul shots, rebounding misses in traffic, and scoring. At one point, when Dakotah missed an outside shot—well off the mark—it looked like Ballard would grab the rebound easily. Four Bruins stood waiting in the paint. But it was Ge'Lawn who collected the ball, wheeling around for a one-handed bucket. Ballard 62, Scott County 61—with 2:44 to go. Anyone's game.

"C'mon now!" Hicks hollered on the sidelines. *"RIGHT HERE!"*

Now was the time for burying Ballard. But then Austin fouled out on the very next possession. Hicks opted to replace him with the rarely used Trey Relford, a junior with enough speed to keep up with Ballard's quick guards. And in the ensuing time-out, the county boys sat before their coach, quiet and seemingly defeated, with two of their regulars, Chad and Austin, finished for the game, and a third, Dakotah, suddenly cold, unable to hit a shot.

"Dakotah," Hicks said, "get your head up, honey."

There was still plenty of time. Trey was going to play defense—"Trey's gonna heat 'em up," Hicks told his team—and Ge'Lawn was going to score, taking it to the hole on the next possession. "Clear that side out for him," Hicks informed the boys. "Ge'Lawn, go to that side, set him up, and go hard with it."

But the play wasn't there. The Ballard defense was sagging on Ge'Lawn, forcing him to fire up a three from the corner. It clanged off the rim, giving Ballard a fast break and a chance to put the game away. The Bruins, however, seemed incapable of closing out the victory. They proceeded to miss a dunk at the other end of the floor and then two free throws. They turned the ball over—not just once in the final two minutes, but four times. And yet, Scott County could not capitalize on Ballard's miscues. Dakotah missed a three, off the rim, and so did Tanner, in and out. Dakotah missed still another three—just short. And for over two minutes, the Cards didn't score. Not once.

The Bruins fans were chanting now, filling Rupp Arena with their big-city bluster. Surely, Ballard couldn't lose now: up three, with the ball, and nine seconds on the clock. Everyone could see that, including the Scott County players themselves. But Billy Hicks still wasn't giving up.

"Finish this thing strong," he told the boys in their final huddle with the Ballard fans chanting over them. "Finish this thing strong here, guys. Hey, guys, I've seen a lot of things happen here. Be tough and battle for the last second."

The players were hardly listening, though, and with good reason. All the Bruins needed to do at this point was inbound the ball, wait for the foul that was coming, make a free throw—one should be enough—and they'd win. Yet on the ensuing inbounds play, a Ballard player, inexplicably, pushed off, committing an offensive foul before the clock even started.

Scott County had one more chance—a chance to cut the lead to one with nine seconds to go. Only it wasn't Ge'Lawn or Dakotah who had been fouled. It wasn't a Scott County star who would be stepping to the line to shoot the front end of the 1-and-1, the biggest free throws of the entire season. It was the little-used backup, Trey Relford, the boy who was seeing playing time only because Chad and Austin had fouled out long ago.

Trey had taken thirteen free throws in a varsity jersey all season—missing seven of them. He wasn't supposed to be taking these shots. But the Scott County junior had no choice in the matter now. Chad, Austin, and Will were watching from the bench. Dakotah and Ge'Lawn were watching from the floor. And nearly 15,000 fans were watching from inside the arena as Trey cupped the ball in his hands, sized up the shot, and let it fly.

It missed. Hard off the back of the rim. Tanner was the first to get a hand on the rebound, skying above the others in the paint. But he couldn't hold onto the ball, which squirted away and landed in the arms of a Ballard player, who began to celebrate as the fans roared.

"We're gonna win this ball game," Hicks had promised the boys in the final minutes. "We're going to win this game right here."

But for once, he was wrong. Ballard beat Scott County, 67–62.

THE COUNTY FANS didn't linger long after the final buzzer. Most were headed for the exits before the team had even left the floor. They didn't need to see the boys getting their semifinalist medals. The boys themselves didn't even want them. Dakotah tore the medal off his neck as soon as it was presented to him. Others dropped theirs after stepping off the court, and the souvenirs clanged around on the floor like lost change. The boys just wanted to get to the locker room, where, alone at last, they began to cry.

In the weeks ahead, everyone would have a theory about why Scott County had lost. Perhaps they had fallen to a better team or perhaps it was just bad luck. Maybe they had gotten what they had deserved or maybe they had been cheated. In their last two games at Rupp, the Cards' opponents shot nearly twice as many free throws as they did—thirty-one more, a lopsided margin that even the best of teams might not overcome. Billy Hicks himself almost complained about the refereeing in the postgame press conference after the Ballard loss, catching himself just in time. "Any questions?" he asked the reporters. "I'll stop right there."

But with his team, in the losing locker room, Hicks gave voice to none of these concerns. He told the boys that they had brought honor to their county and to their school. He told them that he would never forget what they had accomplished together and that he was proud of them.

"Hey, guys," Hicks said. "I've never been prouder of a ballclub."

Yet there was nothing he could say to stop the sobbing. Some boys were trembling now, their young bodies heaving with pain. Others covered their heads with towels and retreated even deeper into the caverns, holing up in bathroom showers and stalls. Somewhere in the building, a pep band was playing and cheerleaders were cheering. There was still more basketball left to be played and reason to shout. But deep inside Rupp, down a concrete tunnel, and behind closed doors, the county boys sat in silence with their heads in their hands, their dreams on the floor, and their cries echoing off the cold, hard tile.

THE CAKE WAS VANILLA with white icing. The balloons were shaped like basketballs and a crowd was gathering now on the floor inside the Scott County gymnasium. The school day wouldn't end for another forty-five minutes. But one teacher had released her entire class to attend the signing ceremony, where Chad, Dakotah, and Austin would officially declare where they were attending college. Kids in other classes excused themselves to be here. And sports reporters made the drive from Lexington to chronicle the moment. They wanted to record what Chad, Dakotah, and Austin had to say. But they also wanted to hear from the boy whose name did not appear on the cake. The reporters wanted to know if Ge'Lawn Guyn had made a decision about his future and if he might be able to share it with them this afternoon. "Ge'Lawn hasn't decided yet," Hicks announced. "But he will be available to talk to you in a minute."

Six weeks removed from the Ballard loss at Rupp, the boys were on the cusp of summer. The school year was almost over and the team's five seniors were about to leave this gym forever. At the signing ceremony, they sat at a table beneath photos of previous Scott County state champions, posed for photos with their parents and coaches, and pretended to sign official documents while the cameras rolled. Then, while others lined up for the free cake, the boys stood up for their interviews, with the television cameras in their faces and the future laid out before them.

DAKOTAH EUTON was making good on his promise. He was going to play basketball at the University of Akron in the fall. He was going to be a Zip. And though opposing fans liked to rip the decision—"What's Akron's mascot?" one fan shouted at the regional tournament. *"The Zits?"*—Dakotah was happy with his choice. As he prepared for his interview at the signing ceremony, standing before the TV cameras in plaid shorts and an American Eagle T-shirt, Dakotah was all smiles, joking with the girls standing nearby. "I'm gonna give you a shout-out," he told them. "A shout-out right now." And others joked with him, chanting his name in the background as if trying to fluster him. *"Eutie! Eutie!"* But once the cameramen readied their equipment and the reporters began asking their questions, Dakotah turned serious.

"I just feel really blessed today," he told them. "I'm really happy with the choice that I made. I think Akron is going to be a great fit for me. I love their coaches. I love the style they play. They got a great team. And I'm just really happy with the way it turned out."

People were always trying to bait Dakotah with questions to get him to lash out at Kentucky fans, to complain about the way he'd been treated, or confess to the bitterness that they believed he must carry deep inside him. But Dakotah never took the bait—not once. He said he'd do it all over again. He said he still rooted for Kentucky to win. The reason, he said, was simple. "I'm from Kentucky." And he wasn't going to let a few "absolutely stupid, crazy fans" ruin that for him.

But in the end, he wanted out. He chose Akron over Eastern Kentucky University because, if he stayed close to home, Dakotah worried he would always be remembered for what he had once been (a Kentucky recruit and failure) instead of what he could be (a Division I college basketball player and star). His high school numbers suggested that anything was possible. Dakotah Euton, it was reported that spring, had quietly become just the fourth high school basketball player in Kentucky history to score 3,000 points and log 1,500 rebounds. And Akron head coach Keith Dambrot, who coached LeBron James in high school, was excited to add the big man to his 2010–11 roster.

"Dakotah," Dambrot said at the time, "is a big, strong, skilled player, with great hands and a soft touch around the basket." He liked the young man's toughness and his knowledge for the game. And Dambrot praised both Dakotah's talent and his character. "Dakotah is a really good kid. I don't think he has a mean bone in his body, really."

The plan was for him to redshirt his first year on campus. But that fall, when Akron's second-leading scorer—six-foot-six, 245-pound forward Brett McKnight—was suspended indefinitely for violating team rules, Dambrot recommended that Dakotah give up his redshirt. The choice, Dambrot said, was ultimately Dakotah's. But Dakotah said he felt cornered. He was a freshman and his coach wanted him to play. "I felt like I couldn't say no," he said. And anyway, if there was a chance to play real minutes, as Dambrot seemed to suggest, then Dakotah wanted it. He wanted to be a leader at Akron, just as he was at Scott County, taking the Zips to as many NCAA tournaments as possible, and leaders, he knew, don't sit on the bench. So, of course, Dakotah gave up his redshirt.

In his first game against Dayton, he showed he could help fill the void left by McKnight's absence, scoring seven points and pulling down four rebounds in ten minutes on the floor. But Dakotah would never again play ten minutes in a game for the Zips. He struggled to get playing time that November and December. And then, to his surprise, McKnight was reinstated, meaning even less playing time for him. It was like he had given up his redshirt—one year of college eligibility—for absolutely nothing.

Dambrot said he felt bad about it. If he thought McKnight, who'd been suspended twice previously, was coming back, he never would have asked Dakotah to give up his redshirt. "I feel bad about him losing a year over it," he explained. "I do." But once McKnight returned, Dambrot said he was obligated to play the best players, which meant McKnight was competing and Dakotah was watching. The Scott County star played one minute for Akron in the entire month of January, just five minutes in February, and not a single minute in the postseason as the Zips won the Mid-American Conference Tournament and earned a slot in the NCAA bracket. Dakotah, apparently, wasn't even good enough for garbage time. At the end of Akron's first-round, 69–56 loss to Notre Dame in the NCAA tournament, Dambrot inserted a freshman and two walk-ons into the game, so that the young men could later say they had played in the tournament. But there was Dakotah, still riding the bench.

"It was just pure business," Dambrot said.

By that time, it was clear that Dakotah wanted to transfer. He was angry about how he'd been treated. "They screwed me out of a whole year," he said. He didn't get along with Dambrot and didn't want to stay at Akron anymore. He wanted to come home, which he did shortly after Akron's loss to Notre Dame, leaving campus before the school year even ended. The basketball player once recruited by the University of Kentucky was now hoping to catch on at a small school close to home. He finally chose Asbury University, a Christian school with an NAIA Division II basketball program, enrollment 1,293, not far from Lexington. In the span of four years, Dakotah Euton had gone from committing to one of the greatest basketball programs in the nation to committing to a school that most people outside the state had never heard of—a tragic fall of epic proportions. And yet, Dakotah seemed genuinely happy about his new school. He had prayed on it, he said, and believed Asbury was the best place for him spiritually. He was thinking a lot lately about life after basketball and felt like he was being led into the ministry. But he was also excited about reconnecting with an old teammate; Austin had signed at Asbury straight out of high school. And Dakotah was looking forward to enjoying basketball again—for the first time in a long time. "Asbury is a place," he said, "where I can go and play basketball and have a little fun." Anyway, it had to be better than Ohio.

"Ohio people," Dakotah said. "They were really rude."

CHAD JACKSON kept waiting all winter for a big basketball program to offer him a scholarship. He felt like he'd earned such attention. In his senior year, he led Scott County in steals, blocked shots, minutes played, and scoring, averaging almost seventeen points a game. Hicks thought Scott County could have beaten Ballard had Chad not fouled out. "Can you imagine," he asked, "if we had Chad down the stretch?" And briefly that winter, an assistant coach from Clemson came calling.

"Boy, that's a good school," Hicks said.

"Oh, yeah," Chad replied.

"Good academics, good climate," Hicks added. "I don't want to get in your business. But it's a good school, a great place. He wants you to call him by Wednesday."

Chad entertained the conversation and, soon thereafter, a Clemson coach even made a trip to Scott County to watch Chad play. But the game that night got snowed out. The Clemson coach was relegated to watching Chad practice—not as helpful. Clemson never offered him a scholarship and Chad kept returning to think about one school: James Madison University, where head coach Matt Brady didn't care that Chad struggled with his outside shot.

As an assistant coach at St. Joseph's University, Brady, a New Jersey native, had a hand in recruiting two guards who went on to star in the NBA: Jameer Nelson and Delonte West. Neither player, Brady said, could shoot well from the outside when they got to college. But both had improved, he said, under his instruction. And now Brady wanted to offer the same assistance to Chad. He was confident that, with work, he could fix Chad's shot; that, with work, Chad could be all-conference and maybe even play professionally some day. In basketball parlance, Chad had a *high-major* body, with *mid-major* shooting skills. Improve those skills and the boy could go far.

Chad, as usual, didn't talk much about the offer or about his decision. Even his mother didn't know what he was going to do. But that winter, he began leaning toward playing for the James Madison Dukes. Chad appreciated the fact that they had been recruiting him for months. He liked that Brady had wanted him long before his breakout senior season even started. And Chad was beginning to buy what Brady was selling. He believed that Brady wasn't just recruiting him, but could help him with his shot and his game, his future.

"I hope we're making progress here," Brady told Chad on one visit to Scott County during Chad's senior year. "And you know what? It would be fine with me if, at some point, you said, 'Coach, I want to come.'"

"That's what I actually wanted to tell you today," Chad replied.

"My man!" Brady said.

"I've made the decision," Chad nodded. "I'm doing it."

"My maaaaaaaaaaaa-aaaaan!" Brady said again.

The forty-four-year-old coach hugged Chad and promised him that he'd get playing time almost immediately. "I'm telling you," Brady said, "you're gonna have an impact on this program." And indeed, early on, Chad did. As a freshman at James Madison, Chad Jackson averaged seventeen minutes a game—a solid start to a college career. And with help from Brady, Chad had improved his shooting, just like his coach had promised. "He was," said Chad, "a man of his word." The hitch had been ironed out for the most part and Chad had never felt more confident about his shooting.

But he didn't mesh with his new teammates. He liked them, Chad said, but he wondered if they cared as much about winning as he did. And like Dakotah, Chad simply missed home. Shortly after the Dukes' season ended, Chad informed Brady that he was leaving. He was moving back to Kentucky, where he'd catch on at Northern Kentucky University, an NCAA Division II program just across the Ohio River from Cincinnati, about an hour from home.

Chad wasn't giving up on his dreams just yet. "If I have a chance to go to the NBA," he said, "that would be great." But his stay at James Madison was over. His last game there was a twenty-point loss to Davidson—the sort of blowout that Chad had never experienced at Scott County. And the Davidson fans let the Dukes have it. As Chad stepped to the foul line late in the game to shoot two meaningless free throws, one fan could be heard yelling above all the others.

"Thanks for the scrimmage, boys!"

WILL SCHU came out for the signing ceremony that day in the gym, eyeing the reporters interviewing his teammates from a chair against the wall. There would be no interviews for him. The stats from his senior season were as pedestrian as he feared they would be. He averaged less than three points and three rebounds a game. He only started once—senior night. And even then, there was some lighthearted debate in the locker room about Will's status for the game.

"Will, you starting tonight?" Ge'Lawn asked.

"No," Will replied. "Probably not," he added. "For real."

But his mother finally wore him down to apply to Berea College, the one and only school that was recruiting him. And during a snow day that February, he sat down on his living room couch to write a 500-word essay about the meaningful contributions that he, Will Schu, was making to the world. Snow was falling outside and the words just started flowing.

One meaningful contribution I have made at Scott County High School is a class that I take called peer tutoring. Every day, I go to that class for the last hour of the day. In that class, I tutor mentally challenged students with learning disabilities. In peer tutoring, I do such things as reading to them, helping with worksheets, or simply just taking them to the gym to play some basketball. Every day, when I go to that class, I feel like I am doing something very good in my life . . .

He finished the essay and ultimately sent off the application. But Will didn't get into Berea. The coach who was recruiting him, John Mills, failed to have his contract renewed that spring. Berea was moving in a different direction, leaving Will with few options. After graduation, he landed a part-time job loading trucks for the United Parcel Service in Lexington. He started off, he said, making $8.50 an hour, but quickly moved up to $9.50 or $10.50, depending on the shift and the job. The money wasn't enough to move out of his mother's house, but it did help him get his own car: a 1996 Oldsmobile Achieva—white, with maroon interior. And that fall, he started taking classes at the Bluegrass Community and Technical College, better known as BCTC, in Lexington. "I kind of wish I was at a bigger school, like a university," he said at the time. "But it's all right, I guess."

He liked the idea of studying business. Maybe one day, Will said, he'd go into business for himself. But Will didn't make it through the school year at BCTC. That winter, he stopped going to class. School, Will said, just wasn't for him, and he set out to find a second job to supplement his income. "Anything, really—short of fast food," he said. "I've applied everywhere, it feels like. Lowe's. Hibbett Sports. Big Lots. Jimmy John's. Kroger's."

He hoped something would come in soon. In the meantime, he thought a lot about basketball. He missed playing and traveling with the team—any team. He thought about calling Coach Hicks and asking if Hicks could help him catch on at a junior college somewhere. But Will never placed the call. He probably couldn't afford junior college, anyway, Will told himself. All the junior colleges he'd ever heard of were too far away. "Like in Florida," he said, "and Texas."

Still, he thought about it.

"I really miss basketball," Will said. "I didn't think I would. But it's driving me crazy. I can't quit thinking about it."

GE'LAWN GUYN didn't cry in the locker room after the Ballard loss like so many other boys. He just sat stone-faced with a towel draped over his shoulders. But that didn't mean he wasn't hurting. At a fast-food restaurant after the game, while the other boys queued up for burgers and fries, Ge'Lawn took a seat near the window. He was in no mood to eat.

"Are y'all in the Sweet 16 tournament?" a curious customer asked him.

"We *were*," Ge'Lawn replied, choosing not to elaborate.

He had missed three of his last four shots in the game, plus a late free throw. But no one could pin this loss on Ge'Lawn. In the fourth quarter, with Chad fouled out and the score knotted up, Ge'Lawn had scored Scott County's final nine points, keeping the Cards in the game down the stretch while his teammates failed to hit a single basket. It was an unceremonious end to a difficult season for Ge'Lawn. And his future now was uncertain. College coaches still wanted to sign Ge'Lawn that spring. But Ge'Lawn was headed to a prep school—a sort of purgatory between high school and college where young men can improve their basketball skills or bring up lagging standardized test scores in order to get into a four-year university. Ge'Lawn hoped to get stronger and needed help with his ACT. After four years of high school, his stats were great. But he still didn't have the scores he needed to go to the college of his choice.

"Talk about what's ahead for Ge'Lawn," one of the reporters asked the boy as a crowd formed around him at the signing ceremony in the gym.

"I'm just gonna wait things out," Ge'Lawn replied.

"What's the advantage of going to prep school?"

"I feel like it's a blessing to get—you know what I'm saying?—an extra year. And still keeping four years of eligibility, college, whatever. I feel like it'll be great. You know what I'm saying? A great thing to do."

"You leaning toward that?"

"Yeah," Ge'Lawn answered. "It'll be great for me. Let's put it like that."

Initially, though, life for Ge'Lawn at South Kent School, an elite academy, in Connecticut, was just hard. The tuition at the all-boys school was pricey and the dress code was strict. Sport coats and ties were required. Ge'Lawn had to do his own laundry and wake himself up for school in the morning—tasks that he had never been responsible for in his life. And above all, the new South Kent point guard was lonely, eight hundred miles from home, with the cold New England winter approaching and not a single teen-aged girl in sight. Alone in his room the first couple nights on campus, Ge'Lawn said he broke down and cried. "I called home a couple of times," he admitted, "saying, 'I don't know if I can do it.'"

But knowing that South Kent wasn't just his best shot, but maybe his last shot, to play college basketball, Ge'Lawn would not quit. He got financial aid to make his enrollment possible. Hicks sent his former player nice clothes for him to wear. And Ge'Lawn, for the most part, did well, bringing up his test scores and running the point for coach Kelvin Jefferson's team. The former Scott County star, with no tendinitis that season, averaged sixteen points, nine assists, and six rebounds a game. Jefferson was impressed. "Honestly," he said, "the sky could be the limit for him." And coaches at the University of Cincinnati were impressed with Ge'Lawn, too. Bearcats head coach Mick Cronin offered him a scholarship and, that November, Ge'Lawn officially signed with Cincinnati. He would be twenty-one years old as a freshman. Still, the Bearcats were thrilled to have him. "Gee is a competitor," Cronin declared upon Ge'Lawn's signing, "flat-out."

The Guyns could not have been happier for their son, who was growing up now in Connecticut. But back home in Scott County, they continued to struggle. Ge'Lawn's mother, Rebecca, suffered a brain hemorrhage in December and had to be hospitalized for days. She recovered, but the family's financial situation remained as tenuous as ever.

The bills kept piling up. On top of the family's usual expenses, George Guyn now had to find a way to cover Ge'Lawn's prep school tuition, which, even at a steep discount, he said, was going to cost the family about $3,500. "Every chance that I get," George said, "I send them some money."

It was just another hard year in a time of hard years. But maybe next year, George said, things would get better. Maybe they'd move to Northern Kentucky and maybe he'd get a job collecting garbage in Cincinnati, where George heard the wages were higher. Sooner or later, George Guyn believed, it would all work out. But until then, he explained, the family would remain in Scott County, teetering on the edge. "This far," George said, "from falling off the Earth."

BILLY HICKS didn't want to be in the pictures. "I ain't much on picture taking," he explained. And it was just fine with him that the television reporters at the signing ceremony had opted not to interview him, worried that he would start rambling and talk forever. This ceremony was for the boys. Billy

Hicks had moved on weeks earlier, starting the day of the Ballard loss at Rupp Arena.

Unlike so many other high school coaches, Hicks didn't come back to Rupp for the state finals that night. He wouldn't be there to watch a tired Ballard team lose, stunned by tiny Shelby Valley, or to witness the Shelby Valley fans weeping over their improbable victory. What mattered to Hicks now was not this season and how it ended for Ballard, but next season and how it started for Scott County. Before he'd even left the locker room at Rupp that afternoon, he was already whispering with his assistants about next year, compartmentalizing the loss by not talking about it at all. He was thinking instead about how they needed to help a sophomore guard improve his defense or how they needed to teach a freshman how to run the point. With Scott County losing four starters—Austin, Chad, Dakotah, and Ge'Lawn—there were whispers that the Cards were going to have a down year, that Billy Hicks, for once, was going to lose. But Hicks wasn't buying it. "You wait and see," he said. "We'll be pretty daggone good."

The following winter was a difficult one for Hicks. Charles Eddie Doan, the team's equipment manager, died in early February, one week before Scott County's regular season showdown with Lexington Catholic. The sixty-nine-year-old, suffering from leukemia, was cut down by strokes at the end, partially paralyzed and unable to speak in the days before his death. Hicks and the other coaches served as pallbearers at the funeral and the boys dedicated the season to him, managing to beat Catholic, 85–81, just three days after they buried Charles Eddie in the ground. Hicks had a hard time getting used to the fact that Charles Eddie was gone. At least once that season, out of habit, he slipped, telling the boys to make sure they tossed their sweaty uniforms in the hamper so that Charles Eddie wouldn't get angry about it. Coach, the boys had to correct him, Charles Eddie was dead. "I've lost two brothers, a father, and I've lost some really good friends," Hicks said. "And God, I really miss ol' Charles Eddie."

But Hicks, as usual, took refuge in the season. It turned out that he was right: the Cards had a good year as usual. Even without the high-profile transfers that everyone complained about, the county still went 23-5. By the regional tournament, the Cards were ranked No. 3 in the state. And then they ran into

Catholic, ranked No. 5. The Knights jumped all over the county boys this time, opening up an early seventeen-point lead. And although the Cards didn't quit, cutting the lead to eight by halftime, they never got much closer, losing in the end, 70–60. Catholic was on its way to Rupp for the third time in four seasons and Hicks was headed home stuck on 781 career victories, just nineteen wins shy of becoming only the second high school coach ever to win eight hundred basketball games in Kentucky.

His wife, Betsy, took the opportunity that spring to remind Billy that he had vowed he would retire once he reached eight hundred.

"Bill," she said, "you told me that. You promised me."

Betsy, a retired teacher, was hoping they'd move somewhere warmer, perhaps South Carolina. But already, Hicks was backing off that promise.

"I can never see myself not coaching in Kentucky," he told her.

He couldn't walk away, even in defeat. Forty-eight hours after the Ballard loss that March, Hicks called the basketball players together one last time. Nearly two dozen boys—from the freshman, junior varsity, and varsity squads— gathered shoulder to shoulder in the locker room to listen to Hicks speak. He told them they'd had a great run, even with the loss to Ballard. He asked them to be grateful for the opportunities they'd had, even though they had fallen short of a state title. And then, one by one, he thanked the seniors for their service, moving down the row and addressing the boys by name. "You'll always be a Scott County Cardinal," he told them. And then, with a wave of his hand, Billy Hicks dismissed the seniors for the last time.

"You can go," he said, simply.

The seniors stood up to leave and the underclassmen roared. They pounded on the lockers and stomped their feet. They clapped their hands and screamed. Dakotah and the other seniors glided out of the room, all smiles. They were free. The metal locker-room door closed behind them with a thud and then Hicks turned to the boys still sitting before him with a simple question.

"About fifty-some points a game just walked out of the room right now," he said. "Who wants 'em?"

Acknowledgments

THIS BOOK WOULD not have been possible without the help of countless people. I must thank, for starters, my agent, Todd Shuster, who believed in this project—and in me—even when I was beginning to lose faith in both. Somewhere in February 2010, right around the time when the Scott County players were wondering whether they'd ever make it to Rupp Arena, I was wondering whether my work chronicling the boys' season would ever end up in print. Thanks in great part to Todd—and to my editor, Yaniv Soha, at St. Martin's—it did. From the moment my book proposal crossed his desk, Yaniv recognized the potential of this narrative, bringing optimism and enthusiasm to every conversation we had about it. And for that, I will be forever grateful.

I am also grateful to the friends who read early versions of the book and offered counsel along the way: namely, Dan Crow, for his wordsmithery; Eric Heinberg, for his honesty; and Andrew Bauer, for, as always, saving me from myself. Each of them sacrificed their time to help me, but they were not the only ones who sacrificed on my behalf. I would be remiss not to thank the following people: photographer and friend Erik Jacobs, who traveled to Kentucky on two occasions that winter, joining me on this journey and brightening my long days with his dry wit; Amanda Seitz, who helped me track down old newspaper clippings about basketball games played long ago, spending hours in the library; friends Antonia Keller and Ian McNulty, who agreed to reschedule their wedding around the whims of a high school basketball schedule; my parents, Keith and Terry O'Brien, who often watched my two young sons while I was away watching other boys, older boys, play basketball; and finally, most importantly, my wife, Eva, who never once questioned why I would want to quit my job at the *Boston Globe* to tell a story from Kentucky. She stood by me from beginning to end, even after the doctors found the tumor—large, but benign—in her abdominal wall, diagnosed her with desmoid fibromatosis, and ordered her to undergo chemotherapy to shrink the mass in the middle of the basketball season. For the record, I'm pretty sure I complained more than she did. Actually, I know I did.

I am forever indebted to Billy Hicks who granted me access to his team for the 2009–10 season, inviting me into his locker room, office, and home. I'll always remember the first time I met him in late March 2009: alone in the gym on a Sunday evening, greeting me with a warm handshake that felt like it might rip my arm away at the elbow, and bidding me adieu two hours later with a slap on the back. Right then, I knew that his was a story that I needed to tell.

And finally, I am indebted to the Scott County players themselves. Even now, years later, I think of them often, hoping they are doing well, on or off the basketball court. But it's the season—the 2009–10 season—that stays with me the most, infiltrating my thoughts and even my dreams. I often think of that most tenuous of times when the players opened their lives to me, enduring my every question with a grace and patience that belied their years and treating me like one of them. No matter what they do, no matter where they go, whether they're playing basketball or not, I'll always be rooting for them.

Notes

THE VAST MAJORITY of the reporting for this book was done on the ground in Kentucky over the course of eight months in 2009 and 2010. With my family, I rented a five-room cabin in rural Georgetown on the back side of a small horse farm, not far from the North Fork of the Elkhorn Creek. I spent my days in Scott County, often in school with the boys, and spent my nights on the basketball court. I was given access to every Scott County practice and game, traveling with the team across the state and the country. I rode on the bus with them and sat on the bench with them. I was in team huddles and time-outs, players-only meetings and private coaches' discussions. I spent time with the players away from the game—in their homes, with their families. And above all, I was just there, in the gym, day after day, filling eighty steno-pad notebooks with notes and recording nearly a thousand hours' worth of interviews, locker-room speeches, and dialogue.

If something appears in quotes in this book, it means I witnessed it first-hand, recorded it, or gathered it from other credible sources, including but not limited to police reports, court files, coroner's reports, other official documents and archival material, as well as television and newspaper coverage of events. On many occasions, during games, I not only recorded the speeches inside the Scott County locker room, but, with permission from the opposing head coach, recorded the speeches inside the other locker room as well, so as to best capture the drama of the game from both perspectives: the winning team and the losing team. Any game action described in the book was either witnessed in person or, in the cases of games played in previous seasons, viewed on DVD. In addition, to ensure that my recollection of contemporary games was accurate, I also watched the video of those games, courtesy of Scott County High, the Kentucky High School Athletic Association, or the Wazoo Sports Network, all of which provided me copies of game video.

No names of any of the players, students, coaches, or other people who appear in this book have been changed. These are real people, living real lives, in Kentucky in the throes of America's Great Recession, working, oftentimes, to realize a singular and powerful dream: basketball greatness.

PROLOGUE

My account of Meet the Cards and the start of the 2009–2010 basketball season in Scott County is drawn from recorded observations while attending the event in November 2009, as well as past media coverage and other reporting. Additionally, Betsy Hicks allowed me to view the letters written to her husband in the spring of 1998 after winning Scott County's first state title.

the most exciting thing around here   Roger Nesbitt, "Scott, Clark counties burning with basketball fever," *Lexington Herald-Leader*, March 16, 1983.

This is not a pep rally   Josh Underwood, "Loss to Oldham County last year a driving force in Scott County's success for 1997–98 season," *Georgetown News-Graphic*, March 13, 1983.

CHAPTER 1: THE STRAW THAT STIRS THE DRINK

My account of Ge'Lawn Guyn, the Ballard–Scott County game, and the day in school leading up to the game is drawn almost entirely from first-hand observations. I spent the entire day with Ge'Lawn, from the moment he walked downstairs in his house that morning until the moment he walked off the court that night, beaten by Ballard.

Best player on the floor . . . straw that stirs the drink   Messages posted on Bluegrassrivals.com, July 28, 2009.

CHAPTER 2: THE FARMER AND THE BEAUTY QUEEN

My account of Toyota's arrival in Scott County is drawn from interviews with key figures, including but not limited to former Gov. Martha Layne Collins, Billy and Marilyn Singer, their son Jon

Singer, former Collins staffers Jiro Hashimoto and Ted Sauer who traveled with Collins in Japan, and Larry Hayes, the secretary of the Collins' Executive Cabinet in the 1980s, who is now serving as the state secretary of the Cabinet for Economic Development.

In addition, I also reviewed documents held in the state's internal Toyota archive and the lawsuits filed in Scott County to stop the project. Finally, I also relied on statewide news coverage of the event, which was covered heavily by the state's two largest newspapers, *The Courier-Journal* in Louisville and the *Lexington Herald-Leader,* and by Georgetown's two local newspapers as well.

Finally, for my description of Kentucky bluegrass, or *Poa pratensis,* I relied both on documents describing the grass as well as several interviews with turf specialists, including Ray Smith and D. W. Williams at the University of Kentucky; Kelly Kearns at the Wisconsin Department of Natural Resources; and Steven Tannas, who authored a study about the spread of Kentucky bluegrass in the North American west.

Wherever he has trodden *Journal of the American Society of Agronomy,* December 1, 1915, p. 257. p. 260.
By the late 1700s, all Kentucky towns Arthur M. Miller, *Geology of Kentucky,* p. 169.
rowdies . . . war on that corner "Citizens complain of rowdies in area near college dormitory," *The Graphic,* November 24, 1983.
Senior skip day has now become high school skip day "Board told absenteeism is severe school problem," *The Graphic,* May 12, 1983.
tell me things are getting better Paul F. Power Jr., "Hundreds wait in line to apply at Clark," *Georgetown News & Times,* July 14, 1983.
The risk of one child being poisoned "Halloween activity outlives its time," *The Graphic,* October 13, 1983.
no one really knows Mark Reese, "County Agent's Notes," *The Graphic,* June 14, 1983.
all the lushness of a burnt marshmallow Paul F. Power, "Wonder Bread years spent in Buckeye State," *Georgetown News & Times,* August 25, 1983.

He could always replace the fish   "Game warden reports more dead fish are found above sewer plant," *The Graphic*, August 11, 1983.

Seventy-five percent of the county's corn crop   "Emergency measure allows grazing on closed acreage," *The Graphic*, August 18, 1983; "160,000 acres affected by continued drought," *Georgetown News & Times*, August 18, 1983.

a fast-approaching disaster   Paul F. Power Jr., "Drought endangers county's top cash crop," *Georgetown News & Times*, August 5, 1983.

told to imagine colder weather   "The Graphic Sportsman," *The Graphic*, August 11, 1983.

Bluegrass Tobacco Festival went on   "Tobacco Festival is held despite last weekend's heat," *The Graphic*, August 25, 1983.

Pearl Price wouldn't listen   Robert Peirce and Michelle Slatalla, "Deadly heat wave claims 28 lives in Louisville area," *Courier-Journal*, July 24, 1985.

betwixt and between   Wilma Norton, "Heat peril subsides slightly, but 4 more deaths reported," *Courier-Journal*, July 25, 1983.

you could have cooked an egg   Wilma Norton and Bob Vonderheide, "Local tolls hits 34 as 2 more victims are found in ovenlike apartments," *Courier-Journal*, July 26, 1983.

That pretty woman   Bob Johnson, "Carroll, Combs lead trek for Collins in GOP country," *Courier-Journal*, October 26, 1983.

22,000 jobs during her first year   "Record 22,009 jobs created in state in '84, Collins says," *Courier-Journal*, January 9, 1985.

neither confrontational nor especially chummy   Lonnie Rosenwald, "Collins' selling style differed from predecessors'," *Louisville Times*, March 22, 1984.

water gets a little old   Diana Taylor Osborne, "Collins feeling better but admits she was apprehensive," *Herald-Leader*, November 28, 1984.

best any offer   "'Every state of union' pursuing Saturn," *Courier-Journal*, December 11, 1985.

Fan-*tastic*   Dee Wilson, "Sources say Kentucky among three finalists for GM's Saturn plant," *Courier-Journal*, February 8, 1985.

Is Tennessee a better place to live than Kentucky? Bob Johnson, "'Off-year' politicking stays on the high road at Fancy Farm picnic," *Courier-Journal*, August 4, 1985.

We would appreciate your informing us Letter from Kaneyoshi Kusunoki, executive vice president of the Toyota Motor Corporation, to Gov. Martha Layne Collins, dated August 8, 1985.

during this time of transition . . . the calendar of events did not mention *The Public Papers of Governor Martha Layne Collins, 1983–1987,* Elizabeth Duffy Fraas, editor, p. 252–53.

plot 57-07 Document titled, "Georgetown-Delaplain Site, Nov. 6, 1985."

If they can isolate you Andy Mead, Cheryl Truman, and Art Jester, "Snags hit in completing land package for Toyota plant," *Herald-Leader*, December 5, 1985.

Quite simply, I'm broke Dee Wilson and Carol Marie Cropper, "Tussle over parcel for Toyota project apparently resolved," *Courier-Journal*, December 7, 1985.

They say it's now or never Cheryl Truman, Roger Nesbitt, and Michael York, "Toyota land package nearly complete; single barrier to deal apparently woman's OK," *Herald-Leader*, December 6, 1985.

Why should I stand in the way Roger Nesbitt, Andy Mead, and Art Jester, "Way appears clear for deal on plant land; legal dispute blocking purchase of parcel for Toyota said resolved," *Herald-Leader*, December 7, 1985.

all this automobile making Andy Mead and Roger Nesbitt, "This turned out to be no ordinary news conference," *Herald-Leader*, December 12, 1985.

a community on the move Hank Bond, "Collins praises Scott County," *Georgetown News & Times*, December 17, 1985.

Will the town be wide-open tonight? "This turned out to be no ordinary news conference," *Herald-Leader*, December 12, 1985.

the $125-million incentive package Dee Wilson, "Collins unveils $125 million incentive package for Toyota," *Courier-Journal*, December 18, 1985.

I am a taxpayer and an American citizen   Beth E. Page, "Collins 'gift' to Toyota," *Courier-Journal,* January 25, 1986.

Japs, Go Home   Carol Marie Cropper, "Rally protests state 'giveaways' for Toyota plant," *Courier-Journal,* January 17, 1986.

Too bad they used kerosene   C. Ray Hall, "Klan keeps fires burning," *Lexington Leader,* July 3, 1978.

My wife doesn't ever want to come back   Betty Winston Baye, "County police probe firebombing of home, suspect racial motive," *Courier-Journal,* July 3, 1985.

in an all-white setting   Gary Pearl vs. City of Louisville and Special Fund, Worker's Compensation Board opinion and award, April 29, 1985.

It serves the people of Kentucky   Gordon Taub vs. Commonwealth of Kentucky, Transportation Cabinet, Department of Highways, deposition of Gov. Martha Layne Collins, June 25, 1986.

CHAPTER 3: COAL DUST AND DREAMS

For my profile of Billy Hicks, his life growing up in Harlan County, and the story of his father Orie, I interviewed at length Billy Hicks, three of his siblings, and Billy's wife, Betsy Hicks, as well as many of Hicks's former teammates, former players, fellow coaches, and others in Harlan County who knew the Hicks family. In depicting the scene at the home where Orie Hicks was shot and killed, I relied on the Kentucky State Police investigation file, news coverage, and a telephone interview with one of the other officers at the house that night, Gillis Gilbert.

Coal production statistics were drawn from the annual reports of the state Department of Mines and Minerals. The Appalachian Archive at Southeast Kentucky Community and Technical College in Cumberland was especially helpful in describing the conditions that coal miners faced in the twentieth century. Also helpful was James K. Crissman's book, *Death and Dying in Central Appalachia,* and Jerry Wayne Napier's dissertation at the University of Kentucky, "Mines, Miners, and Machines: Coal Mine Mechanization and the Eastern Kentucky Coal Fields, 1890–1990."

Coal Land   J. Stoddard Johnston, *First Explorations of Kentucky,* p. 71.

the richest part of the state   Stuart Seely Sprague, "The Great Appalachian Iron and Coal Town Boom of 1889–1893," *Appalachian Journal,* Spring 1977, p. 216.

A. B. McKnight, tippleman . . . Alex Roman, miner   Benham and Lynch Collection of the Appalachian Archive at the Southeast Kentucky Community and Technical College.

scrape them up with shovels   James K. Crissman, *Death and Dying in Central Appalachia,* p. 194.

poor Briscoe Washington   Benham and Lynch Collection, SKCTC Appalachian Archive.

spewing out of the mouth of the mine   Crissman, p. 190.

All we need to settle this thing and mighty quick   Sterling D. Spero and Jacob Broches Aronoff, "War in the Kentucky Mountains," *The American Mercury,* February 1932.

feed a family of five on just $8.83 a week   J. C. Byars, Jr., "Harlan County: Act of God?," *The Nation,* June 15, 1935.

It is not a place for tourists   Boris Israel, "I Get Shot," *The New Republic,* October 21, 1931.

If I was a young man, I'd get me a hoe   Oral history of Hiram Maggard, taken September 17, 1979, and included in the Oral History Collection at the SKCTC Appalachian Archive.

It sounded like the whole world was shooting   Statement taken by Kentucky State Police on October 9, 1972, from an eyewitness to the shoot-out that killed Orie Hicks.

I would do anything reasonable   "EHS Eligibility Still Hanging," *Harlan Daily Enterprise,* October 23, 1979.

Is this real?   John Clay, "Drought is over, and Corbin is delirious," *Herald-Leader,* March 15, 1991.

CHAPTER 4: PRISONER OF THE HYPE MACHINE

My profile of Dakotah Euton is drawn from multiple, lengthy interviews with Dakotah, his parents Clay and Pam Euton, Dakotah's teammates, and two of his former coaches, as well as from statewide newspaper coverage of Billy Gillispie's efforts to recruit Dakotah to play at the University of Kentucky.

My account of the rise and fall of Gillispie himself is drawn primarily from newspaper and television coverage, which was voluminous. Especially helpful was the exhaustive coverage of the *Lexington Herald-Leader* sports reporters, namely John Clay, Mike Fields, Jerry Tipton, and Mary Story; television footage of Gillispie's introduction at Kentucky and his final press conference after his dismissal; and a *New York Times* profile written by Pete Thamel on March 22, 2007, shortly before Kentucky hired Gillispie.

Finally, for my account of the Kentucky High School Athletic Association's investigation into Dakotah Euton, Chad Jackson, and Austin Flannery, I viewed the players' investigation files at the KHSAA, watched their recorded hearings before state hearing officers, and conducted several interviews with coaches, parents, and Scott County administrators about the matter. Especially helpful were my interviews with Scott County principal, Frank Howatt, who met with me at length for several interviews over the course of the reporting of this book.

a Dr Pepper would do   Pete Thamel, "Coach's 'unhealthy' obsession has led to success at Texas A&M," *New York Times*, March 22, 2007.

The number of fans may be thinning   John Clay, "Watch out: At this point, everyone is a target," *Herald-Leader*, February 28, 2007.

I would like to say it doesn't hurt   Jerry Tipton, "Cats stung by fans' booish behavior—Game's 'pro mentality' emboldens local criticism," *Herald-Leader*, December 24, 2006.

I don't know the climate at Kentucky   Mark Mathis, "Season's over, but real drama just getting started," *Owensboro (Ky.) Messenger-Inquirer*, March 19, 2007.

From greatness and invincibility   Marty Fields, "Time for a change in UK basketball," *Herald-Leader*, March 4, 2007.

Barnhart needs to wake up   Troy Thompson, "No more Mr. Nice Guy," *Herald-Leader*, March 4, 2007.

I feel the love already   John Clay, "'Tub-bee, Tub-bee:' Sweet music—Tubby bolts from the Blue," *Herald-Leader,* March 24, 2007.

Hallelujah!   Delano R. Massey, "Classes ignored amid excitement," *Herald-Leader,* April 7, 2007.

He's got the fastest thumbs   Jerry Tipton, "Text messaging might get a thumbs down," *Herald-Leader,* April 15, 2007.

please don't let me be nervous   Jerry Tipton, "Rose Hill star, 16, commits to UK—Euton's early decision part of recruiting trend," *Herald-Leader,* June 19, 2007.

Welcome, young man . . . Billy Clyde rides again   Posts made on the Kentucky Sports Radio blog on June 18, 2007

The slowest player on the court   Mark Story, "World wide wallop: Parents of prized recruits learning how to handle criticism of their sons on Internet message boards," *Herald-Leader,* February 3, 2008.

We looked at the facilities   Jody Demling, "Euton going to Scott County," *Courier-Journal,* March 15, 2008; Mike Fields, "With an eye on UK, Euton plans to transfer to Scott County," *Herald-Leader,* March 19, 2008.

Roughly 70 percent of athletes who transferred   Legislative Research Commission report on the athletic transfers, December 10, 2009.

No, sir. Absolutely not   Joy Berry statement before KHSAA hearing officer on July 9, 2008.

time to get to work   Mike Fields, "Euton, Jackson cleared to play—Scott County transfers ruled eligible," *Herald-Leader,* August 26, 2008.

You all need to settle down   Jerry Tipton, "Fans not happy, but not giving up—Informal survey shows Gillispie should keep job, but also behave better," *Herald-Leader,* March 15, 2009.

CHAPTER 5: THE WORST TIME OF OUR LIVES

For my profile of Will Schu, I relied on multiple, lengthy interviews with Will and his mother Laura Schu, as well as interviews with Will's aunt Sally Schu, longtime family friend Bev McCarthy, former coach David Fooy, other coaches, relatives, and teammates, and people who knew Wilbur Schu before his death, including Tommy

Duke Belt and Ben Chandler. Also helpful in sketching a portrait of Wilbur Schu were stories that appeared about him in both the *Herald-Leader* and the *Woodford Sun.*

For my account about the economic troubles in Scott County, and the rise of the Tea Party there, I relied on interviews with several Toyota workers, elected officials, students, people in line at the local unemployment office, former campaign staffers for both Republican Rand Paul and Democrat Trey Grayson, as well as Grayson himself, Paul's former campaign manager David Adams, and Al Cross, a former political reporter now serving as director for the Institute for Rural Journalism and Community Issues at the University of Kentucky. Also helpful in this section was the media coverage of the state's Tea Party events, which appeared in papers across Kentucky, small and large, in the spring, summer, and fall of 2009.

It's getting scary   Amy Wilson, "2600 show for 100 spots; those in line talk of frustration, desperation," *Lexington Herald-Leader,* March 7, 2010.
more people living in poverty than almost any other state   U.S. Census Bureau, Number and Percentage of People in Poverty in the Past 12 Months by State and Puerto Rico: 2008 and 2009.
The number of Kentuckians on food stamps   Kentucky Cabinet for Health and Family Services.
Kentucky was the saddest state   David G. Moriarty, Matthew M. Zack, James B. Holt, Daniel P. Chapman, and Marc A. Safran, "Geographic patterns of mental distress: U.S. adults, 1993–2001 and 2003–2006," *American Journal of Preventive Medicine,* April 2009.
the Gloom Belt   Jeffrey Kluger, "The Gloom Belt: Kentucky is the saddest state," *Time,* April 15, 2009.
worst time of our lives   "From the courthouse to the statehouse, people 'observe' Tax Day," *London (Ky.) Sentinel Echo,* April 20, 2009.
Unemployment rate in the county had nearly reached 13 percent   Kentucky Office of Employment and Training.

a $4.4 billion deficit Hiroko Tabuchi, "Toyota posts an annual loss," *New York Times,* May 8, 2009.

I'm going to keep making our case Ryan Alessi, "Clinton wins big in Ky.; Obama captures Oregon, edges closer to nomination," *Herald-Leader,* May 21, 2008.

with 41 percent reporting . . . fighting between different races KIP Student Survey Trend Data for Scott County Schools, 1998–2008, prepared by Scott Countians Against Drugs.

You've got the radical left wing in control Carl Keith Greene and Ronnie Ellis, "Seconds anyone?" *Corbin (Ky.) Times-Tribune,* July 6, 2009.

Say it with me, ladies and gentlemen! Greg Kocher, "Anger brews—Irked Kentuckians protest taxes, spending, bailouts," *Herald-Leader,* April 16, 2009.

How's that hope and change working out for you? Karen Richardson, "Obama strategy must be stopped," *Lawrenceburg (Ky.) Anderson News,* November 25, 2009.

This is for Kentucky Mike Fields, "This is for Kentucky: Scott County 72, Huntington 68; Cardinals never trail in knocking off nation's No. 1," *Herald-Leader,* Feb. 3, 2007.

CHAPTER 6: SHORT, FAT GUYS RATING KIDS

For my account of the rise of Rivals.com, I spoke at length on several occasions to Jerry Meyer, as well as to the Web site's original visionaries, Shannon Terry and Greg Gough, and Rivals staffer Tim Watts. I also relied on news coverage about the death, rebirth, and rise of the site.

The description of Jelan Kendrick's announcement that he was committing to Memphis comes from video footage shot by Daniel Cox of the Memphis Roar, a Web site devoted to news about Memphis athletics.

all we do . . . is cover college and high school sports Mike Marshall, "'Lucky' right name for founder of Rivals.com," *Huntsville Times,* August 31, 2009.

They're trying to grow a relationship   Jeff Drummond, "Cats still in the mix for Georgia forward?" CatsIllustrated.com, November 8, 2009.

CHAPTER 7: MAYBE GOD IS AGAINST US

For my profile of Mark Jackson, I relied on interviews with members of the 1986 Woodford County regional championship squad, including Bob Gibson, Robert Greenlee, Mark Moffett, Mike Moraja, and Dante Payne, as well the head coach of that team, Gene Kirk. I also interviewed Mark Jackson's father, Fred Jackson, his middle school coach, Sonny Denniston, and several other people, namely Chad Jackson, and other relatives. I also relied on coverage of the 1985 and 1986 basketball seasons in the *Herald-Leader* and *Woodford Sun*, which together provided a blow-by-blow account of Woodford's unlikely run to the state tournament.

Especially helpful was a *Woodford Sun* profile of Jackson, "Jacket profiles . . . Mark Jackson," written by Mack Calvert on March 6, 1986, which detailed Jackson's basketball career and his plans for the future. The description of Mark Jackson's speech to the fans before going to Rupp Arena is drawn directly from video footage shot of the pep rally in March 1986, preserved at Woodford County High School in the 1985–86 video yearbook, and provided to me by Dave Noble. The footage also included a clip of Mark Jackson's game-changing dunk against Henry Clay in the regional tournament, allowing me to describe the pivotal play in such specific detail.

Court records and police reports form the basis for my reporting on Mark Jackson's criminal problems later in life. The records, on file in Fayette and Woodford counties and open to the public, include two psychological evaluations, a history of Mark's assaults and substance abuse, IQ test scores, and personal statements from Mark Jackson himself, documenting his fall from a high school basketball star to a felon. The following documents found in the court files were especially helpful: two psychological evaluations, one by certified psychologist Katherine D. Peterson and the other by licensed clinical psychologist Harwell F. Smith; a summary of an interview with Mark Jackson, taken by Robert Hobson, a mental health specialist; video footage of Jackson's sentencing hearing; motions filed by the prosecution; a criminal history report; and more than a dozen letters written by friends, loved ones, and former coaches in defense of Mark Jackson.

In describing Mark Jackson's failing health and his ultimate death, I relied on several documents, including: a letter written by his mother Gladys Jackson in February 2000, contained in Woodford case No. 99-CR-00031; Mark Jackson's self-written prerelease probation request sent from prison on February 1, 2002, acknowledging "major health problems," including strokes, and his understanding that "any further drug abuse would be fatal to him due to his deteriorated health," and the Fayette County coroner's report, autopsy report, and toxicology results, which lists the cause of death as "dilated cardiomyopathy due to chronic substance abuse."

All of these records are open to the public.

had to be subdued with a Taser   Georgetown Police Department arrest report, written on October 29, 2009, and filed in Scott County Criminal Court on November 6, 2009, as part of case number 09-M-803 against Chase Jackson for charges of second-degree disorderly conduct and second degree fleeing or evading police.

All my life . . . Woodford County has been in the shadow   Mike Fields, "Woodford romps to 11th region title," *Herald-Leader*, March 15, 1986.

they broke me down   Gene McLean, "For hungry Woodford, what mattered most was the sweet memory," *Herald-Leader*, March 21, 1986.

drinking, smoking marijuana, and using crack cocaine   A psychological evaluation of Mark Jackson, taken by certified psychologist Katherine D. Peterson on May 20, 1993 and filed on June 4, 1993, in the *Commonwealth of Kentucky vs. Mark Anthony Jackson*, Fayette County case file No. 93CR022, details Jackson's history of substance abuse.

a series of violent assaults   Two documents in case file No. 93CR022 detail his history of violence: a Motion to Reconsider bond for Jackson, filed by the prosecution on February 10, 1993, and a psychological evaluation of Jackson taken by Harwell F. Smith, a licensed clinical psychologist, on May 7, 1993.

I am truly scared   Letter written by Mark Jackson to Fayette County Circuit Court Judge Lewis Paisley on April 15, 1993, documented in court file No. 93CR022.

CHAPTER 8: MORAL PEOPLE, MORAL FIBER

For my profile of John Cornett, I relied on news coverage of his efforts to make Scott County wet, as well as interviews with Cornett who met with me at length in his law office, his wife, Barbara, his parents Bob and Jean Cornett, longtime law partner Harold Simms, and others who worked to overturn Georgetown's dry laws, including consultant Dale Emmons, landowner David Lawson, and wet activist Andrea Moss. In addition, I interviewed people who opposed Cornett, hoping to keep Georgetown dry, including Horace Hambrick, a local pediatrician and leader of the dry movement, and the Rev. Tommy Simpson, a minister who served in Scott County at the time of the wet-dry debate.

Details describing the incident involving former Scott County basketball star Bud Mackey come from interviews with Scott County high school administrators Dwayne Ellison and Frank Howatt, news coverage, court documents, as well as a thirty-minute interview with Mackey himself while he was incarcerated at Fayette County jail on a different charge.

For my account of Angie Tedder, the car crash that nearly killed her in September 2009, and the city council debate over selling alcohol on Sundays six months earlier, I relied on several different sources. I interviewed Tedder at length as well as her husband, Ed Tedder, who was driving several cars behind his wife at the time of the accident and witnessed the aftermath. I watched video chronicling Tedder's statements to the Georgetown City Council—both at the time of the council's vote in the spring of 2009 and, months later, in January 2010 when Tedder returned to speak to the council about her injuries. Finally, in describing the crash itself, I relied on the Lexington Police investigation file, case No. 2009169839, which included the following key documents: toxicology results documenting Kenneth L. Carter Jr.'s blood alcohol content at the time of the crash; interviews with eyewitnesses to the crash; photographs depicting the scene and showing the bottle of Jim Beam inside Carter's truck; and, finally, interviews and internal police correspondence, relating to the allegation that Carter had frequented two Scott County establishments that served alcohol on the day of the incident.

What does Cornett not understand   Sally Wilson, "Voters will help keep area dry," *News-Graphic,* February 20, 2000.
to call upon Almighty God   "Day of prayer to be observed," *Georgetown Times,* May 29, 1946.
"T. B." and "V.D."   "Saloons and roadhouses will not get back in Scott County by my vote," *Georgetown Times,* June 5, 1946.
America's favorite neighbor . . . wants to be your neighbor   advertisement, *News-Graphic,* January 10, 1997, and January 12, 1997.
Oh, victory in Jesus   Greg Kocher, "Mercer County votes down alcohol sales," *Herald-Leader,* September 22, 1999.
Let the liquor flow freely   Jim Sanders, "Wet/dry vote would only help Cornett, not Georgetown," *News-Graphic,* February 12, 2000.
How many so-called 'Gay Bars' occupy their streets?   Loretta Tackett, "Alcohol sales would bring a 'slow destruction' to Scott County," *News-Graphic,* March 15, 2000.
Won't it be neat . . . to have all these great bars   Kevin Reber, "Alcohol would bring unwanted bars to town," *Georgetown News-Graphic,* March 12, 2000.
It has been decided twice already   Janet Riley, "How many times must city vote 'no'?" *News-Graphic,* October 22, 2000.

Convictions for driving under the influence . . . fell 38 percent Kentucky State Police annual crime reports, 2000–2009.

Drinking and smoking marijuana were common "KIP Student Survey Trend Data for Scott County School, 1998–2008," prepared by Scott Countians Against Drugs. According to the 2008 survey, Scott County seniors reported doing the following on one or more occasion: drinking alcohol (42 percent) and smoking marijuana (19 percent). Furthermore, more than 70 percent of seniors surveyed reported that it was "sort of easy" or "very easy" to get alcohol and marijuana.

.089, just over the legal limit Lexington Division of Police, Collision Reconstruction Unit Investigation Summary, case No. 2009169839.

CHAPTER 9: THE STREETS GO ON FOREVER

For my profile of George Guyn, I interviewed him at length on several occasions and spent a day shadowing him on the job in Lexington, sitting next to him in his garbage truck during his nine-hour shift. I also interviewed his wife Rebecca Guyn, his son Ge'Lawn, and several men who coached Ge'Lawn in the past, including Daniel Brown, Jarvis Chenault, Weldon Cunningham, and Anthony Hawkins. When writing about Guyn's past as a drug dealer, I relied on interviews with two men who knew Guyn during that time: Tyrone Ballew, one of Guyn's oldest friends who grew up with George in Lexington and is now on death row in Ohio for murder, and Patrick Coffey, a man serving a life sentence in Ohio for the same murder.

I interviewed both men in prison in 2010. And I also relied extensively on police reports and court documents contained in Fayette County criminal case file No. 97CR037, which together portray in great detail George Guyn's life as a crack dealer on the streets of Lexington. Of these materials, a few were especially helpful to me: the six police reports filed between October 29 and November 26, 1996, chronicling the undercover crack purchases that led to Guyn's drug trafficking charges; Rebecca Guyn's letter to Judge Thomas L. Clark begging him to show mercy on her husband filed on February 7,

1997; and video footage of Guyn's sentencing hearing in April 1997. The scene where Judge Clark gives Guyn probation, instead of sending him to prison, is drawn directly from this footage, which allowed me to quote from it and describe it in such detail.

For my account of Charlotte Court and the rise of crack cocaine in America, I relied on newspaper coverage in the *Herald-Leader* as well as other sources, including the *Miami Herald* and *The New York Times*. The following material was especially helpful: the *Herald-Leader*'s in-depth coverage of Charlotte Court's decline and decay and Peter Kerr's stories in *The New York Times* about the national crack cocaine problem. For background, it was also helpful to read two other documents: "The men who created crack," a detailed *US News & World Report* article published on August 19, 1991, and Matthew Clarke's 2005 Gaines Center senior thesis at the University of Kentucky titled "Voices of Home in Bluegrass-Aspendale: Constructing the Ideal." I also used official documents, provided to me by Austin Simms, the longtime director of the Lexington-Fayette County Urban Housing Authority. In addition, I interviewed Simms at length in his office about the rise, fall, and ultimate destruction of Charlotte Court. The project was razed in September 1999.

Finally, for my account of Fight Night, I interviewed several Scott County students about the popular pastime, including Josh Woolums, and attended the fights in the cul-de-sac at the Lane's Run Business Park, which I describe near the end of this chapter.

distinctly substandard . . . wholly unfit . . . a menace to health   City of Lexington, "Public Housing in Lexington, Kentucky," 1954, p. 3.
The best in modern living   "Charlotte Courts to be ready for occupancy in early spring," *Lexington Herald,* December 29, 1940.
Model homes that will rent at nominal sums   "Construction of unit started," *Lexington Leader,* June 23, 1940.
This is my home   "Handbook for Residents of Lexington's Municipal Housing Units," City of Lexington Municipal Housing Commission.

hellhole Geoff Mulvihill, "Goodbye, Charlotte," *Herald-Leader,* September 29, 1999.

If you call the police . . . we'll be back . . . all I need is a chance State of Ohio *vs. Tyrone Ballew.*

you'd think they were selling newspapers Peter Kerr, "Washington Heights: Cocaine trade thrives," *New York Times,* April 1, 1986.

one four-day stretch before Christmas Trish Power, "Boss loses left eye in attack with awl," *Miami Herald,* December 23, 1986; "Man with Uzi speaks convincingly," *Miami Herald,* December 28, 1986; Gary Bogdon, "Suicide averted at bridge," *Miami Herald,* December 24, 1986.

They shoot out here almost every night Barbara Ward and Thomas Tolliver, "Lexington Police open roll call center on day man is shot nearby," *Herald-Leader,* June 4, 1994.

the future of our city Steve Lannen, "Scott County business park has first 2 tenants," *Herald-Leader,* June 18, 2003.

CHAPTER 10: MORE THAN LIFE ITSELF

For my account of Clark County, redshirting, the school board's debate over a new redshirting policy, and the emergence of George Rogers Clark basketball star Robbie Stenzel, I relied on several different sources.

I interviewed Jay and Ann Stenzel at their home in rural Clark County as well as their son, Robbie. I also interviewed Robert E. Lee, the school superintendent at the time of the debate, and two school board members who cast votes on the matter—board chair Judy Hicks and board member Ray Shear—as well as Stenzel's teammate Vinny Zollo, George Rogers Clark's head basketball coach Scott Humphrey, and others who lived in Clark County during the time of the redshirting discussion.

In addition, I reviewed the minutes of the school board meetings where the policy was first introduced, debated, and voted on. And finally, I relied on news coverage of the redshirting policy, namely coverage in the local newspaper, *The Winchester Sun.* Stories written by Jennifer Ginn, the *Sun*'s managing editor, in the summer of 2005 were especially helpful to me.

That's their prerogative   Jennifer Ginn, "Board of education OKs policy to forbid redshirting students," *Winchester Sun*, June 24, 2005.
in the best interests of our son   Jennifer Ginn, "Athletic policy passes; Parent threatens legal action after 4–1 vote for ban on redshirting," *Winchester Sun*, July 20, 2005.
the most poised kid in our program . . . He doesn't play to his age   Mark Maloney, "Mason Co. goes for 5th title in 6 years—Clark Co. edges Scott at foul line in other semifinal," *Herald-Leader*, March 11, 2007.
Hard to make up for that . . . few if any of them are 'true juniors'   Messages posted by anonymous basketball fans on January 31 and February 1, 2010, on Bluegrasspreps.com.

CHAPTER 11: SETTING THEM UP TO FAIL

For my account of life in Scott County High School, I relied on interviews with several students and teachers as well as school administrators, including principal Frank Howatt, director of secondary education for Scott County schools Chip Southworth, and the district's finance director Randy Cutright. Classroom dialogue quoted in this section was witnessed while attending classes at the school—something I did on a regular basis with the permission of Scott County administrators. And my portrayal of the Site Based Decision Making Council meeting, where the issue of athletic eligibility came up, also comes from having attended the meeting. In addition, I interviewed at length two members of the council: Gene Norris and Nancy Curtis.

CHAPTER 12: HOW STUPID DO WE LOOK?

For my account about the rise of Lexington Catholic, I relied on multiple sources. I interviewed Bob Bueter at length on two occasions in his office in Cincinnati, where among other things he showed me the

Lord's prayer that was rewritten in his honor at his departure from Catholic in 1999. I also interviewed several other people with knowledge of Bueter and Lexington Catholic, including but not limited to: current principal Sally Stevens and former principal Sister Lea Paolucci; current basketball coach Brandon Salsman and former basketball coach Danny Haney; the Rev. Walt Bado, a longtime Jesuit who served with Bueter in Lexington; Frank Amato, who taught with Bueter at Loyola Academy near Chicago; Kathleen Quigley, who worked closely with Bueter during his tenure at Catholic; former student Alissa Tibe; longtime teacher Helen Wheat; and Sheila Hardy, a former chair Catholic's board. In addition, I relied on news coverage of Bueter during his time at Catholic, primarily the *Herald-Leader*.

In describing the epic 1998 Catholic–Scott County game, I viewed tape of the game and listened to the radio call, courtesy of Elden May at the Kentucky High School Athletic Association. I also interviewed Hicks, Haney, former Scott County player Casey Alsop, and former Catholic player Steve Searcy's mother, Jo Ann Muir, about that game. In describing Searcy's death, I relied on news coverage and official records, namely the Fayette County coroner's report and autopsy results, which are on file in Lexington, open to the public, and describe in detail the manner and cause of Searcy's death.

The secret in fund-raising   Casey Banas, "School fundraising reaches the big time," *Chicago Tribune*, February 19, 1984.
It's the first job I've ever had   Sacha Devroomen, "Priest returns to state—Lexington taps Ft. Thomas native," *Kentucky Post*, June 19, 1990.

CHAPTER 13: THEY SAID WE WERE SOFT

For my account of Scott County's push through the play-offs, I witnessed or recorded all dialogue and speeches. I was there with Ge'Lawn and Hicks, during their private game-tape session and their dinner at Hicks's house on the eve of the postseason. I was also at the doctor's office with Ge'Lawn, sitting in the room with him and his father when the doctor spoke with Ge'Lawn about his knees. Also helpful in this section was the local media coverage of Lexington Catholic's loss in the district round, namely Mike Fields's story in the *Herald-Leader*, "Generals oust Knights to begin a new day," February 24, 2010, and the radio call of the Catholic-Lafayette game, by Gary Ball and Kirk Chiles.

CHAPTER 14: HOPE YOUR HOPE AND PRAY YOUR PRAYER

For my account of Rupp Arena and Adolph Rupp, the man for whom the building was named, I relied on several different sources. I interviewed the people who currently operate the arena: Lexington Center president William B. Owen, director of arena management Carl Hall, box office manger Jeff Bojanowski, and the Center's longtime director of facilities Merrill Richardson, who has worked at Rupp Arena since it first opened in 1976.

In addition, I relied on media coverage of the arena and the man, published namely in the *Courier-Journal*, the *Herald-Leader*, and *Sports Illustrated*. Especially helpful to me was the Lexington Center's vast internal archives, which were opened to me in 2010 by the Center's marketing director Sheila Barr Kenny. A few *Sports Illustrated* articles were also especially key in writing this chapter: Frank Deford's coverage of Rupp's quest to win the 1966 NCAA championship; Curry Kirkpatrick's controversial 1991 story about that championship, exposing Rupp's alleged prejudices against African Americans; a 1957 profile of Rupp's passion for basketball perfection written by Jeremiah Tax; and a six-page article written for the magazine by Adolph Rupp himself in 1958, explaining in his own words the personal philosophy that led to his success.

General George Custer . . . I'm a little apprehensive   D. G. Fitzmaurice, "Atmosphere a key in Rupp Arena," *Herald-Leader*, July 4, 1976.

We're working in earth-tone colors . . . We couldn't change it   D. G. Fitzmaurice, "Red logo foes make Minter blue," *Herald-Leader,* July 3, 1976.

I appreciate the show of friendship   "Mears likes logo," *Herald-Leader,* July 3, 1976.

So the rich people . . . can have their parties   Steven Anderson, "Injunction eyed; Residents urged not to relocate," *Lexington Herald,* March 18, 1976.

they'd move us cost-free in a trash truck   Joe Ward, "Lexington's poor face housing plight," *Courier-Journal,* July 10, 1975.

If this thing lays a big, fat elephant egg   "Taxpayers to pay if center 'lay egg,'" *Lexington Leader,* July 21, 1976.

Someday I'm going to write a book   Frank Deford, "Bravo for the Baron," *Sports Illustrated,* March 7, 1966.

No nonsense   Jeremiah Tax, "Big Week for the Man in Brown," *Sports Illustrated,* December 16, 1957.

kissing your sister . . . finest team ever assembled   Dick Fenlon and Tev Laudeman, "Rupp, the Baron of basketball, dies," *Courier-Journal,* December 11, 1977.

not just mean, but mean-spirited   Curry Kirkpatrick, "The Night They Drove Old Dixie Down," *Sports Illustrated,* April 1, 1991.

when I go through the pearly gates   Adolph Rupp, "'Defeat and Failure to Me Are Failures,'" *Sports Illustrated,* December 8, 1958.

Sing your song . . . dream your dream   Adolph Rupp quoting from Pakenham Beatty's poem "Self Reliance" in "Defeat and Failure to Me Are Failures," *Sports Illustrated,* December 8, 1958.

nincompoops . . . next game   "Rupp criticizes the 'nincompoop critics,'" *Courier-Journal,* January 24, 1975.

You feel like you need seatbelts   Joe Ward, "Upstairs at Rupp Arena: Are the spectators safe?," *Courier-Journal,* October 25, 1976.

How many hot dogs do you order for 23,000 people?   Steve Wilson, "UK wins 72–64 in arena opener," *Herald-Leader,* November 28, 1976.

It doesn't look anything like Tennessee orange . . . Please, do me a favor   John McGill, "Rupp: Still in the spotlight after 46 years," *Herald-Leader,* July 18, 1976.

EPILOGUE

For the epilogue, I attended the boys' signing ceremony in May 2010 and interviewed all the central characters in the months after the 2009–2010 season ended, following up with them several times over the course of the next year. In addition, I interviewed several other people including: University of Akron head basketball coach Keith Dambrot, James Madison University head coach Matt Brady, South Kent School head coach Kelvin Jefferson, and Charles Eddie Doan's widow, Alma Doan.

Thanks for the scrimmage, boys   Mark Selig, "JMU loses by 20 in CBI; Davidson sizzles to 85–65 victory," Harrisonburg, Va., *Daily News-Record,* March 16, 2011.